The POWER CURVE

SCOTT G. KYLE

CEO and Chief Investment Officer
Coastwise Capital Group, LLC

The POWER CURVE

SMART INVESTING USING DIVIDENDS, OPTIONS, *and* *the* MAGIC *of* COMPOUNDING

NAUTILUS PRESS

New York Los Angeles London San Diego

Published by Nautilus Press,
a division of The Nautilus Works

Scott Kyle is the Principal of Coastwise Capital Group, LLC, a Registered Investment Advisor. Mr. Kyle does not intend to provide personalized investment advice through this publication and does not represent that the securities or services discussed are suitable for any investor. Investors are advised not to rely on any information contained in the publication in the process of making a fully informed investment decision.

This publication is designed to provide accurate and authoritative information in regard to the subject matter covered. It is sold with the understanding that neither the author nor the publisher is engaged in rendering legal or accounting service. If legal advice or other expert assistance is required, the services of a competent professional person should be sought.

Library of Congress Cataloging-in-Publication Data available on request.

ISBN 978-0-9778018-2-4

Library of Congress Control Number: 2009923000

First edition
A C E G I K J H F D B

Printed in the United States of America

To my beautiful wife, Carlie, for her understanding when the daily (and weekend) alarm would go off at an hour only roosters, farmers, and those who recently moved to the mainland from Hawaii would appreciate. Without her love and support this book would remain a lifelong dream rather than a present-day culmination of more than twenty years of investing, trading, learning from making mistakes, studying, teaching, and, most important, being in the game.

To my son, Jet. May you engage in life to its fullest such that you are blessed to experience innumerable challenges and successes along its wondrous journey.

Contents

Preface

Dividends are back with a vengeance and with good reason. After being burned by the technology bubble of the late 1990s, when companies with no real profits saw their stock prices bid into the stratosphere only to crash into the bankruptcy bin, investors are hungry for sound corporations that generate verifiable cash that can be taken to the bank. Tired of false promises and the accounting tricks that implied profits but ultimately led to the downfall of companies like Enron, MCI, and others, today's investors want the security associated with businesses that have consistently increased their earnings over time—and have sent actual checks quarterly to shareholders as proof that the profits earned were legitimate and bona fide. Add to this a low interest rate environment in which investors are seeking the superior income potential that high-yielding dividend stocks offer over traditional income vehicles such as low-yielding bonds. Not only can investors earn more profits today with quarterly dividends, but these dividend checks might be much larger in the future—and the underlying stock could also provide capital gains. Simply put, a portfolio of high-quality dividend-paying companies is increasingly becoming a core component of prudent money management.

Add to this the explosion in the use of options to protect investors against—if not to help them profit from—volatile market moves. The number of investors opening accounts with options trading capabilities has grown exponentially throughout the last decade, and the number of option contracts traded has gone up more than tenfold as well. But often inexperienced investors, insufficiently informed about what they are investing in or how the powerful trading tools at their fingertips work most effectively, take on unexpected risks. They buy high-yielding stocks that they think are safe, only to discover that their expected source of income has disappeared with the announcement of a cut in, if not outright suspension of, the company's dividend. Worse yet, the stock price of the investor's new holding plummets as Wall Street punishes the company that can no longer fulfill its dividend obligations. Add to this the potential pain inflicted by newbie traders who open up new margin accounts to use the latest options trading techniques they learned through an online tutorial or weekend seminar only to see profits wiped out because they did not understand the inherent risks and potential rewards associated with potent options tools.

For the first time ever, in straightforward and accessible language, *The Power Curve* reveals the power behind dividend-paying companies and sophisticated options trading techniques in a way that can lead to immediate profits. While most investment books are either largely academic or entertainment oriented—technical analyses or biographies of the world's great investors—*The Power Curve* offers a practical, easy-to-understand, and immediately applicable guide to investing that was previously the purview of Wall Street hedge-fund hotshots. As with most things in life, success is driven by both science (technical proficiency) as well as art (the learned ability to do things well). The goal of *The Power Curve* is to provide you with both the art and the science necessary for you to achieve superior stock returns over time and to benefit directly from the magic of compounding.

CHAPTER 1

The Importance and Power of Compounding

Why should you bother to push for greater profits with a more active investing and trading program? Historically speaking, equities are already the best asset class when it comes to providing returns over time. Why not just put money in an index fund and sit back? For many with a very long time horizon and no inclination to be involved in portfolio management, a passive index fund approach is perfectly suitable. However, those who have pools of money with a less than "buy and hold forever" time horizon and the temporal resources, as well as the ability and, most important, the desire, can tap into the superior returns that an active trading program can provide. Look at the difference in seemingly small return variations over time shown by Figure 1.1 on the following page.

Two accounts each starting with $100,000 will have dramatically different balances twenty or even ten years later with one account earning a seemingly small three or four additional percentage points per year. This is the power of compounding at work. Incremental differences that would not get your attention in the near term can mean the difference between having to extend your working years and retiring early with security.

Between 1999 and 2009 stocks went approximately nowhere. There were many ups and downs along the way (volatility that you can take advantage of in a profitable way), but a buy-and-hold strategy would have left your brokerage account essentially flat, especially when you factor in inflation. By definition, if you buy the market (and, truth be told, a few mutual-fund holdings are usually a costly way to do just that), your returns will be, at best, slightly south of the market after associated costs. Many smart investors, Warren Buffett among them, believe that the next decade might see returns in the 5% to 8% range, which, after inflation and taxes, will make it hard for many to reach their financial goals. Thus adding even a small level of intelligent trading can get you up the return curve, which, over the years, can make a material impact on the size of your account. Among the four major sources of stock-related gains—long-term capital appreciation (which was viewed as the primary if not sole source of profits in the 1990s), dividends, short-term trading, and income from the sale of options—the latter three sources will likely represent the vast majority of attainable gains in the years to come. My goal is to show you how to make the most of the market's natural fluctuations and to profit from the magic of compounding.

Figure 1.1 **Return Variations over Time**

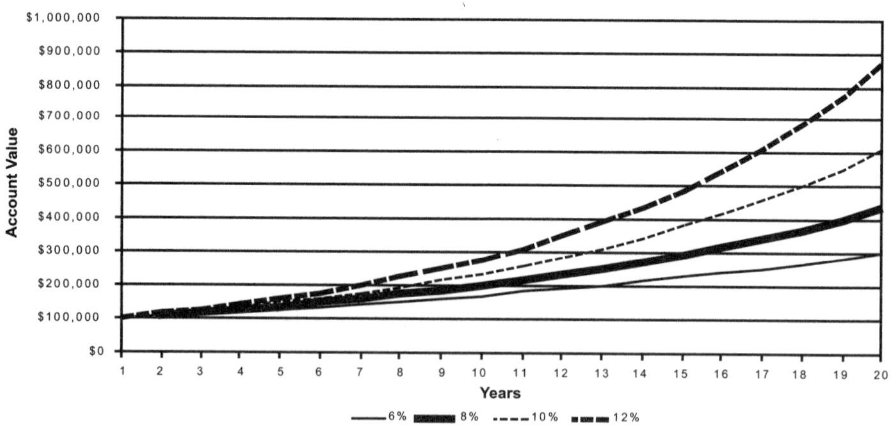

"Compounding Is the Most Powerful Force in the Universe."

Certainly one of the world's great investors had to have uttered this weighty and telling quote. Was it the wise and venerable Warren Buffett? Perhaps the irascible but entertaining Jim Cramer? The legendary and honored Ben Graham? Actually, it was not an investor at all, but a scientist, a particularly famous and important one at that. The man who proclaimed that compounding was more powerful than gravity, electromagnetism, or even atomic friction was none other than Albert Einstein.

Let's look at this force in action.

Figure 1.2 **LOGARITHMIC REPRESENTATION OF COMPOUNDING**

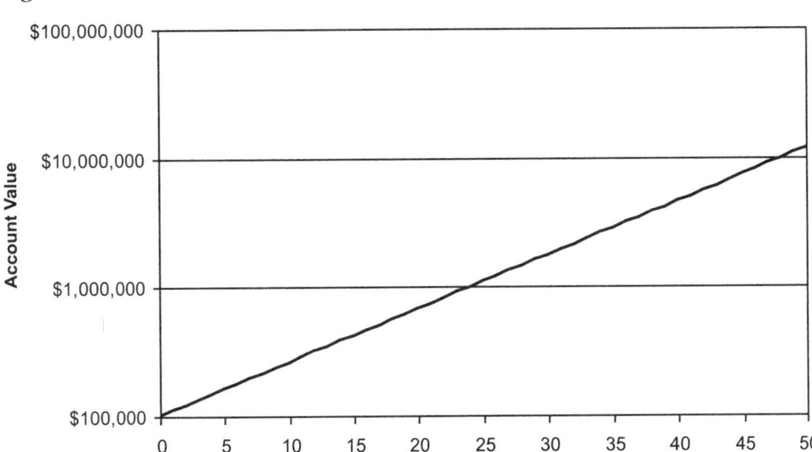

In this representation the vertical axis is skewed so that a given distance always represents the same percentage change. (This means that the distance between 10 and 100 is the same as between 100 and 1,000 since each represents a tenfold growth, although the absolute gains of going from 100 to 1,000 are clearly greater.) You will occasionally see stock-gain charts that use this methodology. Do not be fooled! The real gains (since we are focused on absolute gains) are shown by Figure 1.3 on the following page.

As you can see from the figure, the power of compounding kicks in as time goes on. Investment gains (annual percentage returns) may appear at first glance to improve over time since the chart seems to be flat in the early years and to go higher in later years. In reality, it is the magic of compounding "doing its thing" in subsequent years that makes these gains so large on an absolute basis.

Figure 1.3 **Linear Representation of Compounding**

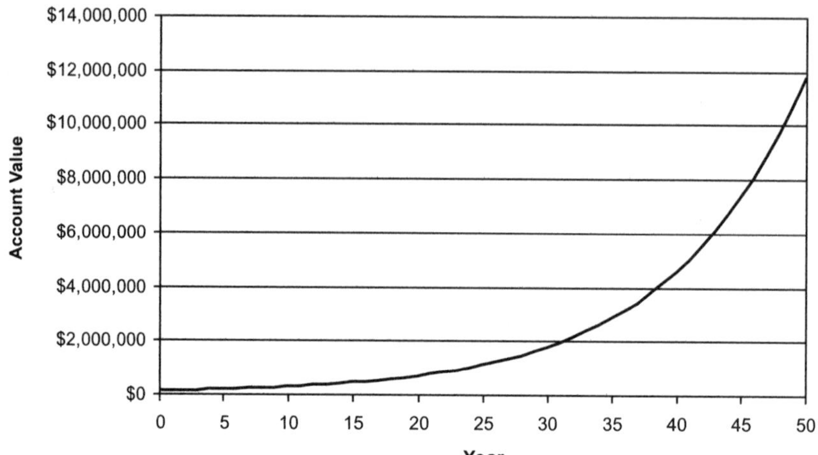

Let's do some basic math. Your account starts out at $100,000. In the first year you make 10%, or $10,000. Now your account is worth $110,000. In Year Two you make another 10%, bringing your total account value up to $121,000. (You made 10% not only on the original $100,000 but also on the $10,000 from Year One, yielding total Year Two profits of $11,000.) In Year Three you make another 10%, in this case $12,100, and so on. By the end of Year Ten your account is up to $259,374; by the end of Year Twenty your account is worth $672,750. By Year Twenty-Six, the amount of gains *per year* exceeds the original investment amount. The power of compounding has taken hold.

Few people appreciate that even small differences in returns can have a dramatic impact on account balances over time as compounding works its mathematical magic. Let's examine four basic return scenarios: inflation as defined by the Consumer Price Index, the thirty-year bond, approximate average historical equities, and what could be classified as superior stock gains.

As you can see from Figure 1.4 on the following page, seemingly small variances in annual returns—a few percentage points—can have a meaningful impact on account balances over time. Just a few percentage points of improvement in annualized returns (from 9% to 12%, for example) can mean the difference between taking a cruise and owning a yacht.

Figure 1.4 **The Impact of Differing Annual Returns**

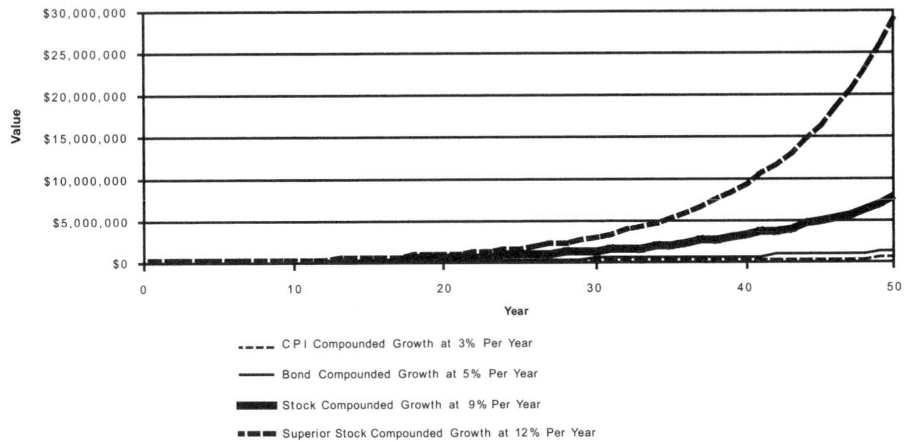

Now that we know how the power of compounding aids in wealth creation, let's see how we can best tap into this force in the equities and **options** markets.

CHAPTER 2

The Role of Dividends in Equity Returns

In the mid- to late 1990s, dividend-paying stocks went out of vogue while capital gains (stock appreciation) ruled. This period of vast underperformance by quality, dividend-paying companies was one of the rare exceptions in the history of the U.S. stock market. Studies show dividends have been responsible for between 40% and 50% of the returns that stocks have provided over the last 100-plus years. Read that again: *Around half of the returns that stocks have yielded over the decades has come from dividends.* Furthermore, high-dividend-yielding stocks have historically provided greater returns to investors than low-dividend-yielding stocks.

In the post-stock-bubble era, dividend-paying stocks came back into style with a vengeance. Investors who were seeing strong capital gains suddenly disappear became interested in the income and downside protection associated with dividend-paying stocks. This became especially true when yields on bonds hit multi-decade lows. Investors were attracted by more than regular checks in the mail and capital gains potential. Over long periods, dividend-paying stocks have provided superior *total* returns over their non-dividend–paying brethren. One important study concluded that dividend-paying stocks returned more than 10% per year from 1972 to 2005 versus a return of just over 4% for non-dividend–paying stocks. Furthermore, returns for companies that paid ever-increasing dividends were more than four times those of non-dividend–paying companies. With quality companies increasing their dividends aggressively, bond yields near historical lows, and equity returns expected to be in the 7% range over the coming decade, stock dividends will play a significant role in portfolio returns once again. Unfortunately just as investors started reaching for yield, many companies began ceasing the very thing investors were seeking: their dividends. To be sure, not all dividend-paying companies are the same. Given the importance of dividend-paying stocks in one's portfolio construction, and with so many income-oriented vehicles to choose from, what should investors look for when considering which companies to purchase?

First some basics. A company's **dividend yield** (aka **yield**) is the amount of dividends paid on a per share basis divided by the company's stock price. For example, if a stock is trading at $40 per share and the company pays an annual dividend (most pay dividends quarterly, so multiply the quarterly dividend by four) of $2 per share, the stock has a dividend yield of 5%. The yield changes, by mathematical definition, with movement in the stock price as well as an increase or decrease in the dividend paid. An increase in stock price absent a commensurate increase in dividend will lower the yield. An increase in the dividend combined with a flat stock price will raise the yield. As we will discuss in more detail below, a company's stock price decreasing, thus causing its dividend yield to increase dramatically, can be a sign of problems and the stock should be watched with a critical eye.

The next thing to know is the company's **payout ratio**. This is simply the dividend on a per share basis divided by **earnings per share (EPS)**. If a company pays out $2 per share annually and has earnings of $4.50 per share, the company's payout ratio is approximately 44%. This is a very important statistic as it indicates how likely the company is to continue to pay, or to increase, its dividend over time. A payout ratio of less than 50% is preferable. If a company's payout ratio starts getting north of 70% due to a decline in earnings, this is a sign that the dividend may ultimately be cut.

Figure 2.1 **History of Payout Ratios**

	Year								
	2000	2001	2002	2003	2004	2005	2006	2007	2008
Dividends (per share)	$0.49	$0.58	$0.68	$0.80	$0.84	$0.89	$0.94	$0.99	$1.05
Earnings (per share)	$1.51	$1.76	$2.06	$2.41	$2.10	$1.83	$1.59	$1.38	$1.20
								DANGER ZONE	
Payout Ratio	32.36%	32.64%	32.92%	33.20%	40.26%	48.82%	59.20%	71.79%	87.06%

Here, Company X continued to raise its dividends even as earnings started to decline in 2004. The result is an increase in the payout ratio. As the payout ratio climbed above 70% in 2007, it served as a warning sign that Company X might cut its dividend because the company is not well positioned to pay out that kind of cash to shareholders.

Companies *hate* cutting their dividend and Wall Street investors despise seeing companies cut their dividends even more than companies hate reducing them. If a company declares a cut in its dividend, you can be confident that the stock price will fall as a result. Don't think for a minute, however, that a struggling company won't cut its dividend. While reluctant to do so, companies take this kind of negative financial action all the time. Even such formerly blue-chip companies as Ford Motor Co. (F), Eastman Kodak Co. (EK), and Citigroup, Inc. (C) have cut dividends. So pay close attention to a company's payout ratio.

There are four important events around the dividend payment: the **dividend declaration date**, **the dividend record date**, the **dividend ex-date**, and the **dividend payment date**. The declaration date, or announcement date, is the day on which the next dividend payment is declared by the board of directors of the company. Typically, companies follow regular schedules when announcing each quarterly dividend. The record date is the date used to determine which shareholders are entitled to the dividend or distribution. The ex-date is the first date on which the stock trades without its dividend payment. In order to receive a stock dividend, you must buy a stock prior to the ex-date. This will ensure that you are a shareholder of record for receipt of the dividend. If you buy the stock on the ex-date or after, you will not be entitled to the announced dividend. Alternatively, if you own the stock and want to sell your shares but still receive the dividend, you must sell on or after the ex-date. Stock prices tend to drop on the ex-date by the amount of the dividend to be paid. For instance, if a company is paying a dividend of $0.50 per share, on the ex-date its stock price will drop by $0.50 in addition to any normal market movement that day. This is simply because the company has taken a piece of itself, namely $0.50 per share of cash on its **balance sheet**, and set it aside to send to investors as a dividend payment. Thus, all things being equal, the company is worth $0.50 per share less on the ex-date than it was on the day before the ex-date, and it trades accordingly. Sophisticated quote systems will even indicate that a stock is up on its ex-date if it falls by less than its dividend payment amount. For example, a stock that drops from $40 to $39.80 on the day it "goes ex" with an anticipated $0.50 per share dividend payment might be indicated to have gone up 0.75% ($0.30 divided by $40) that day. This makes sense as the investor has not lost money; instead his holdings have merely been rearranged. Finally, the payment date is the date when accounts are actually credited with the dividend, or the checks are mailed for those who receive dividends directly rather than having them applied to brokerage accounts.

***Figure* 2.2 DIVIDEND PAYMENT SCHEDULE**

Automatic Data Processing, Inc. (ADP)			
Nov. 11, 2008 Dividend Declaration of $0.33	**Dec. 10, 2008** Dividend Ex-Date	**Dec. 12, 2008** Record Date	**Jan. 1, 2009** Pay Date

SOURCE: EARNINGS.COM

WHY DIVIDENDS MATTER AND WHY INCREASING DIVIDENDS COUNT EVEN MORE

It is important to remember that the payment of a dividend is not necessarily a good thing in and of itself. It is a taxable event for nonqualified accounts in which the company gives a piece of itself back to the investor to spend, invest elsewhere, or put back into the company paying the dividend, typically via a dividend reinvestment plan.

If, for example, a company is paying a $1 dividend and is trading at $50 per share, the stock will drop by $1 per share to $49 per share on the ex-date, barring additional market movement. The investor's account now contains $49 worth of stock and $1 worth of cash, the $1 distribution being taxable. Your $50 of stock before the dividend payment is now $49 of stock, $0.85 of cash and $0.15 in the pockets of the IRS for those in the 15% dividend tax bracket. Doesn't sound like such a great deal now, does it? So why do you hear commentators praising dividends? Clearly it is the company's ability to keep paying dividends that matters, since ultimately there is a direct correlation between ever-increasing dividends and ever-increasing earnings, the latter of which leads to ever-increasing stock prices. Management that knows it has to cut a big check to shareholders every ninety days—and a bigger check every 365 days for those companies that consistently increase their annual dividend payments—will create a culture in which increasing earnings are a priority. In order to fulfill this mission dividend-paying companies tend to outperform the market over time because management has this extra incentive to exercise financial discipline that favors stockholders. Cutting a dividend is paramount to admitting failure, and these companies have set their bars high.

Let's look at the example of Colgate-Palmolive Company (CL) as evidence of the long-term correlation between dividends, earnings, and stock price. In early 2008 Colgate-Palmolive increased its dividend 11%, boasting about forty-five consecutive years of dividend enrichments. At the time the CEO indicated that the new payout "demonstrates the board's confidence in the continued strong and profitable growth of Colgate's global business, our cash-generation capabilities, and our firm commitment to building value." Over the ten-year period from 1998 to 2008, Colgate-Palmolive increased its earnings at an average rate of 9.34% per year. The annualized percentage gain in Colgate-Palmolive's dividend? Surprise, surprise, 9.79%. (The payout ratio fluctuated but only exceeded 50% in one year and otherwise held steady in the 30% to 45% range.) These figures show the strong long-term correlation of earnings and dividend growth for companies which increase their dividends consistently over time.

SOURCE OF FUNDS: ARE YOU A GOOD WITCH OR A BAD WITCH? (YIELD BEFORE YOU REACH FOR THAT YIELD)

There is good yield and there is bad yield. It is vitally important to know the difference at all times, but especially in market environments where product marketers are pushing and investors are reaching for yield, often stretching so far that they fall off the proverbial tree branch. If you hear from analysts or Wall Street pundits something along the lines of, "I don't think the company is going anywhere any time soon, but it has a 5% dividend, so I get paid for waiting," then you are being misled. Some additional background is in order.

Many investors believe dividends are paid out of earnings. They are not; dividends are paid out of cash. A company can have no earnings or earnings that are less than a given dividend payment, and the company can still make its declared payout as long as it has the cash to do so—either cash on its books or access to cash via credit facilities (read: debt). It is a consistent increase in earnings that allows a company to increase its dividend over time. (Note that to minimize the amount of arcane accounting under consideration I am interchanging **cash flow** and earnings that, for companies in most industries, approximate each other over time.)

Often periodicals such as the *Wall Street Journal* (WSJ) will print a table of high-yielding securities—stocks, closed-end funds, and the like—ranked by highest yield. You will occasionally find listed companies and funds yielding 10% or more. It is very important to dig deeper to determine the source of this yield. There are two major red flags that you should look for. The first, as noted above, is when a company is paying out more than it is earning. If its payout ratio is over 100% for several quarters running, then that is exactly what you should be doing, too. To state the obvious, this scenario is not sustainable. A company cannot finance forever a dividend payment through borrowing (and if the borrowing is done from Uncle Sam rather than a traditional financial institution as occurred often in the late 2000s, then the probability of a continued strong dividend policy is even less likely still). If you find a company yielding north of 6%, look carefully at its payout ratio. In most cases it will be at 70% or more, the dividend subject to reduction in the near term. Stay away from these companies as the last thing you want to do is buy into a company just before it slashes its dividend.

Another scenario for a high-yielding security is a fund, usually closed end, that makes a "controlled payout." An example would be a fund trading at $10 per share fixing its dividend payout at $1.30 per share so that the fund yields 13%. Sounds like a great deal, right? Headlines blare: HOW WOULD YOU LIKE TO MAKE 13%? In most cases, however, the fund or the underlying securities it holds are not earning enough to cover the dividend, thus the fund is simply returning principal to shareholders. In other words, the fund is taking money you gave to them and returning it slowly to you over time and charging you a fee for the pleasure. In doing so, the fund is returning to shareholders the very thing the shareholders are counting on to create an income stream. *This is the bad kind of yield.* Buying $10 worth of a security only to have 13% of it given back to you annually in a taxable event is not an optimal investment approach.

Think of what this means in the long term. Let's say I advertised an investment that guaranteed a 20% annual dividend stream. You give me $100 and for five consecutive years I hand you back $20. If I am not earning more on the original money than I am returning to you in the form of a "dividend" then eventually the money runs out and the game is over. The 20% yield provided a total **return on investment (ROI)** of precisely 0% and a negative ROI after taxes. When a company is paying back more than it is earning, the dividend yield will rarely make up for the capital loss and your total position return will be negative.

Here is an example of this concept in practice: In early 2008 Pfizer, Inc. (PFE) released earnings that disappointed Wall Street. Over several years the stock's price had fallen due to declining revenue because of several proprietary drugs coming off patent. Many prominent investors commented, in effect, "For me the attraction is the big dividend." The yield was over 6%, versus money market returns in the 2% to 3% range. The fact that Pfizer was able to continue to pay and even for many years increase (until it decided to do a major acquisition) its dividend in the face of declining sales is a testament to the value and importance of solid financial reserves. Remember, however, that the goal of investing is to get a return on your capital over time—in other words, to have more money in the future than you have today. A big dividend is not in and of itself a good thing. Stating that a dividend yield is twice that of a money market yield is missing the vital point that the capital ownership of Pfizer, or any stock, is subject to decline, whereas a money market fund's principal is fixed. And don't forget, the payment of a dividend reduces a stock price whereas the payment of interest from a money market does not reduce **net asset value (NAV)** below 1.0.

If Pfizer pays out 6% over a year but its stock price declines by 5% after the payment of said dividends, then the investor's total return is only 1%, less than that of a money market paying out 3%. While Pfizer has been in the enviable position of having the ability to consistently increase dividends despite flat or declining revenues and profits, the total return the company provided to shareholders—the bottom line that matters—was *negative* over that several-year period as their stock declined nearly 40% and the dividend did not nearly offset the capital loss. In this case, despite dividend payments increasing from $0.68 per share annualized in 2004 to $1.28 annualized in 2008, the company saw its stock price decline from the mid-$30s to the upper teens during the same time period.

Do not confuse a strong dividend with superior returns per se. They usually do correlate over time, but a strong balance sheet can mask operational weakness in the midterm. The investor must look at what is behind the yield. Is the company or fund earning more than it is paying back in the form of distributions? Is its payout ratio comfortably south of 60% and holding steady or better yet declining? If yes, all is fine. If no, then the yield is artificially high—and the payout will likely be trimmed down or principal is being paid out, or both, leaving the investor with inferior returns.

It is not the fact that a company does pay a dividend that is meaningful, but the fact that it can. Read that sentence again because it contains one of the most important concepts in dividend-stock investing.

The Sweet Spots

If having too much yield is potentially a bad thing, where are the sweet spots for dividend stocks? The optimal yields fall into two areas depending on investor objectives: (1) growth dividend companies that have yields ranging from 2% to 4%, and (2) income dividend companies with yields of 4% to 6%. We will also discuss emerging dividend companies that recently started paying a dividend and/or have a yield of under 2% but are poised to increase their dividend substantially over time.

The Power 100™ is a comprehensive list of dividend-paying companies that meet certain strict financial criteria. This list specifically excludes REITs and utilities, which tend to pay out nearly 100% of their earnings, and focuses instead on companies that consistently increase dividends over time. Many of the high-quality companies discussed here are part of the Power 100 index, but as with any dynamic portfolio, the list is updated regularly to reflect new realities in the marketplace.

Starting with growth dividend companies, there are many high-quality businesses such as Walgreens Co. (WAG), Sysco Corporation (SYY, not CSCO), and Automatic Data Processing, Inc. (ADP) that have yields between 2% and 4%. In many cases these companies have paid and increased their dividends for decades. At the same time, they are companies with good underlying growth rates, and they are investing in their organic expansion with the cash not paid out to investors. These growth dividend companies have characteristics that include: (1) a low payout ratio, typically under 30%, because they tend to be investing a lot in their future growth and thus choose to hold on to much of their excess cash for internal growth purposes; (2) high-dividend-growth rates, often in excess of 12%; and (3) strong financials including high profitability and a solid balance sheet. These are the companies that can give you both capital appreciation and income gains over time.

Growth dividend companies are the kinds of stocks you buy for your young kids' college education—and the income generated by the reinvested dividend payments fifteen years hence could potentially pay the tuition, with the stock likely providing capital gains to boot.

Compare growth dividend companies with classic income dividend companies paying out 4% to 6% yields. The latter would include the usual suspects like financials and pharmaceuticals. Think Verizon Communications, Inc. (VZ), Altria Group, Inc. (MO), Fortune Brands, Inc. (FO), and the like. These companies are characterized by higher yields (often in excess of the yield on the ten-year Treasury), higher payout ratios (usually over 30% but still comfortably under 70%), annual dividend growth in the 6% to 10% range, and strong financials. These are the kinds of companies that will be slow but steady growers, with less capital gains potential than their growth dividend company brethren but with a very strong income potential. You can build a high-quality portfolio of companies from a wide variety of industries with yields in the 2% to 6% range that will satisfy both your current and future income needs and provide good capital gains potential as well. The key is to be patient and let the power of compounding take hold over time.

EVER-INCREASING DIVIDENDS AND COMPOUNDING ON STEROIDS

As will be discussed further in chapter 3, a company's ultimate worth is a function of the discounted cash flows it generates and either pays out in the form of dividends or reinvests in operations for future earnings growth. While your yield at purchase may seem paltry, by taking advantage of ever-increasing dividends—not to mention reinvesting them—you can have a meaningful **effective yield**, which is defined as the current dividend divided by the original stock purchase price. In the figures below we examine the increase in effective yield of a company that starts at a 5% yield and increases its dividend over time—payouts that you keep in cash in this case.

Figure 2.3 **Effective Yield Without Dividend Reinvestment**

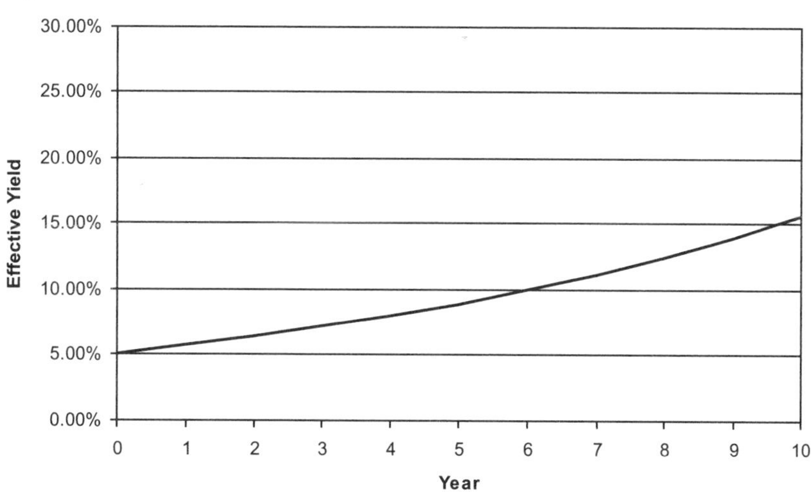

Even if dividends are not reinvested, an investor's effective yield on a security that is increasing its dividend regularly does increase over time. In the above example, effective yield increases to over 15% in ten years for a stock that has a 5% yield at time of purchase and increases its dividend at a rate of 12% per year.

Figure 2.4 **Numerical Calculations of Effective Yield Without Dividend Reinvestment**

Year	Share Price	Number of Shares No Reinvesting	Annual Div/Share	Effective Yield
0	$50.00	2000	$2.50	5.00%
1	$55.00	2000	$2.80	5.60%
2	$60.50	2000	$3.14	6.27%
3	$66.55	2000	$3.51	7.02%
4	$73.21	2000	$3.93	7.87%
5	$80.53	2000	$4.41	8.81%
6	$88.58	2000	$4.93	9.87%
7	$97.44	2000	$5.53	11.05%
8	$107.18	2000	$6.19	12.38%
9	$117.90	2000	$6.93	13.87%
10	$129.69	2000	$7.76	15.53%

If, rather than taking dividends in cash, you reinvested the dividends, then your effective yield would end up being much higher than 15%. How much higher depends on the prices at which dividends are reinvested, but even being conservative, the reinvesting of dividends would add another 5% or more to the effective yield. Why? Because the shares purchased with the reinvested shares would then have dividends paid on them. In the future, when the company increases its dividend as it had done year after year, *all* the shares would pay out a higher dividend.

In the figures on the facing page we show how effective yield grows when the power of compounding with reinvested dividends is employed. In this case, the investor reinvests dividend payments every quarter, and the shares purchased with last quarter's dividends produce even more yield in the future.

In Figure 2.6, assuming the stock price increases at a rate of 10% per year, effective yield has increased to over 26% after ten short years. Of course, what your effective yield will turn out to be is dependent on both the annualized rate of increase of the dividend payment and the price at which additional shares have been purchased. As counterintuitive as it may seem, the stock price going down in the early years increases effective yield in future years as more shares are purchased on which future dividends will be paid—a natural form of dollar cost averaging.

Figure 2.5 **EFFECTIVE YIELD WITH DIVIDEND REINVESTED COMPOUNDING**

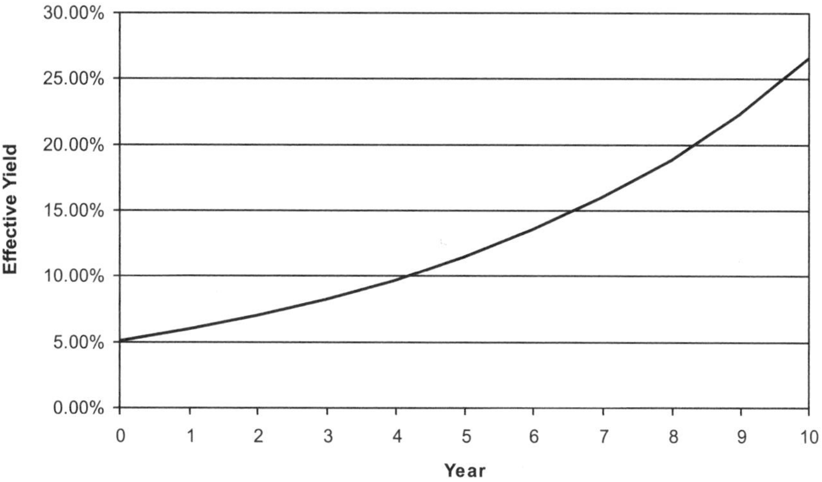

Figure 2.6 **NUMERICAL CALCULATIONS OF EFFECTIVE YIELD WITH DIVIDEND REINVESTMENT**

Year	Share Price	Number of Shares With Reinvesting	Annual Div/Share	Effective Yield
0	$50.00	2000.00	$2.50	5.00%
1	$55.00	2100.00	$2.80	5.88%
2	$60.50	2206.91	$3.14	6.92%
3	$66.55	2321.30	$3.51	8.15%
4	$73.21	2443.82	$3.93	9.61%
5	$80.53	2575.14	$4.41	11.35%
6	$88.58	2716.03	$4.93	13.40%
7	$97.44	2867.34	$5.53	15.85%
8	$107.18	3029.98	$6.19	18.76%
9	$117.90	3204.97	$6.93	22.22%
10	$129.69	3393.43	$7.76	26.35%

You can clearly see the power of compounding when it is applied to the reinvestment of dividends over time. This is the magical power of compounding juiced up more than a Texas-sized Alex Rodriguez.

When you start, the movement is not so dramatic. But as the yield begins to increase and gain momentum, it really starts taking off...to the point where its own momentum keeps it going over time. The last part of that sentence, "over time," is the key. You have to stay in the game to get the benefit of compounding. This is the most difficult part, not putting the brakes on before you have had the chance to really accelerate.

WHEN THE GOING GETS TOUGH, THE WEAK GET CRUSHED

The importance of having quality dividend-paying companies as a core part of your portfolio is a lesson easily forgotten when times are good, but economies and financial markets inevitably hit tough spots. Cash is king. Cash is real. Dividends are real. They are paid out of bona fide cash that has been generated through superior operations. Companies like Walgreens, Sysco, Automatic Data Processing, and Coca-Cola Company (KO) might not be sexy, they may not double in price overnight, but build a portfolio of companies like these, buy them when valuations are reasonable (see chapter 4 on stock valuation), focus your energy elsewhere, and the excitement and potential wealth building associated with quality dividend-paying stocks will emerge over time. You can take that to the bank.

But not all dividend-paying companies are the same, and it can be surprising how quickly a once-safe dividend gets the axe. In 2008, markets dropped dramatically in a very short period of time due to massive economic dislocations in the credit markets, and second- and third-tier companies with weak balance sheets got dropped like the baton of the U.S 4x100-meter relay team. These so-called corrections can be sudden and painful, emotionally if not financially.

The key to being a great investor is to always remember that a storm is just around the corner—you just don't know when it will hit or how severe it will be—and to prepare accordingly. Owning quality dividend-paying stocks as a core part of your portfolio is a great way to have an umbrella at your side, especially during the 100-year storms that inevitably hit every three to five years.

Simply put, if you find a company that has consistently raised its dividend 10%+ year after year, then you have very likely found a company that has also consistently increased its earnings 10%+ year after year. Earnings growth does not have to precisely match dividend growth, but over the years, the two statistics of earnings and dividend growth will generally mirror each other. Most companies that have paid dividends consistently for years have their financial houses in order. So when the *merde* hits the fan and equities are getting pummeled, high-quality dividend stocks will generally outperform. Why? Because when the market waters are rough, investors seek companies that have strong earnings, strong balance sheets, and a dividend yield that creates a "floor" in the stock price—companies that are mature, have a dominant position in their industry, and that can weather the storm.

CHAPTER 3

Fundamental Analysis, Equity Valuation, and Other Stock Selection Criteria

Just as you must analyze the superficial appeal of high dividend yields, you also must do your basic equity research. Options are simply derivates, their value being a function of the underlying security. Before we look at options, let's take a moment to understand fundamental equity analysis and stock valuation as this is the basis for all superior investing.

When it comes to equity analysis and stock selection, you should take the following into consideration: (1) fundamental company analysis, (2) industry analysis, (3) demographic analysis, (4) technical analysis, and (5) macroeconomic analysis. Given the importance of fundamental analysis, we will address this first and then consider the other four main variables in superior stock selection.

GRABBING TIGER BY THE TAIL

How much would you pay for Tiger Woods? This may sound like an unusual question, but it gets to the heart of investing. Say Tiger Woods decided to put his future career earnings up for sale (not unlike how certain musical artists have put their future royalties up for sale using what are commonly known as "Bowie Bonds" after the Thin White Duke who helped to pioneer this security). How would you value that? How much would you pay? As a start, you would assess how much Tiger has made in the past—from endorsements, tournament winnings, and so on. You would then project how much the single-gloved one is likely to make in the future. Will he continue his winning ways? Will the competition catch up to him and his tournament earnings decrease? Will the sport of golf become more or less popular, and will that have an impact on tournament prize money, sponsorship deals, and the like?

After this kind of analysis, you would come up with estimates of likely earnings over the expected remaining years of Tiger's career. Suppose this range is $120,000,000 to $175,000,000. After factoring in and making assumptions (interest or cap rate, and the number of years) about the time value of money (the fact that a dollar today is worth more than a dollar will be in five years), you might value Tiger's career in today's dollars between $55,000,000 and $70,000,000 depending on your interest rate/return assumptions. If Tiger offered to sell you his future earnings for $20,000,000, you would get out your checkbook faster than you can say "hole in one." If he asked for $200,000,000 for his future winnings, you would probably pass in favor of a more attractive investment.

This is, in essence, the process of stock evaluation, except that in terms of companies we usually think on a per share basis. Note that, when they value companies on a per share rather than on a total enterprise basis (what the whole thing is worth), novice investors often draw naïve conclusions about the valuation of a company as a whole. In effect they confuse price and value. How so? An investor sees a stock price of $5.70, down from $8.20, and concludes that the stock is cheap. But if the same investor were told that the total **market capitalization** of the company is $300,000,000, and that the company earns only $5,000,000 on revenues of $100,000,000, he would gain a much clearer sense of how truly expensive the company is. You will, at times, hear commentators say, "Oh, I can buy that stock for about the same price as a cup of coffee, therefore it is cheap." That is missing the point. A $400 stock might be cheap and a $4 stock expensive; what matters is the total company valuation relative to its earnings, sales, margins, earnings growth rate, and other important financial metrics. Whether on a total or a per share basis, whether for Tiger Woods or for a company you are considering putting in your portfolio, the valuation process is the same: analyze historical earnings, project future cash flows, and assess competitive threats and industry trends.

> *The real question is: When is the best time to make an offer for Tiger's future earnings? When is the time to grab the tiger by the tail?*

The financial analysis behind good stock picking is the easy part. There are plenty of people with sufficient IQs who can do the math. Most investors trip up, however, when they let the right sides of their brains dominate their left sides. Once you have a handle on valuing future earnings, when are you most likely to be offered the greatest return on investment opportunity? After Tiger Woods just won his seventh tournament in a row and everyone thinks he is unstoppable? Plenty of people would now be willing to pay a big premium for his future career earnings as they extrapolate recent history far into the future. Or do you make an offer after he misses the cut at a major tournament? Assuming that you do not see any fundamental flaws with Tiger as a golfer—he is in front of a TV on Saturday rather than a gallery of fans because on both Thursday and Friday he was having an off day—you would wait for that unusual opportunity when people were questioning Tiger's skills and the attention was on the hotshot golfer of the hour. Because you have followed Tiger's career closely and know the recent poor performance is an aberration, you have a high level of comfort taking advantage of this transitory situation to buy his future earnings at a discount rather than when he is coming off a winning streak and the price associated with his future earnings is high.

The discipline necessary to wait for a temporary moment of weakness and then to attack sans emotions (but with the confidence that you know the investment well and that the current dip is aberrational in nature) is at the heart of superior investing. Those who behave in the opposite way—becoming interested in a given opportunity only after it has made the front pages as an investment that can do no wrong—invariably do most of their buying high and their selling low, and underperform the market commensurately. The winner in investing is the one who pays the lowest price for the highest-quality company.

Because a company has an ongoing value—an indefinite life—investors are willing to pay a **multiple** of projected earnings rather than merely paying for expected earnings over a given period of time, as would be the case if we bought Tiger Woods's future golf winnings. The question is: How much of a multiple are investors inclined to pay and why? This depends largely on growth rates (top and bottom lines) and profit margins. If a company is increasing its top and bottom lines at 30% per year, an investor might be willing to pay 35 times earnings, whereas the same investor might be willing to pay only 15 times earnings for a company growing at 10% per year. Similarly, investors will tend to pay a higher multiple for a company with large operating margins than for a company with low profit margins. Market valuations also affect individual stock multiples. If the overall market is frothy, investors are willing to pay higher multiples of earnings to own a given company's future cash streams.

Figure 3.1 **IMPACT OF VARIABLES ON P/E RATIOS**

	Low Growth	High Growth
High Margin	Intermediate P/E Ratio	High P/E Ratio
Low Margin	Low P/E Ratio	Intermediate P/E Ratio

Superior returns are achieved when you can find high-margin, high-growth businesses trading at relatively low P/E ratios. Opportunities to find such a combination do not come around often, but they do appear from time to time.

THEY CALL ME PEGGY SUE

By comparing **price/earnings ratios (P/E)** with earnings growth ratios, we can get apples-to-apples comparisons as to how expensive a given company is on an absolute and relative basis. This concept is known as the **price/earnings growth ratio**, or **PEG ratio**. The PEG ratio simply compares a stock's price earnings ratio to its expected earnings per share growth rate. If a company's stock has a P/E ratio of 30X but is growing EPS at 35% per year, its PEG is 0.86 (30/35). Another company might have a lower P/E of 25X but an earnings growth rate of only 10% per year, giving it a PEG of 2.5. Generally speaking, a lower PEG is better as it means you are paying less for earnings growth. PEG is especially valuable for high-growth companies that might appear to be very expensive on a purely P/E basis (think Google) but that might be more reasonably priced when earnings growth rates are factored in. Of course those growth rates must be sustained; a company can see its PEG skyrocket with a decrease in its earnings growth rate. PEG is just one of many valuation tools used to determine whether a company is both a great company and a great stock.

COUNTING CARDS

Several excellent recent books such as *Bringing Down the House* and *Fortune's Formula* have told the stories of people who developed card-counting systems in blackjack that allowed them to beat the house. The simple version of this concept is that the player counts the number of face cards that have been dealt. The fewer the number of face cards dealt, the more likely that a face card will be dealt on the next hand and therefore the higher the "count" is. The higher the count, the more the player should bet on the next hand. The lower the count, the less he should bet. By placing large bets when the count is favorable and smaller bets when the count is unfavorable, the player can maximize his returns. This is pure statistics, plain and simple.

Approaching the stock market as though it were a casino is a misleading way to look at investing. The market's primary purpose is to facilitate financing for corporations and to give investors in turn the opportunity to own pieces of publicly traded companies and receive sufficient returns on their investments over time. But few people know there is an automatic "count" when it comes to making so-called bets in the stock market. What is this count? It is called the price earnings multiple of the market. Here's how it works. The lower the count, the more likely an investor is to have a winning hand over time (i.e., to make money); the higher the count (the P/E ratio) of the market when an investor puts money into an S&P 500 fund for example, the more likely the investor is to receive inferior returns over time. The same applies to the individual stocks that make up the market as a whole.

Early 2000, when the count or P/E ratio for the S&P 500 was over 40X, was one of the absolute worst times to make an investment. Virtually every face card had already been shown, and the probability of a winning hand any time soon was very low. After a long and bumpy ten years, an investor in the S&P 500 would still not have made money on his initial investment. Compare this with time periods when the count for the S&P 500 was, say, in the single digits. Look at the returns provided by the market over the subsequent years and you will find that they were favorable. In 1982 the broad market P/E ratio was well under 10X and the following decade and a half was one of the best performing periods for equities in history.

The reason the average investor vastly underperforms the market—study after study shows that the average mutual fund investor made less than half the broad market gains over long periods—is that he invests more money on average when the count (i.e., the P/E ratio) is high and less money when the count is low—either for the market at large, for a given region/sector, or for an individual security. Investors do the exact opposite of what they should do to optimize their returns. Why? Because that is how most people are mentally wired. The average investor starts paying attention to stocks only after the positive news has made headlines and is already reflected in prices. When the market drops, this investor decides to sell. Then, after the market has rallied and he starts feeling comfortable with equities again he puts money back into the market. It does not help that the major brokerage firms that advise millions of clients have consistently recommended the sale of stocks after they have gone down and advocated buying stocks after they have already had a great run. Similarly, general market commentators advise that investors should "wait for more clarity"—and a rise in the market—before putting money to work after the market has managed to shoot a bogey. Emotionally this might be the comfortable thing to do, but financially it is investing suicide.

The time to buy Tiger Woods's future career earnings is after he has experienced the rare miss of a cut and everyone has written him off as having his best days behind him. Just like the market, Tiger will come back. I can assure you that *Tiger* would invest in Tiger when he is at a low, just like great companies invest in themselves via stock buybacks when they are experiencing temporary hard times. When you own a quality company at a historically low P/E ratio, the increased **operating earnings** of the underlying business, combined with an expanding P/E multiple in general, can lead to superior gains over time.

For that reason, pay close attention to the count. When the market is dealing you a great hand—even though it might look like the casino is on fire—that is when you press your bets. When the count is high, when the market is frothy, that is the time to take some winnings off the table by using some of the trading techniques that will be described in this book. You will eventually be dealt a better investing hand; just be patient. Those face cards still exist in the deck, and you will be amazed that they eventually reappear with regularity. This type of behavior on the margin is what leads to better-than-market returns with lower risk applied.

It takes mental discipline and strength to place your investment "bets" when the market is going down, bleeding red for seemingly endless periods, while headlines and financial pundits proclaim the end of equities. To be sure, you are likely to be "wrong" in the near term as it is impossible to call a bottom, and trends tend to last longer than they "should." But it is when the market is down, when the P/E count is low, that you are most likely to make money in the following three, five, or ten years.

THE FISH IS TALKING BUT IS HE REALLY SAYING ANYTHING?

You probably have heard stock commentators say something along the lines of, "As far as the stock market goes, we are back to where we were in the late 1990s. We've basically gone nowhere in all these years." Just because the market is sporting the same price, does that mean it has truly gone nowhere from point A to point B?

Clearly, plenty of people made a ton of money during the '00s, just as lots of investors suffered losses across the same time period. But as defined by the Dow or S&P 500, the market statistically, mathematically, went essentially nowhere over an approximate ten-year time horizon. Does that mean an investor allocating capital to the S&P 500 in the late 2000s was no better off than one who made the same investment when the S&P was at the same price in the 1990s? Remember, a good definition of investing is the allocation of capital with the reasonable expectation of getting a return on that capital over time. Clearly the entry point—the price we pay for a security relative to its intrinsic value—is one of the driving factors in future returns. Buy a given company at $25 per share and sell it for $30 and your gain is a healthy 20%. Buy the same company at $20 per share and a sale price of $30 turns into a 50% gain, which is a 150% improvement in return. In examining what I refer to as the "ugly math of losses," a seemingly innocent 20% drop in a stock price (from $25 to $20) or some luck combined with patience in attaining a lower entry purchase point can translate into materially larger-percentage returns (in this case, returns increase by 1.5X—from 20% to 50%).

The market as defined by stock prices may not have moved net-net in the approximate ten-year period from the late 1990s to the late 2000s, and the proverbial fish seemed to be spouting only air. But read between the lines and he has a lot to say. In the late 1990s the S&P had a count, or a P/E ratio, in the 40X range. In the late 2000s the P/E ratio was approximately 12X. Many quality companies were earning far more in the late 2000s than eight to ten years before, but buying those earnings in the late 2000s cost you much less than in the late 1990s (see the Coca-Cola example on page 29).

What does this mean in terms of future investment returns, the ultimate criterion? It means what it has always meant, namely that the probability of positive investment returns—five, seven, ten years hence—is greater when you are paying 12X earnings than when you are paying 40X earnings. *That* is what the fish is trying to tell you.

THE SINGLE HABIT OF HIGHLY EFFECTIVE INVESTORS—ANOTHER LOOK AT THE COUNT

In *The 7 Habits of Highly Effective People,* Stephen R. Covey discusses the idea of creating a matrix with "to do's" that fall into one of four quadrants: not important and not urgent, not important and urgent, important and not urgent, and important and urgent. Most people, he suggests, focus on things that are not important but rather happen to be in the person's face—e-mails that pop up and so on.

Similarly, highly effective investors have habits that separate them from less-successful investors. Very few investors are born with these behavioral traits—the appropriate mind-set, discipline, long-term thinking, and the like—and most need to learn them, or to "un-learn" bad investing habits. Here is a simple construct that will help get you 90% of the way to making good investment decisions and, more important, to avoiding bad ones.

Draw a square and divide it into four quadrants. Label the top row of the large square "good stock," the bottom row "bad stock," the top left half-hand column of the square "good company," and the right-hand column of the square "bad company." Now we have a matrix with the upper left quadrant being "good company/good stock," the upper right-hand quadrant being "good stock/bad company," the lower right-hand quadrant being "bad stock/bad company," and the lower left-hand quadrant being "good company/bad stock."

Figure 3.2 **Framework for Investment Quality**

	Good Company	Bad Company
Good Stock	Best 1	Second Worst 3
Bad Stock	Second Best 2	Worst 4

By "good company," I mean a company that has consistently made profits, that has a strong balance sheet, and that is a leader in its industry. By "good stock," I mean that the price of the stock relative to the value of the company is favorable—using, for example, the price/earnings ratio.

The goal of a highly effective investor is to reside in the "good company/good stock" quadrant. The next best quadrant is "good company/bad stock." "Bad company/good stock" is a little worse, and the place where you do not want to be is the "bad company/bad stock" quadrant.

Taken to this extreme, the point becomes clear. Let's look at this matrix in a time of excessiveness in the investment world—the late 1990s and early 2000s. Coca-Cola is a prime example of a good company/bad stock in the late 1990s. It consistently increased its profits from 2000 to 2008; yet in 2008 its stock was down approximately 50% from its high in the late 1990s. Why? Simply put, while Coca-Cola was still a great company, it was a bad stock when it was selling more than 70X earnings (compared to approximately 15X in 2008 when it was both a great company and a great stock). The stock was too expensive to provide adequate returns in the short or medium term; its count was unfavorable. Will Coca-Cola eventually provide positive returns to investors who bought it in the late 1990s? As a good company, it likely will within another three to five years—ten to twelve years after the stock hit its previous high. (This is especially true once we factor in reinvested dividends; these have continued to increase each year despite the stock's decline. Why? Because earnings have been increasing, thus the company can afford to increase its dividend. That is a hallmark of a good company.) Coca-Cola has a strong franchise; it is in a good industry; the company has a rock-solid balance sheet. None of these factors has changed or will likely change for years. The price you have to pay for this greatness, however, changes from time to time. Catch Coca-Cola or other strong companies when they are both good companies *and* good stocks, and you will increase your chance for good investment returns over reasonable time periods.

In the good stock/good company quadrant in the late 1990s were stocks like Altria (formerly Philip Morris), which was left for dead in the late 1990s, no one caring a whit about the company's solid and ever-increasing dividend, high profit margins, and international growth prospects. While highflyers were crashing all around it, Altria was expanding profits and seeing its stock price light up throughout the '00s.

Compare the Coca-Cola scenario with a company like JDS Uniphase Corporation (JDSU). In the late 1990s, the company fit squarely in the bad stock/bad company quadrant. Why? There are a myriad of reasons, but on the bad stock side, valuations were off the chart, the company was not making any real profit, and the closest thing the company ever made to a dividend was a reverse stock split, which are not words you want to hear. By 2008 the stock was sporting a single-digit handle (under $10 per share). Will those who bought the stock in 2000 at a split-adjusted price of over $1,200 (no, that is not a typo) per share ever break even? Likely not while they are alive. Bad stock, bad company.

POWER TIP

Being There

The market at large, not to mention individual securities, can produce well over a typical year's worth of gains in a very short period. Witness Microsoft Corporation (MSFT) in 2006 going from the low $20s to the upper $20s in a matter of months. In anyone's book a 30% gain represents a solid annual return. This large, well-established company saw its stock price increase by several years' worth of gains in a few months' time. The key is, you have to be there for the gains. Spikes in stock prices invariably come when you least expect them, when things look the bleakest, *when emotionally it is the toughest time to own stocks.* But that is when the real dollars are made.

Do not forget that the fundamentals of a business do not change day-to-day with swings in the market price. When you are feeling apprehensive about your holdings, adopt the perspective of the company as opposed to the stock. Ultimately, you own a piece of the business. It is the performance of the company that matters over time, and the stock price will eventually reflect the company's financial fundamentals.

A Physical Education (More PE)

I learned this positive lesson in a very real way from 2000 to 2002 as the U.S. public markets were heading south during most months. I owned shares in a small but highly profitable sports magazine. The board of directors made the decision to distribute by way of a dividend all the excess profits (read cash flow) each month. As markets around the world—and the value of people's stock portfolios—were plunging, this little business was sending me what seemed to be larger and larger checks every thirty days. How could this be? The market was getting pummeled; shouldn't all businesses have been on the ropes? Nope. For most publicly traded securities—even stocks of top-quality companies and companies caught up in the premature hype of the Internet—prices in the late 1990s had gotten ahead of what revenues and earnings could justify. Even if top and bottom lines were plugging away at a company, multiple contractions (i.e., declining P/E ratios) had the prices of stocks hurtling erratically. However, in owning a privately held business with no public listing (private equity, or PE, not to be confused with P/E), I had no stock ticker flashing in my face. The only financial indicators I could use to assess the business were the financial metrics that ultimately mattered—revenues, cash flows, and operating margins. Had I been watching a wildly gyrating stock price, I am sure a seemingly good offer would have tempted me to sell and I would have missed out on those big dividend checks and future capital gains.

Bottom line: Block out the white noise, focus on the fundamentals, keep your time horizons in mind, remember that a stock price is not a company—and be patient. When you least expect it, your company—as long as it is a quality one—will see its stock spike over a matter of weeks or months, sometimes providing a year's worth or more of gains in a period not much longer than a typical European summer vacation. You want to be there for the gains; you have to be there for the gains. A couple of months can go by quickly and this can rapidly heal the pain inflicted by short-term market drops. The question is: Will you have the emotional fortitude, confidence, patience, and intelligence to put money to work when there is blood in the streets—to buy low and sell high?

ADDITIONAL CRITERIA FOR STOCK SELECTION

Now that we have reviewed the components of stock valuation and key fundamental indicators, let's examine the more refined criteria an investor should consider when selecting stocks for a portfolio. While every investor needs to develop his own set of variables to fit his investment knowledge and style, some important metrics to consider are dividend-payment measurements including duration, number of years payment has increased, and payout ratio. Let's also look at profitability metrics including ROI, ROE, return on assets (ROA), return on sales (ROS), and other industry-relevant measures as well as capital structure soundness including balance-sheet strength and debt ratios.

When it comes to dividends, a history of five years or more of heightened dividends is a good place to begin your research. For income dividend companies, 5% annual increases should be the minimum. For growth dividend companies, dividend growth rates closer to 10% or more should be viewed favorably. In terms of the payout ratio, a company that has consistently paid out less than 60% of its earnings in the case of high-yielding stocks and less than 40% in terms of lower-yielding **growth stocks** is a good starting point. If you see the payout ratio jump and stay high, this is a warning sign of earnings challenges at the company and further investigation is warranted.

An investor must also consider several important valuation metrics, depending on the type of industry that the investment target is in. The most widely examined valuation metric, and certainly a good place to begin our discussion, is that of the price/earnings ratio, or P/E. P/E ratios should be compared to the company's historical P/E range, to those of the company's peers, to the market as a whole, and to the company's growth (PEG ratio). A lower P/E ratio, combined with a favorable (as in low) PEG ratio, makes for a good investment candidate. For example, if Company X is trading at 13X earnings and its historical P/E range is 12X to 20X, the company is trading near the low end of the range. If the broad market is trading at 17X, then the target company is also trading at a discount to the overall market. If the company's earnings are growing at a faster rate than that of the overall market as defined by the S&P 500 (assuming the target company is a large-cap stock), then you are getting faster-growing earnings and paying less per dollar of earnings than you would for the broad market. In addition, if the company's earnings growth rate is in excess of its P/E, its PEG ratio is less than 1.0, which is also favorable. Finally, if the company sports a P/E ratio that is at the low end of its peers, then all valuation metrics are favorable.

Other traditional valuation metrics include **price-to-book** and **price-to-sales** ratios. For companies within the retail industry, price-to-sales is an important ratio. For companies within the financial industry, comparing a company's price to its book value is an important step because financial companies tend to trade at some multiple of **book value**. In general, when financial companies are trading at less than book they might be compelling buys, whereas when they begin trading at 1.5X to 2X book they are heading toward overvaluation. As with all industries, market leaders tend to trade at a premium vis-à-vis their peers. For example, Goldman Sachs, Inc. (GS) has traditionally traded at around 0.5X book higher than its competitors, a multiple largely justified by its superior management, trading prowess, and ability to avoid the major mistakes to which its peers have fallen prey. A company's strength within its industry must therefore be weighed when considering these financial metrics. There is a reason why a given company is number one in its industry. Investors are almost always better off buying the preeminent company in an industry rather than the second or third best competitor. Companies with dominant market shares—the so-called best of breeds—are well positioned to take advantage of their weaker brethrens' challenges. This is another lesson I learned firsthand during my days as CFO of The Active Network, Inc. throughout the late '90s and early '00s. We were the 800-pound gorilla, and when the Internet bubble burst, we had more say than Don Vito Corleone in terms of who would live and who would die in the industry. Many a competitor came to visit our "house," kissed our proverbial ring finger, and left empty-handed after being told in effect that a man's business was up to him but theirs was not a business that we wanted to enter into. Our answer was often no and once we made up our mind we didn't change it. In addition to possessing greater market share, a market leader can be the company with the greatest sales or profitability. Other competitive advantages include patents, trademarks, and brand identity.

Return on equity (ROE) is another consideration when measuring the financial strength of your investment targets. A company's return on equity is the amount of earnings per share divided by its equity per share. You should look for high and consistent ROE, preferably above 10%.

Finally, an often overlooked but vital financial criterion is that of balance-sheet strength. Most investors focus on a company's profit and loss (P&L) statement because this is where all the "action" is. However, a company's balance-sheet strength, or lack thereof, often determines the company's ability to survive and possibly thrive during inevitable industry-specific or macroeconomic downturns—those twenty-five-year floods that happen every three to five years.

POWER TIP

The Importance of Balance Sheets—The Lesson of Merck

Investors put most of their emphasis—and time—into assessing a company's profit and loss statement. To be sure, the 1990s was the decade of the P&L when top-line growth was in the spotlight. While this is certainly an important financial consideration, a company's balance sheet is just as, if not more, important in determining a company's ability to provide returns to shareholders over time, especially during such challenging periods as the '00s, the decade of the balance sheet.

Look at the case of Merck & Co., Inc. (MRK). In brief, this company was a disaster from mid-2004 to late 2005. Key drugs came under fire from regulatory authorities, a myriad of lawsuits was filed by patients, and the government sued the company over tax issues. Moreover, the pharmaceuticals industry was in a funk due to the dearth of new blockbuster drugs and the competition from generics.

Given this, you would think Merck might be on its way out à la a bad automotive or airline company. Yet, a short two years later the company's stock was higher and the company's dividend intact. Why?

Figure 3.3 **Balance-Sheet Strength in Action**

SOURCE: FINANCE.YAHOO.COM

Examining Merck in the mid-'00s as it struggled with legal and operational issues, if Merck had a weak balance sheet—if it were highly leveraged with little to no cash on its books—it probably would have been "game over" for the business or, at a minimum, the stock price would have collapsed. Such was the case for many overleveraged companies that went from the heavens to the dustbin in the late '00s. Yet several years after the company took the biggest body shot it had ever experienced, Merck was going strong, its stock having rebounded nicely and a solid dividend being paid quarter after quarter. Compare this example with the dividend cuts made by automakers Ford and General Motors Corporation (GM) during the same time period. Why did these companies feel compelled to do what all companies loathe to do, cut their dividend? Predominantly due to their weak balance sheets. This is an important lesson when it comes to equity analysis and financial appraisal. When in doubt, invest in companies with rock-solid balance sheets; look for the industry leaders, the best-of-breed companies that will not be the ones to fail when the inevitable business and financial challenges arise. This focus on quality companies with solid balance sheets will, in and of itself, be a large source of risk reduction when it comes to portfolio construction.

Now that we are convinced that we have to look beyond the P&L to determine a viable investment candidate, what are some basic balance-sheet items that can give us confidence or pause? Just as individual consumers who are leveraged up with mortgages, car loans, and credit card debt are at risk for a single bad financial event putting them over the edge, so too are companies with weak balance sheets just a recession or a delayed product launch away from financial disaster. What are some metrics that we can examine to see whether a company is close to a precipice or standing on solid ground?

The balance sheet summarizes a company's assets, liabilities, and shareholders' equity. Basic balance-sheet considerations include the **current ratio**, which is the current assets divided by current liabilities. While acceptable current ratios vary industry by industry, you should generally seek companies with ratios in the 1.5 to 2.0 range. Too low a ratio means that the company may have challenges meeting its short-term obligations whereas a ratio which is too high may mean the company is not using its current assets efficiently. The **working capital** ratio looks at current assets minus current liabilities. This figure will help you determine whether a company is able to meet its near-term obligations. A higher number is preferable, which makes intuitive sense. **Leverage** is a key measure of a company's capital structure. Does a company rely solely on its own equity to finance its assets (in other words, is it debt free?), or does it also employ debt? If the latter, how much debt is on the company's books? By dividing long-term debt by the company's total equity, you can determine a basic level of leverage. While some level of leverage can help to improve a company's return on equity (assuming the capital is deployed in a way that the return on the capital exceeds the cost of the capital), a company with too much leverage puts itself at risk of not being able to meet its obligations if its operations suffer an unexpected disruption. Unlike the profit and loss statement, the balance sheet can seem complex and murky, thus most novice investors avoid balance-sheet analysis entirely. While you do not have to read every footnote of the quarterly 10-Q, by focusing on basic and understandable measures, you will increase the probability that the company you invest in will continue to send you checks for years to come as their asset-and-liability house will be in order, thus securing both their own and your financial futures.

The Big Picture

Macroeconomic analysis—using economic indicators such as GDP rates, inflation levels, interest rates, and unemployment rates—is considered by many fundamental investors to be the least important consideration when making long-term stock selections. No one can consistently forecast major economic barometers. As the old saying goes, economists have predicted nine of the last five recessions. Even if you dedicated your entire professional life to studying, understanding, and predicting various economic criteria, you would be wrong most of the time when the news was actually released (to be later revised in most cases). Even if you manage to get a data point correct from time to time, accurately predicting both the timing and magnitude of the event in question (e.g., the unfolding of a recession within a certain time period) creates additional challenges. Further, and more to the point as an investor, you must also accurately predict the market's reaction to such events. Consistently doing so in such a way that the undertaking adds true value to your portfolio is a near impossibility. While it is true that certain sectors tend to outperform in a recession (health care, consumer staples), the drivers for a given economic cycle tend to differ each time, and the economy has a way of surprising even the smartest academics, let alone investors. Less than 5% of your investing-related time, if any time at all, should be dedicated to macroeconomic considerations.

Technical Analysis—Bottom's Up

Generally speaking, the longer the holding position, the more company fundamentals matter and the less technical variables are part of the equation. Conversely, the shorter the holding period, the more technical indicators matter and the less fundamentals play a role. Do you have a ten-year time horizon for holding stock? If so, fundamental factors such as stock valuation and competitive position within an industry should dominate the analysis. Looking to buy or sell an equity option to expire within a few days? Then fundamentals are of little consideration and technical analysis is paramount.

Figure 3.4 **Fundamental versus Technical Analysis Time Frame Considerations**

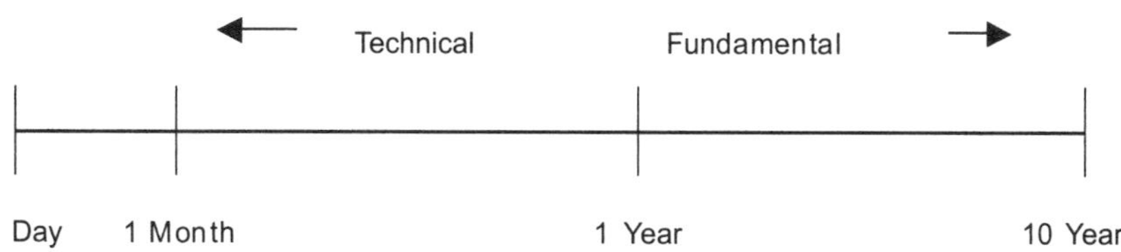

Entire books have been written on technical analysis, so I would recommend picking up one of the better tomes if you have a penchant for reading this sort of thing. Technical analysis, by and large, consists of looking at charts and retroactively justifying the movement in a stock's price. This approach pays no consideration to what is happening with a given company on an elemental level. If a chart shows an upward trend and a stock breaks above a given resistance level, a technical analyst might well recommend the stock *after* it has gone up, regardless of whether the fundamentals have changed during the interim. Technical analysis is principally beneficial when used in conjunction with fundamental analysis to determine whether a stock has created what is called a "bottom." As value investors, we are often looking for that otherwise solid company which has fallen on hard times. Value investors tend to be early. The time that it will take to turn around the situation in question is often underestimated. Therefore, it can be helpful to look at a chart to see if the company's stock price has stabilized before taking a position. After consistently finding myself early to the party, I began to incorporate more charting into my repertoire for the sole purpose of trying to identify true bottoms.

***Figure* 3.5 Charting a Stock Hitting a Bottom**

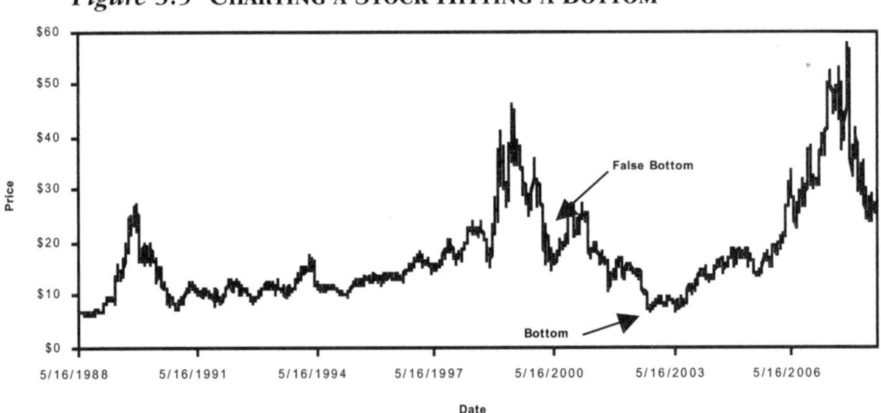

Another technical tool that can be helpful, especially when the use of options is part of your portfolio construction, is the volatility indicator VIX. VIX measures the implied volatility of the S&P 500 over thirty days (the VXN tracks the NASDAQ 100, whereas the VXD measures the implied volatility of the Dow Jones Industrial Average). Individual stocks also have their own historical and implied volatility measures. Given the relationship between high volatility levels and low stock or market prices, a high VIX or individual stock volatility reading can be a useful piece of information in validating a favorable entry point.

Trading volumes as well as insider trading (when executives of the company either buy or sell their own company's stock) are two other technical indicators that can provide insight as to whether a stock has formed a base. Often sell-offs in a given stock or the market as a whole are accompanied by very large volumes—panic selling by investors who "cannot take it anymore," or who must sell because they are getting margin calls from their brokers, or who need to raise money to pay their bills. Sales often beget sales for those in a position of weakness. Look at average daily trading volumes for a given stock. A new low with a larger-than-average volume can be a positive sign that the selling has been exhausted and a bottom is being created. Furthermore, smart company directors and senior executives will sell large blocks of stock near the tops and will put their own money to work during low points. While not a definitive indicator in and of itself, these technical indicators can provide clues as to future stock behavior.

***Figure* 3.6 VOLUME AND PRICE OVERLAY**

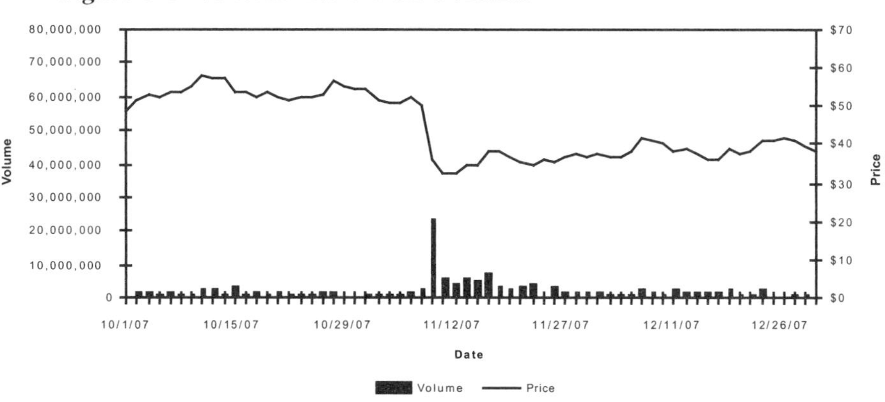

In the three days from November 7 to November 9, 2007, Company X stock fell 37.6% with an average three-day volume of 11,083,900. In the three days leading up to the plunge, the three-day average volume level for Company X was 1,724,167. This is a prime example of a huge volume increase accompanying a large price decline.

Similarly, you can examine charts to see where a stock or **exchange traded fund (ETF)** has traded over a certain time period. Often when a security has dropped in price, it is tempting to get in on the rationale that, if the stock has dropped 20%, it must now be of compelling value. Without a longer-term price appreciation perspective, however, one can lose sight of the fact that the security may have previously run up several hundred percentage points, and thus a 20% drop off its recent highs represents only a small portion of the total decline potential inherent in the security, based on the longer-term run-up.

***Figure* 3.7 SHORT-TERM PERSPECTIVE ON STOCK DECLINE**

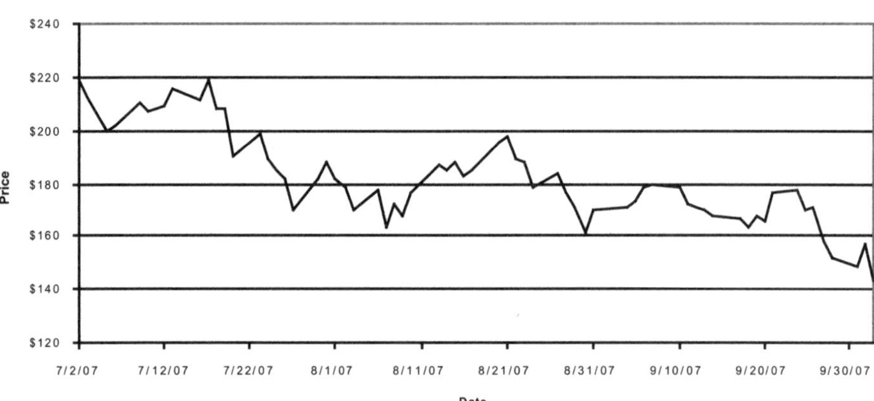

***Figure* 3.8 LONG-TERM PERSPECTIVE TO ASSESS STOCK DECLINE**

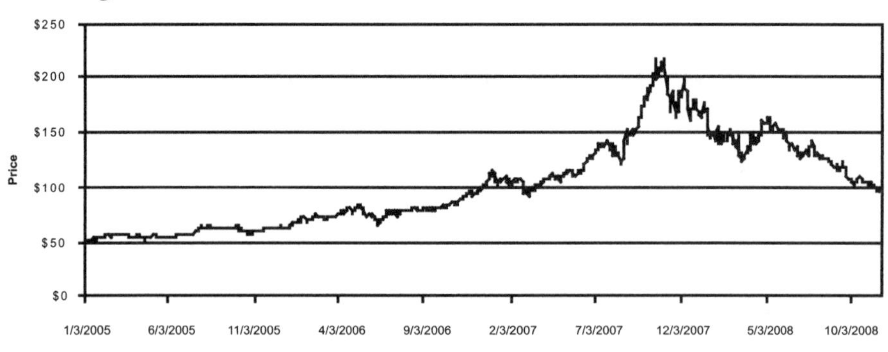

The fact is, stocks can drop by 20% repeatedly. A $50 stock dropping 20% goes to $40. A 20% decline from there puts the stock at $32. Another 20% slump puts the stock at $25.60. Ask someone how much a stock that has dropped 20% three times has declined in total and the typical answer will be 60%, or for the more sophisticated, "more than 60% given the math of compounding." Wrong both times. The stock has not even declined 50% yet. The math gets even uglier. Another 20% drop puts the stock at $20.48, and a fifth decline of 20% puts the stock at $16.38. That is five 20% drops and the stock is "only" down 67% door-to-door. Another 20% drop puts the stock at $13.10 and down a little over 73%. That means a whopping incremental 20% plummet only decreased the total loss by a little over 6% on an absolute basis. (When you look at the math behind making up for losses, you will quickly see that being down 70% versus being down 60% is a much larger difference than it appears.)

Therefore, charts can put into perspective how much stocks have run up and how much they can fall. When you are in the heat of the stock market day and you see a stock or sector "crack" 20% and are tempted to jump on this opportunity, check a longer-term chart to put the near-term price movements into a longer-term perspective.

In summary, technical analysis has a limited place in stock selection, thus, as with macroeconomic analysis, it should consume less than 10% of your total money-management-related time if your time horizon is a year or longer, and perhaps 10% to 20% of your time if you are predominantly a trader rather than an investor. And you can certainly outperform the market with zero technical analysis incorporated into your stock selection process. There are few to no purely technical analysts, or chartists, who consistently outperform the market year after year, so use technical analysis as a "validator" of your fundamental analysis and focus your time and energy on areas where true value can be added to your portfolio.

We the People

Demographic analysis is the practice of looking at long-term trends in society and the economy at large to identify industries or companies that will benefit from broad shifts in such things as migration, and the ratio between urban and suburban dwellers. One example would be the aging of America. Statistics about the number of baby boomers entering retirement, for example, might support an investment in health care companies that would benefit from increased prescription drug use.

Getting Industrious

Industry analysis is the next criterion to use when building a portfolio designed to outperform the broader market. Now we are starting to get into areas beyond fundamental/valuation analysis that truly merit the majority of our time and attention as investors. Being in the right industry or sector is a vital starting point to obtaining superior returns. Even for those who focus on individual stock selection as opposed to building a portfolio of ETFs, industry analysis is essential for increasing the probability that they are at least playing in the right field.

Figure 3.9 **INDUSTRY SECTORS**

1. Consumer Discretionary
2. Consumer Staples
3. Energy
4. Financial
5. Health Care
6. Industrials
7. Information Technology
8. Materials
9. Telecom Services
10. Utilities

SOURCE: MORGAN STANLEY CAPITAL INTERNATIONAL AND STANDARD & POOR'S

Of course the above sectors can be broken down in more detail. For example, within the financial grouping, you have brokerage, mortgage, thrift, insurance, REITs, regional banking, and the like.

What should you look for in industry analysis? One simple but effective framework is known as the Five Forces. This approach analyzes: (1) competition within the industry, (2) potential for new entrants, (3) power of suppliers, (4) power of customers, and (5) threat of substitute products. Add to this technological change that makes a given offering or process obsolete (the disruption principle).

For competition, examine how many competitors there are within the industry. How large are they? Are they well financed? Is the industry fragmented (e.g., laundry, with hundreds or thousands of competitors) or concentrated (such as the auto industry with its small number of players)? Is this an industry that requires a significant amount of capital to enter, like the aviation industry, or are barriers to entry quite low, as is the case with most dot-coms?

Other considerations include geographic area. Is the industry local in nature? National? Global? What is the industry size? What are the trends? What is the outlook? How is the regulatory environment?

Demographic and psychographic attributes of the industry and its customers are also important. Demographic information includes population and household size, median income, age, sex, race; psychographic considerations include lifestyle information, tastes, and buying habits.

Most people have other full-time jobs, families to look after, and hobbies to enjoy. Taking the time to become an expert in so many areas is difficult if not impossible. Thus, fundamental company analysis is where the vast majority of investing research time should be dedicated. At the end of the day, it is how much a company earns—and how much you paid for those earnings—that largely determines investing success.

CHAPTER 4

Keeping Your Options Open

The focus of this chapter is on how to use options to generate income, enhance returns, and provide downside protection. Sounds easy enough. In reality, options can be complex and confusing, if not outright intimidating. Many people think of derivatives in general or options in particular as risky. To be sure, any vehicle can be a source of danger depending on how it is used. A knife in the hands of an ill-intended robber is dangerous; a blade in the palm of a talented surgeon can be lifesaving. The purpose of this chapter is to provide you the tools to use options in conjunction with quality dividend-paying companies to your financial advantage.

An option is a derivative, which is simply a fancy term for the fact that the option's movement in price is a function of an underlying security, be it a stock, ETF, index, or other investment vehicle. The easiest and best way to think about options is to compare them to insurance. When you buy fire insurance, for example, you sign a contract (the policy) and pay money (the insurance premium) in order to be protected against the occurrence of a fire for a specified period of time (the duration of the contract). If the event does occur prior to the expiration of the contract period, then you receive whatever your contract calls for (e.g., the replacement cost of your house).

The insurance company hopes the event you are protecting yourself against never occurs. If your house does not burn down, the insurance company keeps the entire premium you paid without making any payments itself, an outcome that adds to the company's profits. Of course accidents do occur and insurance policies are paid out periodically. The insurance company's goal is to write enough policies and price them in such a way that after collecting all the premiums and paying out all the claims—and paying operating costs—it ends up with a big profit.

Let's apply this analogy to options. Say you are planning to buy a house in the next year. You anticipate the house will cost $100,000. You intend to borrow 75% of the cost, thus you need $25,000 as a down payment. You own 1,000 shares of Company X, which currently trades for $27 per share. For tax or other reasons you do not want to sell your shares today—perhaps you think Company X's stock will go up in the coming months or maybe you want to wait until your holding period exceeds one year so that you are subject to capital rather than income gains. However, this is your sole source of funds for the down payment on that home and you want to be sure that you have at least $25,000 when it comes time to purchase the house. How do you ensure if not insure this outcome? You can buy stock insurance; in this case you can buy a **put option**, which gives you the right, but not the obligation, to sell a stock at a given price during a specified period. For those speculating on price appreciation, a **call option** gives you the right to buy a stock at a given price for a certain time period.

Back to our soon-to-be home owner. In this case you might buy Company X insurance to be sure you will receive at least $25 per share for your stock during the course of the contract. In other words, you would buy—pay a premium for—a put option that would give you the right, *no matter what happens with Company X's stock price* (i.e., even if it were to burn to the ground), to sell the stock for a fixed price while the contract is in effect. Were the company to go bankrupt and the stock to fall to zero, you have locked in a preset sales price of $25 per share. In order to buy 1,000 shares' worth of protection, the put buyer would need to purchase ten contracts, as each option contract represents 100 shares of the underlying security. For an option priced at $0.50 per contract, you would be fully covered by paying $500 (10 contracts X 100 shares per contract X $0.50

per share = $500 of premium paid). By entering such a put option contract, a Company X investor is certain to have at least $25,000 of stock when it comes time to make the down payment. Whether this insurance is worth it, whether the contract is of good value, is up to the buyer of the insurance.

As with stock, options have a **bid price** and an **ask price**, the former being the price at which an option can be sold and the latter the price at which the option can be bought. The difference, or delta, between the bid and ask is the **spread**. You will often also see the term **last** listed on a quote screen. This is simply the price at which the most recent trade was made. This may differ substantially from bid/ask quotes for relatively illiquid options. (For portfolio valuation purposes, you should use a mid-point between bid/ask rather than the last trade price.) A typical option might be trading at $0.80 by $0.90, meaning that you could sell the option for $0.80 per contract and buy the option for $0.90 per contract. Often you will see such wide spreads in options—sometimes 30% or more—whereas highly liquid securities such as IBM stock might trade at $110.08 X $110.09, a .01% spread. In options trading in general, and particularly in cases where liquidity is low, it is vital that orders be placed on a **limit order** rather than a **market order** basis. If you are not **filled** at your initial limit price, the spread will often narrow, at which point you can alter your limit order to see if you will get filled there. As with most things in life, you won't get anything unless you ask!

When stocks traded in fractions, options premiums traded in one-eights. The introduction of decimal pricing helped to narrow spreads in options, which are inherently less efficient in terms of bid/ask spreads than equities due in part to their lower liquidity.

Figure 4.1 **Spreads Associated with Option Increments**

Options Trading In	Bid	Ask	Spread	% Spread
1/8	1/2	5/8	1/8	25%
Dimes	$0.50	$0.60	$0.10	20%
Nickels	$0.50	$0.55	$0.05	10%
Pennies	$0.50	$0.51	$0.01	2%

As options began to trade in smaller units the spread percentages decreased dramatically, increasing options' market efficiency and improving their cost effectiveness.

The stated price per share at which the buyer can purchase (in the case of a call) or sell (in the case of a put) a given stock is called the **strike price**. Typically strike prices are spaced in 2.5 or 5 point increments. For example, a stock trading at $38 per share will have options with strike prices of $32.50, $35, $37.50, $40, $42.50, and so on. Not long after penny increments were introduced to options, $1 strike-price steps were made available on selective stocks trading under $20 per share. More recently $1 increments were made available to strike prices above $20 per share on certain securities.

The date on which the contract ends is called the **expiration date**. Most options expire on the Saturday following the third Friday of each month, with trading ending at close of day that Friday. There are important exceptions, however, as noted below. Some securities have options that expire each month, while others have option expiration dates that are quarterly. You can also buy or sell an option mid-cycle, as options are traded on all market days. This means that you can establish virtually limitless positions that take into consideration intra-month events such as earnings announcements. Certain widely traded options, such as the ones that trade on the very popular SPYs, have what are called "weeklies," or options that expire every week rather than every month.

There are two main types of expiration, **American-style** and **European-style**. American-style options can be exercised at any time by their owners, while European-style options can only be exercised on their expiration dates. This is an important consideration for options that become in-the-money prior to expiration and can be assigned prematurely (in the case of American-style). Furthermore, most European-style options are **cash-settled based**, meaning the owner of the option gets credited cash (or is debited) in the amount equal to the difference between the index's closing price and the strike price of the option rather than receiving any securities. The owner of an American-style option, however, must buy or sell the stock depending on whether he is a holder of puts or calls, and then buy/sell the newly acquired underlying security in order to profit accordingly. Most individual stock equity options, as well as those available on ETFs (e.g., SPY, which is the S&P 500; QQQQ, which is the NASDAQ 100; or DIA, which is the Dow Jones Industrial Average), trade American-style through the end of trading on the third Friday of each month. Most index options (e.g., SPX, NDX), however, trade European-style and stop trading at the end of the day on the Thursday before the third Friday of each month.

It is important to note that the price for which the European-style options settle—or the **settlement price**—is determined on the Friday morning following the end of trading on Thursday and may differ dramatically from the final price the day before. If, for example, you own contracts of the $1,950 strike price calls of NDX (which trades European-style) and the NDX closes at $1,955.45 on the third Thursday of the month, you might think you are headed for a payday since your calls are $5.45 in-the-money. Let's say, however, that some bad corporate or macroeconomic news comes out after the bell on Thursday, leading to a big down opening on Friday. The settlement price of the NDX on Friday morning might be under $1,950, leaving your calls worthless. This is an important consideration when deciding whether to close out options prior to expiration. In effect, you enter a "blackout" period for about sixteen hours, with events occurring during this period that could affect your pocketbook though you are unable to manage the position—not just because market hours are over, but because it is "game over" for the particular option (but the score is still being tallied). Remember, however, that just because a European-style option cannot be exercised prior to expiration does not mean it cannot be traded prior to expiration. It can be traded any time the market for options is open, with European-style options often trading until 4:15 P.M. EST rather than 4:00 P.M. when most equity markets close for business. As a good rule of thumb, if you are short index options that are within 2% of being in-the-money, it is best to close them out before the blackout period between Thursday's close and Friday's open. While, statistically speaking, it will not happen often, all it takes is one 3%+ overnight move to wipe out all the gains you made from letting your near-the-money options expire. It takes a lot of nickel gains to make up for one multi-dollar loss, and the period around options expiration is not called the "witching hour" for nothing; the third Thursday and Friday of each month tend to be some of the most volatile periods. (I draw the analogy of using options actively to what my friends who are commercial pilots describe as a "typical" flight. There is a lot of activity at takeoff—when you put the positions on—and landing—options expiration—but in between you spend much of your time checking the weather or in our case doing your fundamental analysis.) So do the smart thing and pay your broker a commission for the pleasure of buying back out-of-the-money and about-to-expire European-style index options for a nickel and change. You will be glad you did on the one morning a year you wake up to some dramatic event that causes the market to open at a dramatically different price than the previous session's close.

POWER TIP

Tickers for Settlement Prices of Major Indices

Index options, which trade European-style, stop trading on the third Thursday of each month (Tuesday for VIX options). The prices at which they settle, however, are based on the Friday morning prices (Wednesday for VIX). These prices are published the morning after the respective option expiration. Note that you will sometimes need to put a $ sign before the ticker.

NASDAQ 100: NDS
Russell 2000: RLS
VIX: VRO
Dow Jones Industrials: DJS
S&P 500: SET

The ability to buy and sell options with varying expiration dates at varying strike prices allows the options trader to fine-tune his hedging, trading, or speculating strategies. Note also that there is limited **counterparty risk** in trading options, meaning the person or institution with whom you have entered into the transaction will not fail to fulfill their contractual obligation. In general, when agreements involve only two parties, then counterparty risk is at its greatest; when a well-established and financially sound intermediary is involved, counterparty risk is mitigated. In the case of listed derivatives, the exchange's clearinghouse is the counterparty to each option sale or purchase, eliminating the possibility that you will be unable to sell the stock on which you have purchased put options. This structure is more important than it seems on the surface, and it is certainly in stark contrast to the myriad of transaction failures that occurred during the credit bust of the late '00s when many investors and traders alike found themselves in transactions that fell apart due to counterparty risk.

OPTIONS LEVELS AND QUALIFICATIONS

There are four different levels of options trading. A broker determines the level for which an investor qualifies depending on the nature of the account as well as variables that include the investor's lifetime trading experience, **net worth**, income, number of trades made per year, and average trade size. For qualified accounts (IRAs, etc.), the types of options you can trade are limited by law, regardless of how much experience you have or how large the account is. These limits are meant to protect investors from taking on too much risk in their retirement accounts. The following represents the various options levels and what types of trades can be conducted given the level of options-trading authorization:

Level 0: This level allows for covered options and protective options, long stock/short calls (covered calls), long stock/long puts (protective puts), short stock/short puts (covered puts), and short stock/long calls (protective calls).

Level 1: This level allows all of the level 0 transactions plus long options, long puts and calls, long straddles, long combos, long strangles, and cash-secured equity put-writing.

Level 2: This level includes all transactions in levels 0 and 1 plus spreads, credit and debit spreads, diagonal call and put spreads, and ratio spreads.

Level 3: This level includes all transactions in levels 0 to 2 plus uncovered options, uncovered puts and calls, short straddles, short strangles, and short combos.

It is important to know the level for which you qualify and the types of options that you can trade. Note that some firms use the scale 0 to 3 while others use 1 to 4. Even for investors who otherwise qualify, brokerage firms often require an initial minimum equity account value of $25,000 or more for the sale of options. Note that some of the more aggressive techniques detailed in this book (e.g., naked calls) are only available to those who qualify for the highest level of options trading. Be sure to consult your broker or financial institution to determine the tools you can use in your trading program.

TRADING OPTIONS

Option **chains** are listed on the **CBOE** (Chicago Board Options Exchange) and other popular Web sites and the following information is provided: underlying security ticker symbol, strike price, expiration date, and type of option (call or put). For example, DLQGE stands for "Dell Computer July '08 expiration $25 strike price call." An option chain might also include a final letter after a dash. This letter indicates which exchange the option trades on (B for Boston, E for CBOE, P for Pacific, A for Amex, X for Philadelphia, and so on). To add more confusion to this alphabet soup, sometimes the first two or three letters in the option chain will be different even if the underlying stock is the same. For example, whereas the July '08 $25 Dell calls are DLQGE, the July '08 $20 Dell calls have the ticker symbol DLYGD.

It is also not uncommon for option chains to change in the middle of the game. Options that have far-dated expiration periods will often see their chains altered as the expiration goes from twelve months out to nine months out. This is necessary since, for example, an option for a given security expiring in January 2010 cannot share the same chain as an option expiring in January 2009. Finally, since many option chains have five letters as mutual funds do, sometimes you will use what seems to be a viable ticker symbol only to receive the message "ticker not valid" when attempting to make a trade. When

Figure 4.2 **Option Codes**

Codes to Determine Expiration Month of Call or Put

	JAN	FEB	MAR	APR	MAY	JUN	JUL	AUG	SEP	OCT	NOV	DEC
Calls	A	B	C	D	E	F	G	H	I	J	K	L
Puts	M	N	O	P	Q	R	S	T	U	V	W	X

Codes to Determine Option Strike Price

A	B	C	D	E	F	G	H	I	J	K	L	M	N	O	P	Q	R	S	T
5	10	15	20	25	30	35	40	45	50	55	60	65	70	75	80	85	90	95	100
105	110	115	120	125	130	135	140	145	150	155	160	165	170	175	180	185	190	195	200
205	210	215	220	225	230	235	240	245	250	255	260	265	270	275	280	285	290	295	300
305	310	315	320	325	330	335	340	345	350	355	360	365	370	375	380	385	390	395	400
405	410	415	420	425	430	435	440	445	450	455	460	465	470	475	480	485	490	495	500
505	510	515	520	525	530	535	540	545	550	555	560	565	570	575	580	585	590	595	600
605	610	615	620	625	630	635	640	645	650	655	660	665	670	675	680	685	690	695	700
705	710	715	720	725	730	735	740	745	750	755	760	765	770	775	780	785	790	795	800

U	V	W	X	Y	Z
					2.5
7.5	12.5	17.5	22.5	27.5	32.5
37.5	42.5	47.5	52.5	57.5	62.5
67.5	72.5	77.5	82.5	87.5	92.5
97.5	102.5	107.5	112.5	117.5	122.5
127.5	132.5	137.5	142.5	147.5	152.5
157.5	162.5	167.5	172.5	177.5	182.5
187.5	192.5	197.5	202.5	207.5	212.5
217.5	222.5	227.5	232.5	237.5	242.5

this occurs, call your broker and have him manually enter the trade for you, but be sure to get your online commission rate (every penny counts).

After some practice you will begin to recognize options chains, but you should continue to be careful when you enter your orders for a particular options trade. You do not want to end up selling Dell July $25 puts when you meant to buy Dell July $25 calls. (If you do not have a given contract open, a sophisticated trading platform will not let you sell an option to close because you cannot sell to close a contract you have not bought to open—see below.) Finally, when you enter a ticker symbol to get a quote (as opposed to when you are making a trade), you will often have to add ".O", as in "DLYGD.O," because this designates the ticker chain as an option quote.

In looking up option quotes, you will see, as with stocks, the **volume** of contracts traded. You will also see a term called **open interest**, which is the total number of contracts not yet exercised or expired and which should not be confused with volume. Open interest gives you a sense of the liquidity associated with a given option. A low or zero open interest position generally means that there is little activity in the option. Spreads for such options are generally large, and thus you should place limit orders rather than market orders so that prices received are not surprisingly different from published bid/ask spreads. (That said, when calculating your potential return from a buy write, for example, only the amount you receive for selling the call matters in determining if the return potential is favorable. Even if after selling the option you show a loss by virtue of the option being priced at the ask post-sale, eventually the options price will come in and you will capture the entire profit potential associated with the price you received for your option sale.) In addition, large trading volume relative to open interest is an indication of high activity and interest in the company on which the options are being traded.

As discussed above, the buyer of an option pays a premium to the seller of the option. This premium has three components: the **total premium**, the **intrinsic value premium**, and the **time value premium**. Let's examine each. The total premium is just what the name implies: It is the amount paid for the option contract. The

intrinsic value is the amount by which an option is **in-the-money (ITM)**. Let's say you buy a put option for $2.50 per contract, giving you the right to sell Dell stock at $25 per share (the strike price). At the time you buy this put, Dell is selling for $24 per share. Under this put scenario, the option is in-the-money, thus the intrinsic value of the option is $1, which is the strike price minus the share price. Since the total premium is made up of the intrinsic value and the time premium, the remaining $1.50 premium must be time premium. Only when options are in-the-money do they have intrinsic value. Options that are sold **out-of-the-money (OTM)** have no intrinsic value, only time value. In the example above, if Dell were selling for $26 per share when you bought the $25 put, the cost of the put would have been perhaps $0.80, the entire premium being time value.

Figure **4.3** **TIME VALUE VERSUS INTRINSIC VALUE FOR PUTS**

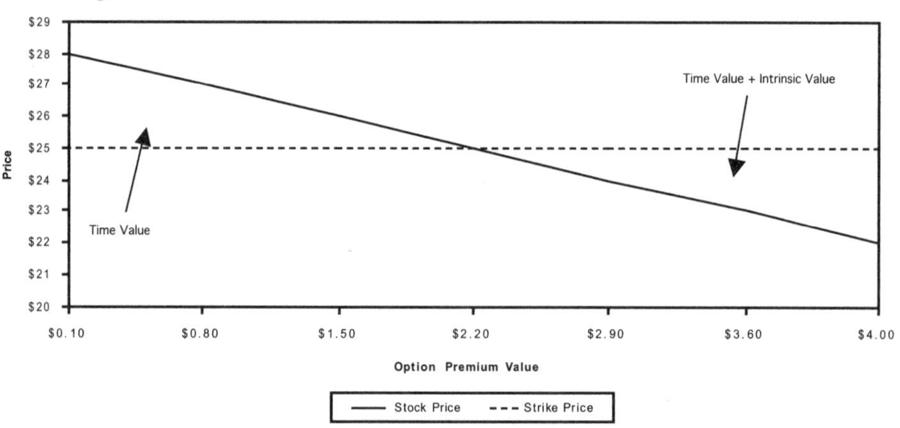

In basic terms, call option buyers want the underlying stock to go up; this is a bullish or "long" bet. Conversely, put option buyers want the price of the underlying security to go down in order to profit from the position. This is a "short" or bearish bet. When you buy an option contract you are **buying to open**. If you sell this contract, you are **selling to close**. If you sell the option short instead of buying a put or call long, you are **selling to open**. For example, if Dell is trading at $28 per share and you want to own 1,000 shares of the stock, but only at a lower price, you may sell ten contracts of $27.50 puts to open. If the put option price is $1.20 of premium per contract, you will receive $1,200. If the underlying stock price goes up and the short put contracts begin to lose value, you might choose to **buy to close** the contracts, thus completing the transaction (selling high, buying low). Alternately, you can wait until expiration date to have the option expire worthless if the stock is trading above the strike price in the case of holding a put short.

Figure 4.4 **Option Transactions**

	Long	Short
Put	Buy Put to Open Sell Put to Close	Sell Put to Open Buy Put to Close
Call	Buy Call to Open Sell Call to Close	Sell Call to Open Buy Call to Close

Trading Places

Selling options can be confusing at first since selling a put to open seems like a "double negative." If you are getting confused, place yourself in the position of the option buyer. In buying a put, you want the stock to drop in order to profit. If you are the seller of the put, you want the opposite to occur, the stock price to go up. Using the insurance example, the seller of the option has in effect sold insurance to the buyer of the option, the seller betting that the event being protected against (in this case the stock price falling below the strike price) never occurs.

Rather than buying an option to close that you originally sold to open, you might also let an option contract expire if the stock price is above the strike price (in the case of a put) or below the strike price (in the case of a call). Put another way, if an option is out-of-the-money at the time of expiration, you do not need to close out the contract; rather, you can simply let it expire worthless and save the commission dollars and the nickel or dime per share you will need to pay when OTM about-to-expire options are trading at $0 X $0.05 or $0.10. If an option is in-the-money—the stock price is below the strike price in the case of a put or above the strike price in the case of a call—you might choose to become **exercised**, or **assigned**, which means you are required to buy the stock if you have sold puts or sell the stock if you are short covered calls (if you are short naked calls, you become short the stock upon expiration, which is the mirror image of being required to buy the stock if your short puts become assigned). Any option that is in-the-money $0.01 or more at the time of expiration will be subject to being exercised. This threshold is down from $0.05 effective mid-year 2008, so this should be taken into consideration when deciding whether to close open positions prior to expiration.

Note that whether you are long or short an option, you do not have to get assigned—or exercise the option—if it is in-the-money. You can always close out the transaction prior to expiration without ever owning the underlying security. For example, if you bought Dell $25 calls long for $0.75 per contract and the stock is trading at $28 per share just prior to expiration, you can sell the calls at a profit that will be equivalent to your exercising the option and selling the stock at the then market price. In the case of selling the option, its value would be approximately $3.10 just prior to expiration ($3 of intrinsic value and a few pennies of time value). If, instead of selling the call option in the secondary market for $3.10, you exercised the option, you would buy the stock at $25 per share and either hold the shares or immediately sell the stock at $28 per share (the then market price), which would again yield an approximate $3 per-share profit.

Let's Roll

In addition to either closing out your option contract prior to expiration or exercising it upon expiration, another alternative is to **roll** your option to a later-dated expiration period. Rolling an option involves

Figure 4.5 **Closing an ITM Option Contract**

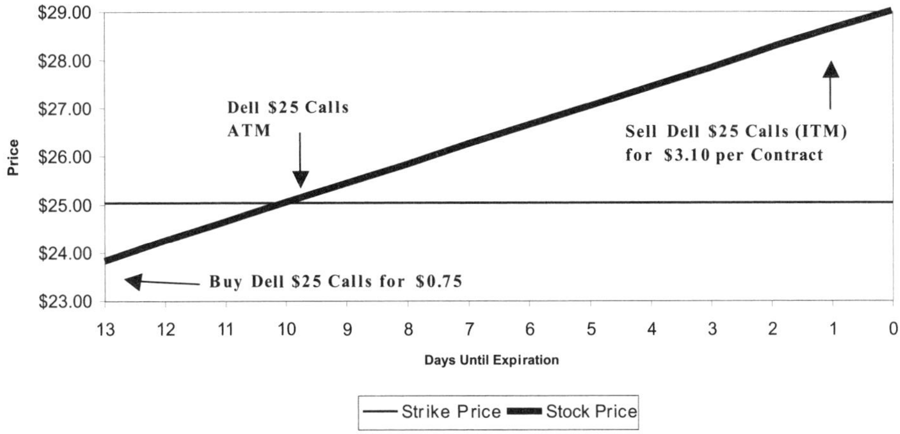

Price
$29.00
$28.00
$27.00
$26.00
$25.00
$24.00
$23.00
Dell $25 Calls
ATM
Sell Dell $25 Calls (ITM)
for $3.10 per Contract
Buy Dell $25 Calls for $0.75
13 12 11 10 9 8 7 6 5 4 3 2 1 0
Days Until Expiration
Strike Price
Stock Price

POWER TIP

Gimme Credit

When you sell an option, your account gets credited immediately with the premium amount sold and you can invest this cash in other securities. This is a technique Warren Buffett has used that is no different from when he sells insurance premiums as a means to generate cash to invest in the stock market. You can have your credited cash earn interest, you can use the cash to buy a put for downside protection, you can go out and spend it, you can buy additional shares...you can take a friend out to dinner. The cash is immediate, it is real. Enjoy!

buying the about-to-expire option to close and concurrently selling to open a later-dated option either at the same strike price (a straight time roll) or a different strike price (to **roll up and out**). This is an advanced technique that can optimize the benefits associated with receiving time premium. For example, if you have sold an OTM $27.50 put and the stock price has dropped to $26.50, the option price will be trading for a little over $1 just prior to expiration. Rather than being assigned or permanently closing out the position, you might choose to buy back the put and roll it out to a later-dated expiration date, receiving what is called a **delta premium**. You might also hear the term **credit spread**, which represents the net gain from proceeds received by way of selling an option with a higher price less the money spent in concurrently buying back the original option at a lower price. While the difference is subtle, I am differentiating between the common trading practice of simultaneously buying/selling two options with different strike prices for a net credit and the technique of closing one option out and selling a later-dated option to take its place. The latter, which we are terming the delta premium, is simply the difference between the price of the about-to-expire option premium you are buying to close and the price of the later-dated option premium you are selling to open for the later-dated option. By definition, all the delta premium in this example is time value premium since the options are in-the-money. The goal is to buy the put back for $1.10, for example, and to sell a later-dated option for $1.50, gaining a net credit to your account of $0.40 per share, which represents the thirty or sixty days of additional time premium. You would typically do this if you still felt bullish on the underlying stock but did not want to own it and thus chose not to get assigned.

On the call side, if you have bought a stock at $28 and sold the $30 calls for $1.50 of premium, the stock might close just below $30 at time of expiration. If you are hesitant on the stock or if the market is behaving bearishly, you could roll down rather than rolling out or up by selling the ITM $27.50s for the most significant protection (remember, you have already collected $1.50 premium, so your effective purchase price has been lowered to $26.50, thus even selling the $27.50s at this time allows for profits on the position even though your stock purchase price was $28 per share). Clearly, your upside potential is limited here, but you are giving yourself some solid downside safety. The middle-of-the-road tactic would be to sell the later-dated $30 strike price calls. If, however, you are feeling bullish on the stock you can roll the options up and out by selling the $32.50s, which will offer you the least amount of premium but the greatest amount of upside capital potential. When deciding what strike price to sell next, you are weighing the trade-offs of maximum gains/least protection associated with a higher strike price versus lower gains/maximum protection that the ATM or ITM calls afford you.

There will also be times when the call you sold earlier is trading for pennies several weeks before expiration. If you sold a call for $1.00 per contract and it is now trading at $0.05 X $0.10 a week or more prior to expiration, you have already captured in excess of 80% of the total profit potential associated with this position. Rather than waiting until expiration to pick up the final nickel or two, consider rolling the option to a later-dated expiration period once you have captured 80% or more of the profit potential associated with the about-to-expire option. In waiting until expiration, you are giving up premium associated with options set to expire in sixty or ninety days. Simply put, you have only a dime or two to gain from the option you currently hold short, whereas you may lose much more than that in waiting until expiration, the later-dated options declining from $1.80 to $1.35 during the two-week period you are waiting for your (negative) ten cents to turn into zero.

Do the Write Thing: Being Covered and Getting Naked

As we have learned, options can be either bought or sold. When you buy an option you are **long** the option. As with selling equities short—borrowing shares you do not own in hopes of buying them back at a lower price—when your first transaction is to sell an option you are short the option. A short option can either be **covered** or **naked**.

An example of the former would be a **covered call** option, also known as a **buy write**. This occurs when you own a stock long and sell, or **write**, calls against that long stock. For instance, if you own Company X stock long at $27 and you sell the $27.50 calls short for $0.80 per contract, the call is covered because the short call position is offset by the long equity position. (If no long equity position existed, the call would be naked rather than covered.) In this case, you are trading potential upside for some income and downside protection. If the stock closes below $27.50 at the time of expiration, you earn the entire premium and continue to own the stock. If, however, the stock is above $27.50 at expiration time, you are required to sell your stock at $27.50 even if the stock is trading substantially higher.

Figure 4.6 **Covered Call Scenarios**

Closing Price at Expiration	Outcome	Total Position Profit	Profit Source	Opportunity Cost (of Selling Stock Instead of Options)
$27.00	Option expires worthless.	$0.80	Full premium from option sale	$0.00
$27.50	Option expires worthless.	$1.30	Full premium from option sale + $0.50 capital gains	$0.00
$28.00	Option is exercised. Forced to Sell Stock.	$1.30	$0.80 + $27.50 - $27	$0.00
$28.50	Option is exercised. Forced to Sell Stock.	$1.30	$0.80 + $27.50 - $27	$0.20
$29.00	Option is exercised. Forced to Sell Stock.	$1.30	$0.80 + $27.50 - $27	$0.70
$29.50	Option is exercised. Forced to Sell Stock.	$1.30	$0.80 + $27.50 - $27	$1.20

Covered calls limit your profit potential but still provide downside protection. Were the stock to close sharply down, you still benefit from the full premium of the option sale. However, if the stock were to close above the strike, your upside is limited to the premium you receive from the sale of the option, plus the strike price (the price at which you sold the stock to the option buyer) less the original stock purchase price—in this case $27. If the stock were to close above the strike and you had not sold options, your upside via capital gains would be unlimited.

Let's look at how covered calls work by examining a $50,000 portfolio. At its starting point, your portfolio shows $50,000 of cash and no other positions. In order to get some equity exposure, you buy 1,000 shares of broad-based ETF X trading at $49 per share. Now your portfolio shows a long position of 1,000 shares of ETF X at $49 per share for a total value of $49,000, plus $1,000 of cash. In order to generate income and provide some hedging, you sell short 10 OTM calls, specifically the $50 strike price calls for $2.30 of premium per share. What does your portfolio look like now? After the sale of the short calls, $2,300 of cash is deposited immediately into your account so that your cash balance is now $3,300. There is also an offsetting debit to the account, specifically a short position in the amount of ($2,300). This short position with a negative balance is just like any other position in your account. It can gain in value by becoming less negative or drop in value by becoming more negative.

Figure 4.7 **Transaction Impacts on Positions**

	Step 1	Step 2	Step 3
Action:	Start Portfolio	Buy ETF	Short OTM Calls
Positions:	$50,000 Cash	$49,000 ETF $1,000 Cash	$49,000 ETF $3,300 Cash ($2,300) Short Calls on ETF
Total Portfolio Value:	$50,000	$50,000	$50,000

Your Portfolio: Shorting Calls

Three possible outcomes exist from this position: ETF X stays flat, ETF X decreases in price, or ETF X increases in price above $50 per share. Let's examine each scenario. If the ETF price is still $49 per share at the time of expiration, then the short position will be worth $0 (up from –$2,300) and you will have collected the premium as profit. At this point you can elect to sell additional option premium via later-dated options or hold the position unhedged if you feel its capital gains prospects are sound. If the ETF price is below $49 per share at the time of expiration, you have still made $2,300 from selling the short call and you simply have an unrealized capital loss on the equity position itself. However, if the ETF is trading above $46.70 per share, you are still ahead on the total position as the $2.30 per share collected reduces your break-even point to $46.70, and, in any case, you are better off for having sold the calls. Finally, the stock price could be above $50 per share at the time of expiration. In this case, unless you close out (buy back) the option prior to expiration, your stock will be sold, or assigned, and you will have gained $1 per share, or $1,000 on your equity, in addition to the $2.30 per share for the covered calls. In summary, the sale of calls on long positions in your portfolio is a conservative way to generate income and provide some downside protection. This strategy works particularly well for volatile positions that have recently had a big run-up and from which you are considering taking profits. If you want to own a stock for the long term and think it has considerable additional upside potential, you should not sell covered calls because you risk missing those future gains if you are forced to sell the stock. At a minimum in this scenario, you should only **hedge** part of the position (e.g., sell only five call contracts representing 500 shares if you own 1,000 shares of the stock).

Options provide flexibility, precision, and predictability; you can choose exact strike prices and expiration dates. You can elect to hedge a position in its entirety, or in any percentage thereof (e.g., if you own 1,000 shares of a given stock, you can sell a single call to hedge 10% of the position, two calls to hedge 20%, or any number of calls up to ten, which will make the long position fully covered). To focus on growth, buy growth stocks and sell few or no calls. To maximize income and downside protection, buy quality dividend-paying stocks and sell options that are very close to the money. You can focus on capital preservation and income by selling at-the-money calls on part of the position, and on capital gains by selling OTM calls on the remaining number of shares. While you cannot predict nor control future stock price movements, you can know with certainty the outcome of various options scenarios based on closing equity prices.

Figure 4.8 **COVERED CALL GAIN/HEDGE SCENARIOS**

		Expiration Date				
Strike Price		**May**	**June**	**July**	**August**	**September**
$42.50	Premium Earned	**$2.00**	**$2.75**	**$3.35**	**$4.80**	**$5.75**
	Max Gain	$0.33	$1.08	$1.68	$3.13	$4.08
	Max Gain %	0.75%	2.45%	3.80%	7.09%	9.24%
	Effective Sale Price	$44.50	$45.25	$45.85	$47.30	$48.25
	Effective Hedge	4.53%	6.23%	7.58%	10.87%	13.02%
$45.00	Premium Earned	**$0.45**	**$1.32**	**$1.93**	**$3.50**	**$4.50**
	Max Gain	$1.28	$2.15	$2.76	$4.33	$5.33
	Max Gain %	2.90%	4.87%	6.25%	9.80%	12.07%
	Effective Sale Price	$45.45	$46.32	$46.93	$48.50	$49.50
	Effective Hedge	1.02%	2.99%	4.37%	7.92%	10.19%
$47.50	Premium Earned	**$0.09**	**$0.52**	**$1.01**	**$2.43**	**N/A**
	Max Gain	$3.42	$3.85	$4.34	$5.76	
	Max Gain %	7.74%	8.72%	9.83%	13.04%	
	Effective Sale Price	$47.59	$48.02	$48.51	$49.93	
	Effective Hedge	0.20%	1.18%	2.29%	5.50%	
$50.00	Premium Earned	**$0.03**	**$0.20**	**$0.48**	**$1.64**	**$2.60**
	Max Gain	$5.86	$6.03	$6.31	$7.47	$8.43
	Max Gain %	13.27%	13.65%	14.29%	16.91%	19.09%
	Effective Sale Price	$50.03	$50.20	$50.48	$51.64	$52.60
	Effective Hedge	0.07%	0.45%	1.09%	3.71%	5.89%

An uncovered short call sale is a different matter entirely. If you do not own Company X long and you sell the $27.50 calls, you have sold the calls naked. In this case—as with shorting a stock—your downside potential is unlimited, as Company X stock can go higher over time. However, selling calls short and naked can be considered a slightly less-risky version of shorting stock outright. How is that? Simple. Let's say two traders think Company X's stock price is headed south and want to make an aggressive bet on such an outcome. Trader A sells short 1,000 shares of the stock outright at $27 per share. Trader B sells ten $27.50 call contracts (the equivalent of the same 1,000 shares) for $1.20 per contract. For every penny the stock goes up over $27 per share, Trader A begins to lose money. His losses start immediately as the stock price heads north. Trader B, on the other hand, does not start losing money until the stock gets to $28.70 per share, which equals the strike price plus the premium he has collected. That represents his break-even point. Only after the stock climbs 6.3% does Trader B begin to lose money.

But there is no such thing as a free lunch. Trader A can make up to $27 per share on the short equity position—the price at which he shorted the stock down to zero—whereas Trader B has capped his gains at $1.20 per share, the amount he received for selling his naked calls. So, while these two short positions—the naked calls and the outright equity short—have similar characteristics and a common objective, the dynamics of each position differ starkly.

Figure 4.9 **Profits from Shorting Stock versus Shorting Calls**

Stock Price	Trader A Profits (per share)	Trader B Profits (per share)
$0.00	$27.00	$1.20
$25.50	$1.50	$1.20
$26.00	$1.00	$1.20
$26.50	$0.50	$1.20
$27.00	$0.00 Break Even	$1.20
$27.50	($0.50)	$1.20
$28.00	($1.00)	$0.70
$28.50	($1.50)	$0.20
$28.70	($1.70)	$0.00 Break Even
$29.00	($2.00)	($0.30)
$29.50	($2.50)	($0.80)
$30.00	($3.00)	($1.30)

On the short put side, none other than Warren Buffett has used the sale of short puts to lower his effective purchase price, increase his returns via premiums collected, or both. Here is how it works. Let's say a stock is trading at $32 per share and you have a generally positive outlook on the company and its share price. However, you think there is a chance that the stock price will go down in the near term, and in any case you would prefer owning the company at a lower entry point. To achieve this objective, you can sell out-of-the-money puts to lower your effective purchase price. If you sell the ten contracts of the $30 strike price puts and collect $1.50 per share, you have effectively lowered your purchase price to $28.50 per share.

Figure 4.10 **Short Put Profit Scenarios**

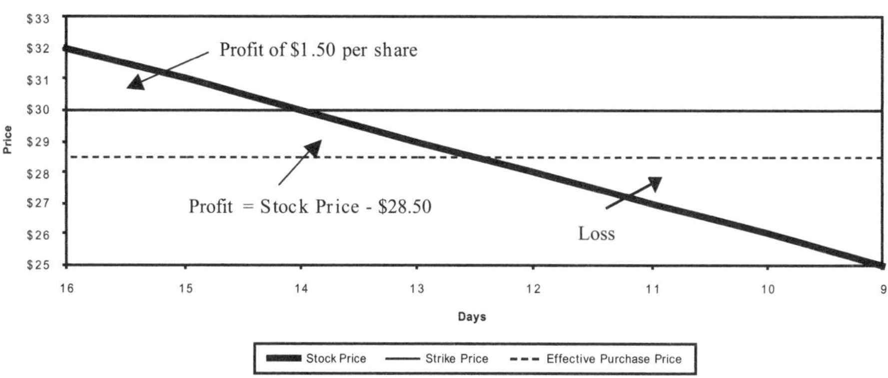

What are the possible outcomes under this scenario? The stock could close above $30 per share at time of expiration, in which case you profit from the maximum potential gain of $1.50 per contract X 100 shares, or $1,500 on ten contracts sold. If the stock price closes below $30 at time of expiration, then you are required to purchase the stock at $30 (assuming you do not roll the option). Since you have collected $1.50 per share of premium, any closing price above $28.50 represents profit. While a closing of the stock price below $28.50 would yield a near-term loss, the sale of a put on a stock that you otherwise wanted to own effectively lowers the purchase price and by mathematical definition increases the likelihood of superior returns over time. In this case, your effective purchase price was lowered by nearly 11%, from the then market price of $32 down to your effective entry price of $28.50.

What strike price puts should you sell? The more comfortable you are owning the stock, the closer to the money your short put sales can be. For example, if a stock is trading at $46 per share, you could sell the $45 strike price and collect a larger premium than if you sold the more conservative, farther out-of-the-money $42.50 strike price for less premium, the former yielding you perhaps $1.30 of premium whereas the latter might get you $0.65 per contract. If you would prefer not to own the stock, but want to use the sale of short puts as a means to add profits to your portfolio, focus on selling puts that are farther out-of-the-money.

However, when you sell naked puts, you should assume for the purposes of entering the trade as well as for portfolio accounting and risk control considerations that you will be assigned on the put. Your sales of short puts are just a more conservative version of your traditional long equity position. Therefore, always employ the same discipline and fundamental research.

(Don't) Sell Me Short

Short puts can also be used as a hedge against short equity positions, just as short calls can be used as a hedge against owning stock long. This strategy is referred to as a **sell write**. In this case, a trader enters into a short equity sale by borrowing shares, selling them, and buying them back at a lower price, thus profiting from the price difference. This is simply the mirror image of buying stocks long with the goal of selling them for a profit at a higher price. Whether you first buy low and then sell high, or first sell high and later buy low, the profit objective is the same. To hedge a short equity position, a trader might sell a put and collect the premium. The net effect is to cap the upside of the short position while providing a small hedge in case the stock goes against the trader. For example, if you have a bearish take on Dell and want to short the stock but hedge your short position, you could sell short 1,000 of Dell at $27 while simultaneously selling ten contracts of the $25 puts. If you collect $1.50 of premium per share, your upside would be limited to $3.50 per share, which is the difference between the $27 price at which you sold the shares and the $25 strike price plus the $1.50 premium.

Figure 4.11 **SELL WRITE PROFIT SCENARIOS**

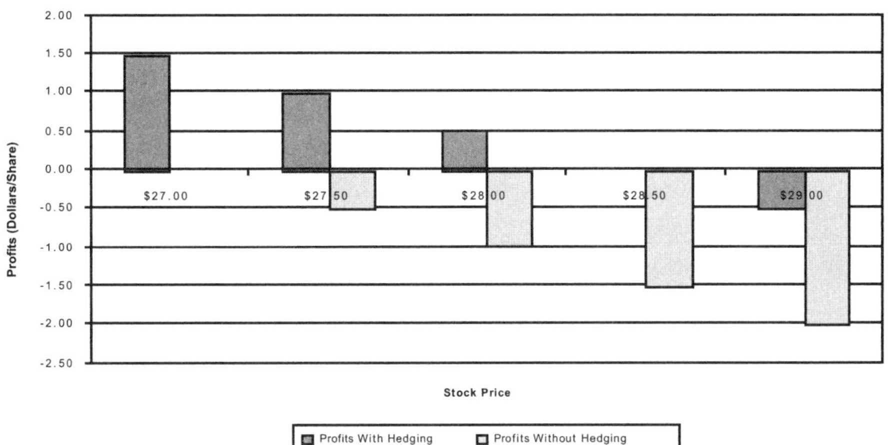

This graph depicts the various profits attained from different stock price movements, given a short sale of stock. The stock is shorted at $27 a share. Assuming the position was not hedged with the short sale of puts, and if the stock price stayed at $27, profits would be zero. The investor would have borrowed shares, sold them at $27, and then bought them back at $27. If the stock price increased to $28, his loss would be $1 per share. If, instead of being naked short equity, the investor had shorted the $25 puts to hedge his short equity position, he would have gained a premium of $1.50 a share. This premium acts as a cushion against losses on the short equity position in case the stock price rises. It also serves as a source of external discipline to take profits on a given position just like a short call against long stock. A sell write in effect "forces" you to take profits on a short equity position when the underlying security has fallen to a predetermined level. Without this external source of discipline, you might hold on to your short position for too long and miss the window to take a profit should the market rebound. If the stock price were to stay at $27, the investor would have borrowed shares, sold them for $27, and then bought them back for $27. This time, however, because he shorted the puts, he would have gained that $1.50 premium. If the stock price were to increase to $28, the investor buys the shares back at $28 for a capital loss of $1. But with the cushion from the premium, his profits are at $0.50 ($1.50 premium – $1.00 capital loss).

If Dell goes up, the sale of the short put provides a $1.50 per share cushion so that losses are only incurred once Dell goes above $28.50 per share. Losses would occur immediately for short sellers experiencing a rise in the Dell share price without a short put hedge position.

POWER TIP

Don't Get Stung—Let Options Be Your Pilot

Most people hire personal trainers not because they are clueless about how to use weight machines, but because they need an external source of discipline to keep making smart physical choices. This function of a personal trainer offers real value. The sale of covered call options can be like your personal trainer—it impels disciplined sales at predetermined levels. When you might otherwise hold on to a stock for too long, the sale of an out-of-the-money call forces you to sell high, to take some profit chips off the table. For this reason alone, options can be a valuable tool in your trading and investing repertoire.

OTHER COMMON OPTIONS TRADING TECHNIQUES

There are a myriad of ways to use options, on their own or in conjunction with equities, to profit. One common technique is called a **straddle**. This is the simultaneous purchase or sale of put and call option contracts with the same terms (strike price, expiration date, underlying security). First, the straddle purchase: A trader buys an equal number of Company X July '08 $25 puts and calls. You would enter into this transaction if you felt that the stock was going to make a big move but you were not certain in which direction. Traders often enter into such positions prior to earnings announcements when the declaration of actual earnings could differ markedly from expectations, leading to large movement in the stock. The breakeven for such a straddle position would be the addition of the premiums paid. Thus, if Company X stock were trading at $24.80 per share prior to expiration and the trader bought ten $25 strike price put contacts for $1.10 (of which $0.20 is intrinsic value) and ten $25 call contracts for $0.70, the stock would have to move $1.80 in either direction from the strike price for the combined position to be profitable. Thus, if the stock closes at expiration between $23.20 and $26.80, the position will have lost money. (A close above $26.80 or below $23.20 would put the position in a profit.) Losses are limited to the premium paid for the combined options.

Conversely, an uncovered straddle sale is entered into when a trader simultaneously sells the same number of calls and puts with the same terms without owning the stock. The seller of a straddle believes that the underlying security will remain relatively flat and therefore the premiums sold will collapse in value. Using the above example, if Company X closes between $23.20 and $26.80 the straddle seller will have made money on the transaction. To profit from the position, the seller of the call and put would buy back the option that is in-the-money and let the option that is out-of-the-money expire. In turn, if Company X stock is trading at $25.75 just prior to expiration, the straddle seller would buy to close the short call option for approximately $0.75 per contract and let the short put expire worthless. In this case the total profit would be $1.10 + $0.70 of options premium sold minus $0.75 per contract to buy back the ITM calls. Losses in this case are limitless as the stock has no maximum it can gain and the seller of the options is short calls that have unlimited downside potential.

Figure 4.12 **UNCOVERED STRADDLE BREAKEVEN**

Stock Closing Price	Put	Call	Cost	Profit
$22.50	ITM	OTM	$2.50	($0.70)
$23.00	ITM	OTM	$2.00	($0.20)
$23.20	ITM	OTM	$1.80	$0.00
$23.50	ITM	OTM	$1.50	$0.30
$25.00	ATM	ATM	$0.00	$1.80
$25.75	OTM	ITM	$0.75	$1.05
$26.00	OTM	ITM	$1.00	$0.80
$26.80	OTM	ITM	$1.80	$0.00
$27.00	OTM	ITM	$2.00	($0.20)

A **strangle** involves the combination of a put and a call with different strike prices but the same expiration date. In the case of a buy strangle, a trader buys the same number of OTM call and put contracts in hopes of very large movements in the underlying security. The cost of this premium is less than that of a straddle; however, the underlying security must move in a greater amount for the position to be profitable. Using our example above, a straddle buyer buys an equal number of the July $22.50 puts and the $27.50 calls for premium amounts of $0.40 and $0.30 respectively, the total cost of the position being $0.70 per contract. The position becomes profitable when the underlying security increases to a price that is greater than $28.20 or less than $21.80.

POWER TIP

ATM Is the Ultimate ATM

When you own a stock long and have sold a short call against that long position, your best-case scenario is that the stock closes just at-the-money at time of expiration. For example, if you bought Company X for $32.20 per share and sold the $32.50 calls, a closing price of $32.49 or $32.50 would optimize the premium sold for the next-dated option. In this case, option ATM truly becomes a bank ATM machine.

Stock Closing Price	Premium in $32.50 Calls
$31.50	$0.40
$32.00	$0.75
$32.50	$1.00

The same strategy applies to a strangle sale, but from the perspective of a seller. In this case, the upside of the premium seller is lower and limited to $0.70 per contract. However, the underlying stock price must move even more before the seller of the strangle goes below breakeven.

Da Bulls!!! (And Da Bears)

Other common options trading techniques include the **put bull spread**, the **put bear spread**, the **call bull spread**, and the **call**

bear spread. A put bull spread involves selling a put at a given strike price (a bullish bet) and concurrently buying an equal option contract quantity on the same security with the same expiration date but at a lower strike price. In essence, the long put hedges the short put so as to cap the potential losses associated with the put sold. Of course, buying the long put insurance lowers the profit potential of the position by the amount paid for the OTM long put.

A put bear spread, as the name implies, is a bearish bet that is hedged. In this case, a long put is purchased with the simultaneous sale of a put that is farther OTM. This helps to finance the long put purchase, but also caps gains to the delta between the two strike prices after factoring in the cost (or gain) from the option sale and purchase.

The same methodology applies on the call side. A call bull spread involves the purchase of a call at a given strike price (a bullish bet) accompanied by the sale of a call at a farther OTM strike price. You would enter a call bull spread position if you felt a given security was going to increase in price but that the increase would be limited. If you were bearish on a given stock but wanted to cap your downside, you would enter into a call bear spread, which would entail the sale of a given call option along with the simultaneous purchase of a farther OTM call.

Figure 4.13 **Call Bull Spread**

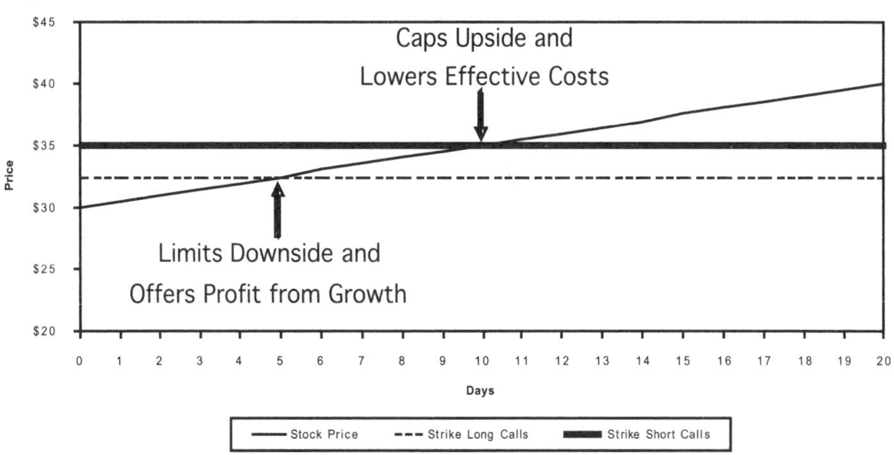

These represent the bulk of the basic options trading techniques. There are others with fancy names like "Iron Condors" and "Butterfly

Spreads," but the options strategies covered in this book are sufficient to take a myriad of positions that will provide upside profit and/or downside protection as dictated by a given investing or trading strategy.

VOLATILITY—THE VIX

There is an important concept within options called **volatility**, which can be defined as the amount by which an underlying security is expected to fluctuate in a given period. In layman's terms, some stocks move all over the place while others have a propensity to hold steady. Various factors contribute to this. How big a company is in terms of revenue and market capitalization can play an important role, larger companies generally being less volatile than their small-cap cousins. Older, more established companies (independent of market cap size) tend to see fewer swings in their stock price than newer listings because their earnings patterns have been demonstrated and there is less chance of a surprise in reported profits. The industry in which a company operates also plays a role in terms of options volatility, or "vol," as it is referred to on Wall Street. Stocks in high-growth industries and sectors that are less predictable in terms of product cycles (e.g., biotech) tend to be more volatile than industries like utilities, which typically have steadier, more foreseeable revenue streams.

The country of origin might also affect a stock option's volatility level. Stocks of companies based in more mature and stable economies like that of the United States are likely to be less volatile than those in emerging, potentially unstable countries like Venezuela or Malaysia. Finally, world events, be they economic, social, or political, can impact the volatility of markets at large, not to mention the individual stocks that are subject to those global macro events.

Individual stock option volatility levels (both historical and implied) can be found in sources like the CBOE. This is a great resource for seeing whether implied volatility for a security on which you are considering selling options is near a high or low vis-à-vis its historical range. For options sellers looking to optimize premiums earned, this is as useful as seeing whether a stock is trading near the high or the low of its P/E range.

Let's put things in perspective and wrap some science around the art. Historically, the **VIX**, which measures the near-term (30-day) expected volatility of the S&P 500 and thus is a tool for measuring **implied volatility**—as opposed to a **historical volatility**—has ranged between about 9 on the low end to just over 80 on the high end. An inverse correlation tends to exist between the VIX and the stock market: when the market drops fast, the VIX goes up; when the market goes up, the VIX drops. This holds true especially in the extremes. Whether the VIX is leading or following the market is unclear on any given day. However, when the VIX reaches extreme levels it has proven to be an excellent contrarian indicator of future market movements. Post-9/11, for example, the VIX spiked dramatically to then record highs in the 50s. Between 2004 and early 2007, as the stock market moved north in a consistent, steady fashion, the VIX lingered near historic lows of around 10, occasionally spiking to the upper teens during market sell-offs or major political scares. During the peak of the financial/credit crisis in the fourth quarter of 2008, VIX hit an all-time high near 90. The VIX can be thought of as a "fear gauge"; when people are afraid, when stocks are going down, when there is bad news on the front page of the *Wall Street Journal* and the *New York Times* (and especially *Business Week,* the ultimate contrarian indicator), the VIX tends to be higher, and premiums for options (especially puts) are more expensive.

Volatility is neither absolute nor constant; it is ever-changing. A stock's historical volatility may be X whereas its implied volatility may be X + Y. An implied volatility that is higher than historical volatility might be driven by global macro factors, industry-level forces like new regulation, or company-specific forces like expected changes in management or the prospect of a takeover. For that matter, implied volatility might be, and often is, greater for puts than for calls, even on the same company. For example, if a stock is trading at $12.50 per share, you might think that call and put options on the stock with the same expiration date that are equally out-of-the-money ($10 puts that are 2.5 points, or 20% OTM, and $15 calls that are also 2.5 points/20% OTM) would have the same premium level. You should not be surprised, however, that premiums for puts are often more expensive than premiums for calls under this circumstance. People are willing to pay more to protect against the downside than they are to gain from the upside. Or, on a behavioral economic level that focuses on emotional drivers such as fear and greed, people hate to lose money more than they love to make money. Thus, put premiums are bid up higher than call premiums, especially during tumultuous times. This concept is key to making profits so we will return to this later in depth.

Figure 4.14 **Asymmetrical Premium of Equidistant Calls and Puts**

Beginning in early 2006, the CBOE introduced options on the VIX. This means that you can speculate on volatility levels or hedge your option positions. For example, if the VIX is very low, around 10—and you believe the VIX will go up—you can now buy a call on the VIX. Similarly, you can buy puts on the VIX if the VIX is high and you think it is headed lower. Why might you want to buy a call on the VIX other than to speculate on its direction? If, for example, you have a lot of short put (bullish) premium on your books and you are concerned about being so exposed to rapid downside market movements, you can buy a VIX call that will hedge your short premium. In this case, if the broad market drops sharply, the gains on your VIX calls will help to hedge, or offset, the losses on your short put premium that would be caused by both adverse directional movement (down) as well as unfavorable volatility/VIX-induced premium movement (up), both of which would cause short puts to become more negative.

Be advised that trading VIX options is an advanced technique. Not only is the sale of a put on an index that is inversely related to broad market movements the ultimate triple negative (like when a politician says, "I don't necessarily disagree that we shouldn't invade Iran…"), but there are also some characteristics of VIX options that differ from traditional equity options. First, they trade European-style, thus they cannot be assigned prior to expiration. Furthermore, since the VIX represents no underlying security, all settlements are in cash. In addition, expiration dates are typically on the Wednesday prior to the third Friday in each month rather than Thursdays (which is the case for most European-style index options), and therefore the last time you can trade the option is the Tuesday before the Wednesday expiration date. To that end, a VIX option holder is subject to overnight market and VIX movements between the final day the VIX can be traded and its settlement price the following morning. If you are short VIX calls and a major negative event occurs the Tuesday evening prior to settlement Wednesday, VIX might spike dramatically overnight so that your thought-to-be-safe short VIX calls will now be ITM and your account will be debited for the difference between the strike price you sold and the VIX settlement price.

One other critical nuance of VIX options is that they do not contain the inherent time premium traditionally found in options. For most options, a trader can expect to get a delta premium for selling later-dated options if the underlying security price is near-the-money as expiration approaches. If you have sold the April $15 strike price puts on Company X and the stock is trading at $14.90 on the day of expiration, a trader could expect to buy back the April $15 puts for about $0.30 and sell the May $15 puts for perhaps $1 or more. *This element of time value does not exist in VIX options.* The VIX is a measure of implied volatility. Thus, if the market is predicting greater volatility in the future, the price of the later-dated VIX put options might actually be less. (Note: If your head is spinning at this point, don't worry; this is an advanced concept that takes a while to get your brain around.) If you sold the April $15 VIX put options and the VIX is trading at $14.90 approaching expiration, the April $15 puts might be trading for $0.30 and the May $15 contracts might be trading for less than the April $15 puts that are about to expire. Therefore, the ability to roll options for a delta premium can be limited. In addition, current trading volume levels are limited—and bid/ask spreads wide—so trading the VIX options is fairly inefficient today at best. Consequently, if you use the sale of VIX options to speculate, you should do so very selectively, since rolling options that are set to expire in-the-money might cost you money (i.e., you will receive a delta premium debit rather than the expected credit). You might want to choose price targets and only sell options when the

VIX hits that target. For instance, only sell puts if the VIX drops below 12 and only sell VIX calls if the VIX gets into the mid-30s or whatever level is consistent with recent ranges. But the purchase of VIX options to provide a near-term hedge on one's portfolio of short premium can be effective because the VIX can move dramatically in a very short period, especially to the upside when markets move down quickly and violently. To be sure, the purchase of VIX calls can be a more effective and efficient way to protect your portfolio than even the purchase of OTM long broad-based index puts as VIX options change in price immediately with a dramatic decline in the market whereas stocks might have to move 5% or more before your long puts start making you money.

In conclusion, the VIX is an important tool and indicator when considering various options strategies, as well as an important variable.

THE PRICING OF OPTIONS

Now that we have learned the various macro issues that can impact volatilities in the stock market, let's discuss what micro considerations can affect the volatility of a given stock. For that we will go back to our insurance analogy.

Let's say you are considering buying fire insurance for your house. You live in a place with cold and wet winters and hot and dry summers. More fires start in the summer than in the winter because the brush and tinder that grows during the rainy season becomes dry and susceptible to flames during the summer. Since the probability of a fire is higher in the summer, a six-month policy covering April through September will be more expensive than one that extends from October to March. If a rash of fires breaks out in your area, premiums will rise. Want to have a policy to protect you for two years rather than six months? It will cost you more. Are you insuring a mansion or a small condominium? The house that is worth more will cost more to insure. These are the essential variables that go into the pricing of an option: the likelihood of the event occurring, the length of time being covered, and the value of the underlying asset.

But just how directly does movement in the value of an underlying security affect the prices of options? If a given stock moves 5%, will all of its corresponding options also change 5% in value? Let's examine this question closely.

The term **delta** is defined as the amount an option price will change given a one-point change in the price of the underlying security. Delta values range from 0 to 1 for long call options and short put options (bullish options) and a value range of -1 to 0 for long puts and short calls (bearish bets). If a stock moves three points and the option delta is 1, the option will also move three points. While the exact calculation of delta is beyond the scope of this book (see the additional resources section for information on where useful measurement tools can be found), as a rule of thumb, a stock that is **at-the-money (ATM)**—its price being at or near the option's strike price—will have a delta of approximately 0.5. As a stock's price moves farther and farther OTM—falling below strike price in the case of a call and rising above strike price in the case of a put—delta approaches 0. As a stock price becomes increasingly ITM—rising above the strike price in the case of a call and falling below the strike price in the case of a put—delta approaches 1.0 as shown in the following figure.

Figure 4.15 **Short Put Deltas**

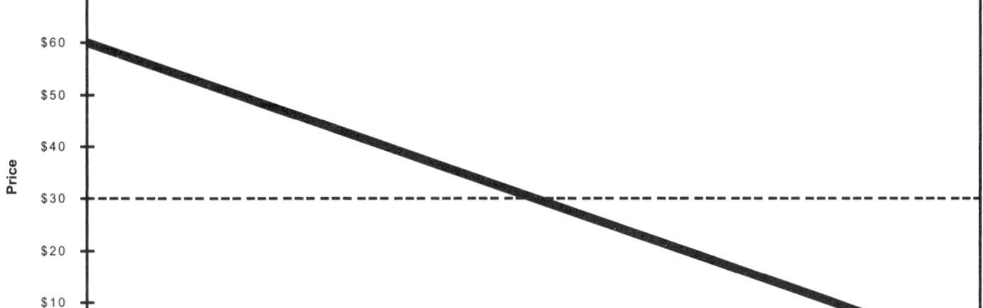

As shown above, when the stock price is greater than $30, and the put is OTM, the delta approaches 0. When the stock price is less than $30, and the put is ITM, the delta approaches 1. When the option is ATM, with the strike price equaling the stock price, the delta is approximately 0.5. Compare this with the dynamics of deltas in the context of call options.

Figure 4.16 **CALL DELTAS**

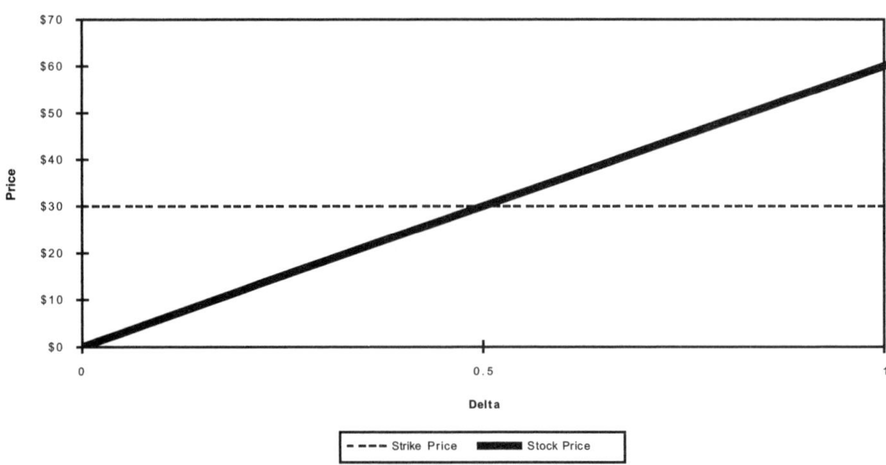

In the case of a call, when the stock price is greater than $30, the call is ITM and the delta approaches 1. When the stock price is less than $30, and the call is OTM, the delta approaches 0. When the option is ATM, in this case when the stock equals the strike at $30, the delta is on the order of 0.5.

In effect, options "self-regulate" in that, as stock prices go down, your long exposure (via short puts) increases as deltas approach 1. Conversely, as a given stock price goes up and a short call becomes increasingly in-the-money, the short call delta approaches 1 and the combined position gets increasingly short. And that is the essence of buying low and selling high.

Here is an analogy to put the concept of deltas into perspective. Let's say you are playing tug-of-war. You start out with one person on each side, Person A on the left and Person B to the right. When Person A (the stock) tugs, Person B (the option or derivative) feels 100% of the effect of the tug. In this case, delta is 1, the option being fully ITM and behaving just as the underlying stock acts; the option "feels" the full force of the stock's "tug." Now let's say we have twenty people on each side. When Group A pulls, the impact of this movement will still be felt almost entirely by the first few people in line in Group B. Will person twenty at the end of the line and perhaps fifty feet from the center—the position that is far out-of-the-money—be affected by the force of the tugs in the same way as the person near the center—at the strike price—will be? We know that those closest to the center will feel the tugs' effects more than those who are at the tail end of the tug-of-war game.

Another way to think about deltas is to consider the play in a steering wheel. If you are in an SUV and you turn the wheel, you will feel some looseness, or play, in the steering wheel. The steering wheel in your hand moves slightly before it causes the vehicle's wheels to turn. This would be the equivalent of a low delta, an option with a strike price that is far OTM relative to the underlying stock price. In contrast, if you are driving a high-end sports car then every movement in your shoulders and hands is transmitted to the steering wheel and then directly to the car's wheels. The yield of output to input is extremely high. This would be an in-the-money option with high delta values. There are even rumors out there that the military is developing technology that will allow a jet fighter pilot's thoughts to be translated directly into a plane's movements; talk about delta force!

To see this in action for yourself, check out a good Web site, www.cboe.com. Look up Google, Inc. (GOOG) or another security that has had a big move on that day. You will see that deep ITM options have moved in almost the same magnitude as the stock, whereas the OTM options have moved far less. If, for example, Google drops from \$530 to \$522, an eight-point drop for the day, then the \$560 ITM puts will increase by close to \$8, whereas the \$520 puts (ATM) will have moved perhaps four or five points. Farther OTM \$450 puts, the ones near the tail end of the tug-of-war game, will have moved only a fraction, perhaps less than a point. The delta for the far OTM puts is very low, in the range of 0.1 or even 0.05, so the impact of a price move on these options is muted, whereas the ITM puts have a delta of close to 1 and move in a way similar to the underlying stock itself.

Of course, deltas are not static. In the case above, as Google moved from \$530 to \$522, the delta for the \$520 puts increased from around 0.3 to 0.5. If Google were to continue to decline to \$490, the delta of the \$520 puts would accelerate to 0.8 or even 0.9. At that point, the \$520 puts would act almost in the same way as the underlying stock. Remember that deltas capture expected movements in options relative to their underlying stock at any moment in time, but they are constantly changing with this movement; you need to factor this dynamic nature accordingly when assessing the impact that stock movements will have on your position values.

Just to hammer home this important concept, let's go back to the insurance analogy. Each put option represents an insurance against a certain event occurring. Those who purchased the $520 puts are trying to protect against the stock price dropping below $520. Investors who purchased $450 puts are trying to protect against the stock dropping below $450. If Google drops from $530 to $522, the probability of the stock price dropping below $520 goes up quite a bit, whereas the $450 strike price is still a long way off. Therefore, the price of the $520 insurance will go up significantly as the stock price approaches $520 whereas the same drop to $520 will have little impact on the $450 puts. The price of this insurance will remain relatively cheap. Only as Google starts approaching $450 will these options start reacting more meaningfully to movements in the daily stock price.

THAT'S JUST GROSS: NOTIONAL AND DELTA ADJUSTED EXPOSURES

In the world of stocks, **exposure** refers to the size of the "bet." Investing and trading in equities and options is nothing like gambling, but we'll use betting tables as an analogy only to bring clarity to a complex subject.

Let's say you go to Vegas with $100,000 in your pocket. If you step up to the roulette table and put all $100,000 on black, then you are 100% long black; you have 100% exposure to black. If you borrow $50,000 from the house and put $150,000 on black, then you have 150% exposure to black. If you put $50,000 on red and keep $50,000 in your pocket, you have 50% exposure to red. If you decide to sit out a spin of the wheel and make no bet at all, your exposure is 0%. This brings up two important concepts of exposure: gross and net. The former is the total of all long and short exposure, while the latter represents the addition of long and short exposure (short exposure being expressed as a negative value).

Using our roulette analogy, if you put $50,000 on black and $50,000 on red, your **total exposure** (aka **gross exposure**) would be 100%, but your net exposure would be 0% (not counting the green squares on the wheel). This is the equivalent of being neutral in the market, or having an equal amount of long exposure (hoping stocks will go up) and short exposure (betting stocks will decline in price). Even with a neutral portfolio, you can still have lots of "bets" on the market. Of course, betting on both black and red on the same wheel makes no sense, as these two outcomes are mutually exclusive, the losses on one side of the transaction negating the gains on the other, whereas in the stock market your longs can go up concurrently with declines in shorts. But what if you were to line up dozens of roulette tables, each with an independent outcome? Now you could win on both your black bets and your red bets at the same time. Suppose that you had ten tables in front of you and that you knew half of them were tilted so that black came up more than 50% of the time, the other half of the tables being positioned so that red was the predominant outcome. In this case, you would put half your positions on black for the wheels that favored black and half your money on red on the wheels that favored red. You would have 100% exposure to the roulette wheel even though your net exposure was 0%. Your total roulette portfolio would be indifferent to whether black or red came up in general, as long as black came up on your black bets and red was the winner on your red bets. You could win simultaneously on black outcomes and red outcomes while not putting all your money on either black or red.

There are six ways to incur exposure in stocks and options. The three ways to attain long exposure are: (1) buying stocks long, (2) selling puts short, and (3) buying calls long. The three ways to get short exposure on your books are: (1) selling stocks short, (2) buying puts long, and (3) selling calls short. In equity investing, if you have a $100,000 portfolio and you buy $100,000 worth of the S&P 500 via an ETF like the SPYs, you have 100% long exposure. If you borrow $50,000 from your broker by going on **margin**, and you add it to your $100,000 of SPYs, then your total exposure is 150% long. If you buy $40,000 of the SPYs and keep the rest of your portfolio in cash, then you have 40% long exposure. If you take your entire $100,000 and short the SPYs, then your portfolio exposure is 100% short. Portfolio exposure can range from 100% or more short to 100% or more long (given the ability to borrow), and everything in between.

Hence, any given portfolio has gross (total) exposure, **gross long exposure**, **gross short exposure**, and **net exposure**. If you take the $100,000 portfolio described above that is 100% gross long via SPYs and sell short $40,000 of stocks that you think will underperform relative to the S&P 500, you have created a portfolio that has 140% gross total exposure (100% long exposure + 40% short exposure) but 60% net long exposure (100% long exposure minus 40% short exposure). In this scenario, though you have a long bias, you are relatively indifferent to the overall market direction per se; you just want your long bets to go up and your short bets to go down. One interpretation is that this portfolio is riskier than a 100% long-only portfolio in that your long exposure can go down and your short exposure can go up, with you losing both ways. But a portfolio with 60% net exposure will tend to decline less than the broad indices during down market conditions if the choice of underlying securities has been made intelligently.

If you wanted your portfolio returns to be independent of market direction and dependent solely on stock picks, you could go long $75,000 of certain stocks on which you were bullish, and short $75,000 of stocks you expected to decline, thereby setting up what is called a **market neutral** portfolio. In this case, though your portfolio gross exposure is 150%, your portfolio net exposure is 0%. Though you have placed more than 100% worth of bets, the total portfolio construction is theoretically more conservative than if you were 100% long the market (and certainly more conservative than if you were 150% long the market).

It is this ability to place more than 100% worth of "bets" while constructing a portfolio with a net exposure of less than 100% that allows sophisticated professional investors to outperform the market with less risk, a key concept explored in more detail below.

Options Exposed

When you go long or short stocks, your exposure is long/short dollar for dollar the security being traded. The same does not hold true for options-induced exposure. Therefore, we need to introduce a few other types of exposure.

The first, **notional exposure**, can be defined as the total face value of the option if it were fully assigned. This is the equivalent of gross, or total, exposure for stocks. For instance, in the case of the purchase of ten Dell $25 put contracts, the notional short exposure is $25,000. The purchase of five Dell $30 calls would provide $15,000 of notional long Dell exposure. The sale of twenty Dell $22.50 puts would yield notional long exposure of $45,000, and so forth. Think of notional exposure as the face value of the contract.

Easy enough. But as we have learned, most options do not behave on a one-for-one basis with the underlying stock, so we must adjust the notional exposure for the delta of the option, giving us **delta adjusted exposure**—a very important concept for portfolio construction and risk management when options are involved. As noted, a stock with a price far out-of-the-money vis-à-vis the option strike price will have a delta close to 0. For example, if you have sold ten Dell $25 puts when the stock is trading for $28 per share, the delta will be approximately 0.2. While the notional long exposure is $25,000, the delta adjusted exposure is only approximately $5,000. If the stock moves up $1, instead of your gaining $1,000 as you would if you owned 1,000 shares of Dell long, your short put position will gain only $200, or 20% of the movement in the underlying security. Because the delta is 0.2, the option price will move only 0.2 points for every one point the stock moves. Similarly, if Dell were to drop from $28 to $27, someone owning 1,000 shares of the stock long would lose $1,000 on his position, whereas the seller of ten short put contracts, while having the same notional exposure as the person owning the shares long, would lose only approximately $200. Note that for short call options and long put options, the delta is negative in that the option loses 20% of its value as the stock price rises. In other words, stock price and options price are inversely related in those two circumstances, whereas with short puts and long calls, a rise in the underlying stock also increases the value of the option.

Figure 4.17 **Portfolio Exposures**

Sample Portfolio: $100,000

1. 1,000 shares Co. X at $29 per share
   = 29% Gross Long

2. 1,000 shares Co. X at $29 per share + 5 contracts $30 short calls
   = 29% Gross Long + 15% Gross Short
   = 44% Total Gross

3. 1,000 shares Co. X at $29 per share + 5 contracts $30 short calls
   = 14% Net Long

4. 1,000 shares Co. X at $29 per share + 5 contracts $30 short calls
   = 35% Delta Adjusted

Animal House

The dynamic, ever-changing nature of deltas brings us to the Greek letter **gamma**. This is simply the rate at which delta changes. Gamma is expressed as a positive number in the case of long options and as a negative number in the case of short options. Gamma increases and peaks as a stock price approaches a strike price, and decreases to 0 as options become increasingly in- or out-of-the-money. An option that goes from way, way OTM to simply way OTM will see its delta change very little and that will be reflected by a low gamma. A stock price approaching a strike price, however, will have a very high gamma as the delta indicators accelerate rapidly. Once the option is deep ITM, gamma again approaches 0 because underlying stock movements have little impact on a delta hovering close to 1.

Note that as expiration gets closer, the gamma of an ATM option will increase very quickly. If a stock is trading at $24.50, its $25 call options that are expiring within a couple days will have a delta of approximately 0.5. Upward movements in the underlying stock will have a dramatic impact on the delta of the ATM call options. Conversely, if the option has a long time until expiration, the same movement in the underlying stock will have less of an impact on delta, thus gamma is lower. Compare this to OTM options and their behavior at differing intervals in regards to expiration. As noted, an OTM option that is about to expire has a very low delta, something near 0. For this option, gamma will also be very low. If, however, the OTM option has a long time until expiration then gamma will be higher even when delta is low. This is, in effect, the opposite of gamma behavior in ATM options.

If you take only one thing away from this discussion it should be that delta values accelerate very quickly as stocks approach option strike prices and even more so the closer you get to expiration. So watch your about-to-expire ATM options closely as they are "in the game."

Contact

The next term we are going to examine is **vega**, which can be defined as the amount by which an option price changes when volatility

Figure 4.18 **CHARTING GAMMA WITH STOCK PRICE OF $50**

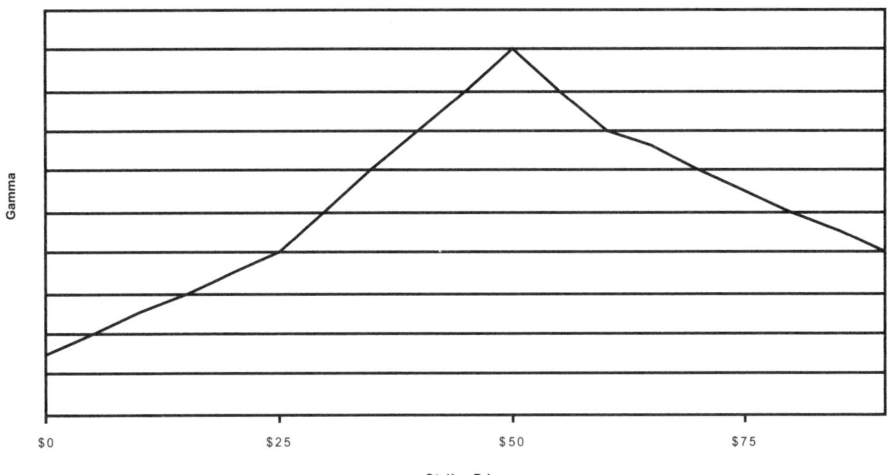

changes—specifically implied volatility (as opposed to historical). Vega is always a positive number and is also referred to as **tau** (not to be mixed up with tao, which, when pronounced properly, is easily confused with Dow). Options premiums are driven by a myriad of variables including volatility of the underlying security. If an event drives up the implied volatility of a given stock, its options premium will increase even if there is no movement in the stock price itself. For example, the floating of a takeover rumor of Company X on a strong down day in the market, which offsets the takeover rumor in the near term and causes Company X stock to close flat on that day, would foster an overall increase of premium in Company X's options—the calls in particular. This is the essence of vega.

For the owner of options, a decline in volatility is a source of risk, while volatility increases can enhance profit. The seller of options has the opposite risk/reward profile pertaining to vega. In terms of price movement, vega is at its peak when options are ATM and at its nadir for very far ITM or OTM options. A change in volatility will have little impact on deep ITM options, whereas for near-to-the-money options, volatility will have a big effect on premium levels. In terms of the amount of time left in an option cycle, vega is largest for far-dated options and lowest for options about to expire.

Figure 4.19 **Charting Vega with Stock Price of $50**

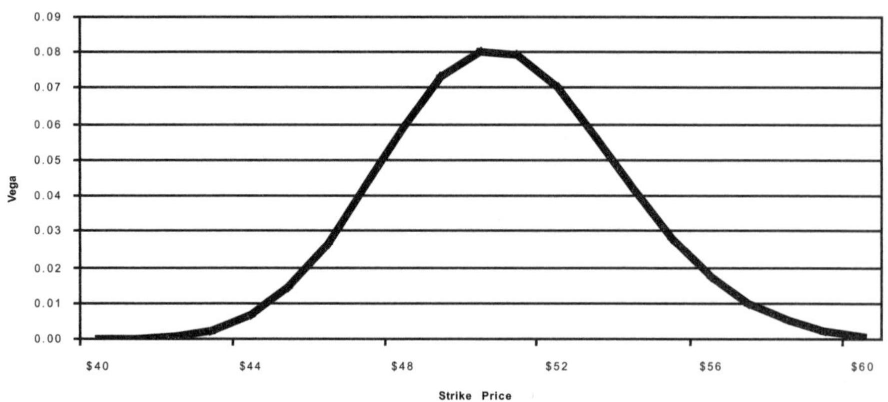

For short put options sellers, an up day can provide a triple treat in terms of profits. First, your short put will lose value (become more profitable) by way of direction gain. Next, the passage of time will cause decay. Finally, most up days for the broader market are accompanied by a drop in the VIX. Thus, short premium can collapse rapidly when you have all three sources of profit (direction, time, and lower volatility) working in your favor.

LET'S GET WASTED

The notion that options are a wasting asset is an important one. Over time the inherent value in options erodes (specifically the time value premium). The decline, however, is not linear but almost exponential.

For example, assume you buy an OTM put that has twenty days left until expiration. If time decay were linear, the option would lose 5% of its time value each day. Its intrinsic value will go up and down depending on how far ITM, if at all, the option is. But the option does not lose 5% of its value per day over those twenty days. Instead, it loses less than 5% per day in the early days and more than 5% per day as the expiration date approaches.

Going back to the insurance analogy, let's say you were about to hop on a plane and an enterprising insurance salesman convinced you to buy flight insurance for $100 (the premium) for a four-hour flight (the expiration period). He then decided to join you on the flight and plopped down in the seat next to you. As a smart guy always looking to make a profit, he offers to buy the insurance back from you fifteen minutes into the flight, or 6% of the 240-minute flight time. If the decaying value of the insurance were linear, he would offer to buy the insurance back for approximately $94 since 6% of the flight minutes have elapsed. But, being prudent and realizing a whole lot could still go wrong in the flight, you tell him you will only sell it back for $98. He declines, and you hold on to the insurance.

Figure 4.20 **Time Decay of Options**

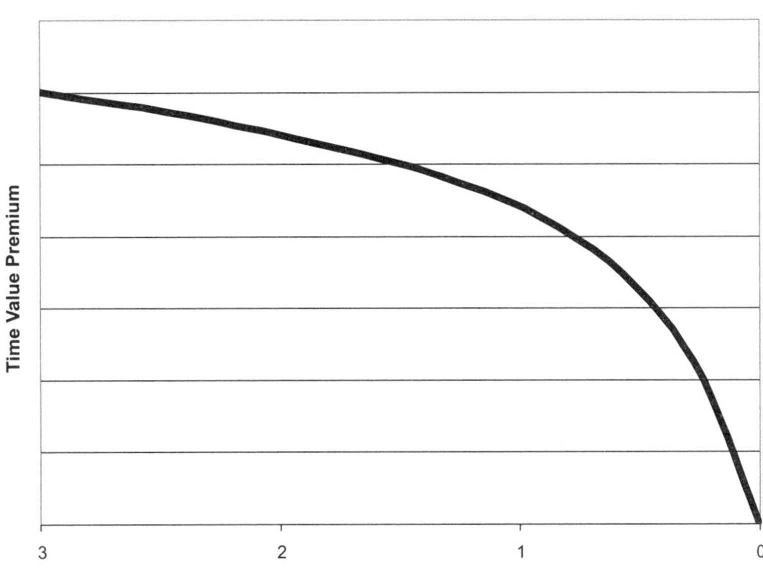

After a bad meal and a short film, the halfway point of the flight passes. Mr. Insurance turns to you and offers you $50 to buy back the insurance. "A fair deal," he says. "No way," you reply. "Even though the flight is halfway through, I still want to hedge against the event the insurance is protecting me from, so I will only sell you the insurance back if you pay me $60." No deal.

The flight continues, the pilot informs you that you are well into your descent and that you should be on the ground and at the gate in about ten minutes. Buckle up those seat belts and turn off those BlackBerries. "Ahh, we have made it," says Mr. Insurance. "I'll buy back your policy for two cents on the dollar—there are only ten minutes left in the flight so you are lucky I will pay you anything at all." "No way," you reply. "I'll take $15 or I am holding on. You know how tricky landings can be." "How about $8," he haggles. "That is double what my rate sheet says that I should pay you based on the fact that only 4% of the flight is left." Again, no deal.

Fortunately, your pilot is well trained and the landing is smooth. Now you are confident that all will be okay, so you turn to Mr. Insurance to consummate a deal. After all, you have not been told "buh-bye" just yet, so you should be able to get something for your policy. But Mr. Insurance is on his cell phone, so you can't get his attention. "Can I sell you my policy for $10 now?" you ask as the plane comes to a peaceful stop and passengers start to gather their belongings. "How about $5?" you inquire desperately as you see the gateway approach the plane. Mr. Insurance is still on his phone . . . time is running out. The cabin door opens and passengers start filing out just as Mr. Insurance gets off the phone. "How about $2 to buy my policy back—I could still get hit in the noggin by some overhead baggage that shifted during flight." "I'll give you five cents," he replies. "But only ten minutes ago you were willing to pay me $8. How could the value have gone down so quickly?" "Tough break," beams Mr. Insurance as he quickly folds five crisp $20 bills into his pocket.

You have just learned the lesson of nonlinear time-value decay. In some cases, when earnings reports are released the evening before expiration, as Google typically does each quarter, premiums hold much of their value until the bitter end—right up until expiration—driven largely by higher-than-average implied volatility right around earnings time. In that case, the time-decay graph appears even steeper than for most options expiration cycles as traders are willing to pay for options all the way up to expiration. Then, once the earnings news is released, options premiums collapse as traders conclude that extreme movements in the stock price are not in the cards. One conservative way to take advantage of this phenomenon is to sell at- or even in-the-money covered call options just prior to earnings. The profit stars align perfectly when earnings are announced one to two weeks before options expiration which can actually yield a scenario where slightly ITM options actually provide strong annualized returns. For example, if Company X is trading at $15.30 the day before it is to release its earnings, you might be able to get $1 or more for the $15 calls about to expire in two weeks. Of course, fundamental analysis comes first, but if the company does not disappoint heavily, you have positioned yourself well—and conservatively—to earn a quick 5% raw return. Look out for these opportunities because they occur regularly if you are paying attention to the earnings calendar juxtaposed to the options expiration cycle.

TAKING A ROMAN HOLIDAY

Three-day weekends are beautiful things for sellers of options. Not just because they offer time to enjoy the beach on a summer holiday, but because the stock market's being closed represents a great source of profit for people who are short premium with time decay constantly working in their favor. Time is the friend of options sellers and the enemy of options buyers. You have probably heard the stock market adage "Sell in May and go away" that refers to professional investors' tendency to sell their book before heading to the Hamptons. And, not coincidentally, the traditional broad market summer doldrums are usually followed by a post–Labor Day year-end rally. In the case of options, any time you get a chance to put short premium on the books prior to a long weekend, sell on Friday and go away, all else being equal.

The Greek that measures the time decay of a given position—which is another way of saying the time risk associated with being the buyer or seller of an option—is called **theta**. Theta is typically noted as a negative number. An option with a theta of -0.18, for example, will lose $0.18 per day regardless of whether the option is a call or a put. Of course, time decay is not linear; premium decays more quickly as the option approaches expiration. Options with the largest theta are ATM options approaching expiration. Theta is at its lowest for very long-term options, especially deep in- or far out-of-the-money ones. As with the other Greeks, theta can be measured on an individual position or on an entire portfolio-based level. In essence, calculating theta will tell you the amount of profit (for those who are short premium—a positive theta position) or loss (for owners of options—a negative theta position) due to time decay on a daily basis.

The Sweetest Thing: The Optimal Spot for Options Time Horizon

What is the optimal time horizon for selling options? Thirty days? Sixty days? A year? More? Less? First, some mathematical analysis. By definition, the return on an annualized, as opposed to absolute, basis is greater the nearer term the option is sold. Thus, while an investor will collect more absolute premium for calls sold ninety days out than for calls sold only thirty days out, the annualized return for the thirty-day calls is higher than that of the ninety-day calls given the accelerated decay toward the end of an option's life.

Figure 4.21 **OPTION TIME FRAME RETURN ANALYSIS**

Days Until Expiration	Premium	Absolute Return	Annualized Return
30	$0.85	2.69%	37.51%
60	$1.50	4.75%	32.11%
90	$2.20	6.97%	30.93%

In addition to their greater annualized returns, shorter-term options also provide more flexibility, in that they can be rolled, allowed to expire, or otherwise adjusted as needed with near-term broad market or stock-specific movements. Finally, the higher volume of nearer-term options traded means that their spreads tend to be narrower than the spreads of their long-dated counterparts with lower liquidity. Thus, favor nearer-dated options when looking to sell calls or puts.

What about **LEAPS**, or long-term equity anticipation securities? While OTM LEAPS puts are certainly a conservative way to enter a long-term stock position, they offer the combination of limited upside (limited to the amount of the premium sold, as is the case with all short put options) and all of the downside; the stock can go to zero. But if your bullish thesis was correct and the stock goes up over the long term, you do not participate in the gains beyond premium collected. By their nature, LEAPS offer little time-decay benefit in the near term, thus you get neither the advantage of near-term time decay nor the potential for capital appreciation inherent in longer-term equity holdings. LEAPS puts also offer less flexibility to take advantage of or respond to nearer-term broad market or company-specific events—actions that occur regularly and that often present profit opportunities or reasons to become more defensive with regards to a given position. For example, if you sell near-dated OTM puts and the stock moves up on an expected earnings report, your less-than-sixty-day options might decline in value from $1 to $0.30 in a short period of time and allow you to buy them back at close to 80% of their profit potential, given tight spreads. Then, if the stock declines again, you could resell puts for a higher premium level than your recent buy-to-close purchase. The same OTM LEAPS might drop in value from $3.50 to $3.20 and, given wide spreads, the repurchase of the put might be a break-even undertaking at best.

In conclusion, the sweet spot for maximizing profits and flexibility in options sales is in the thirty- to ninety-day range. How far out you sell an option might be driven by your return objectives; or it might be a function of the premium available at any given strike price. For example, let's assume you purchased Company X long at $22 per share and concurrently sold a thirty-day short call option with a strike price of $22.50 for $0.80 per contract. If the stock closes at $20 per share at time of expiration, you might need to go sixty or ninety days out to get a decent premium for the $22.50 strike price, the new thirty-day $22.50 call options having little or no premium left in them.

***Figure* 4.22 Near versus Far OTM Return Profiles**

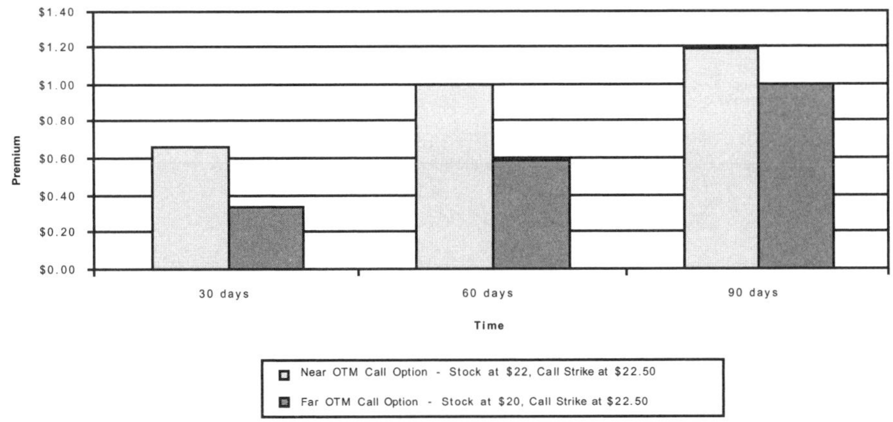

In this case, going out ninety days makes the most sense as this balances annual and absolute returns. When using options to add incremental profits to your core holdings, you can pick and choose your spots to collect premiums when the return profiles are favorable.

CHAPTER 5

Optimizing Options

Now that we have learned the basics of options and the forces that drive their movements, let's look in more detail at practical ways to apply options to portfolio construction and trading.

The Replacements

Let's say you purchased a stock for $48 per share and simultaneously sold the September $50 calls for $1.20 per share. At the time of expiration the stock is trading at $50.30 per share, or slightly ITM. There is likely to be premium in the $52.50 later-dated strikes, so if you still feel bullish on the stock, you might want to close the September $50 calls for $0.40, or whatever they are trading for (still making $0.80 per share on the short calls), and roll into the October $52.50 contracts. This provides further upside capital gains potential while still offering some downside protection via the short call. And, if the ex-date for the company's next dividend is prior to the third Friday of October, then you have the potential to make money on the $52.50 calls, the stock, and the dividend. This is a nice triple treat. By definition, the farther OTM the call option sale is, the "looser" the hedge is and the more you are relying on capital appreciation for gains. By contrast, at- or near-the-money calls provide a "tighter" hedge that shifts profit potential away from capital gains and toward premium collection.

POWER TIP

Getting Burned by Your Ex

Often you will own a dividend-paying stock long and be short covered calls against the security that become ITM. The person on the other side of your short call position—the owner of the call—will likely want to exercise his option to purchase the stock (now that the stock price is above the strike price) at a time when he can capture the dividend. Therefore, if your goal is to hold on to the stock and earn the upcoming dividend, be sure to either close your short call option position entirely or roll it to a higher strike price or a later-dated option or both—or risk getting burned by the looming ex-date. The only saving grace in getting prematurely assigned on an option, be it due to the buyer of the option looking to capture the dividend or the option simply being so deep in the money prior to expiration that the buyer of the option chooses to exercise, is that at least you are earning the entire profit potential on the position in less than the expected option period. Thus, your annualized returns increase because your holding period has been shortened.

But what if the stock price is $52 approaching expiration? You do not want to roll to the $52.50 calls, but you would have to go too far out time-wise to get a decent delta premium on the $50 strike price. (In other words, since the option is well in-the-money, there will be very little time value premium in the later-dated $50 calls.) One technique is to sell puts to replace the stock that was just (or is about to be) **called away**. If you purchased 1,000 shares at $48 per share and sold the September $50 calls for $1.20, your effective sale price is $51.20 at time of **assignment** and your total profit is $3.20 per share, or 7% ROI **raw**. Rather than rolling the calls for little to no time premium, you can sell the October $50 puts, likely collecting another $1 to $2 per share of premium. Thus, if the stock price drops and you are subsequently assigned, you would buy the stock at the equivalent of $50 minus the premium you collected, or $48.50 per share if you got $1.50 for the puts.

This is a more conservative, effective, and profitable way of maintaining exposure to a covered call position that has become ITM at expiration.

At times stocks trade in ranges. Within a portfolio of twenty to thirty stocks, certain positions are stronger and others weaker at any given time, either for transitory but fundamental reasons (such as an industry performing better during certain parts of the economic cycle), or for nonfundamental reasons that are reflected in the market regularly. Taking advantage of the ranges—effectively and repeatedly buying more shares when the price is lower and selling them when the price is higher, either directly or by way of short options—can add incremental profits to a portfolio while lowering risk.

POWER TIP

The 80/20 Rule

What types of annualized returns should one look for between dividends, capital appreciation, and options premiums when considering selling covered calls? While everyone has a different perspective and risk/reward profile, a good starting point is if the sale of a call leads to a position with 20% or more annualized upside, then the call is worth selling. The 20% annualized return can be made up of any combination of capital gains (or even a loss, if the call option sold is in-the-money), dividends, and the option premium itself. Remember that the sale of a call provides the additional benefit of some downside protection, so even if a 20% annualized return figure seems too small in and of itself, you need to give the position credit for the fact that it has less risk than an unhedged long-only stock holding. Therefore, if you purchase a stock for $24.50 per share and sell a $25 strike price call for $0.85 which expires in three months' time, the annualized return potential for this position is approximately 23% assuming the stock has a 4% yield. When VIX is very high, the annualized returns a trader can get from fairly tight call sales can easily exceed a 20% annualized return objective, so take advantage of these rich premiums on high-quality companies.

Delta Force

In general, maximum delta premium credit occurs when the stock is at or very near the strike price sold. When there is still time before expiration, there is always a trade-off between capturing additional time decay in the option you currently hold short (and optimizing theta) and the loss in delta time premium the more a given stock becomes ITM. The closer to expiration, the more the position has captured all possible time decay, thus the more important it is to roll when the option becomes ATM or ITM. The optimal outcome is that a stock closes just below a given strike price (in the case of a short call) or just above (in the case of a short put). This scenario allows you to capture the entire directional and time premium for your current short option, and in turn to sell the next dated option at its maximum premium for your chosen strike price.

If you have let a short put get ITM and are considering rolling it to a later-dated expiration date so as to avoid getting prematurely assigned as well as to capture at least some delta premium credit, you are in essence making a bet on what the stock price will do between today and expiration. Let's say you are short April $90 puts on Company X, which is now trading at $85 a few days before expiration. Your puts are trading for about $6.20 per share, the intrinsic value of $5 + $1.20 of the remaining time premium. A few days before expiration you could close the puts for $6.20 and sell the next month's same strike price options for about $8.50, or a delta credit of $2.30.

Three basic things could happen between now and expiration if you decide not to roll the option today but rather to wait until closer to expiration (with the intention of rolling the option if it is still ITM). First, the underlying stock price could head farther south and you could wake up one morning to find yourself prematurely assigned. In this case, you either hold the stock long and unhedged, immediately sell calls against the position (there will likely be good premiums in the $90 calls' not-too-far dated), or sell the stock and reenter a later-dated short put option to replace the stock. This is the worst-case scenario because, after commissions and spreads, you will have little, if any, delta premium credit.

The second possible scenario is that the stock moves very little and you roll for a delta premium before being assigned (whether at expiration date or before). This is the middle best case. The optimal scenario is that the underlying stock rallies as expiration nears. The closer the stock price approaches the strike price, in this case $90 per share, the higher your delta credit will be. The scenario in which you make maximum profits is the one in which the stock closes at $90 so that your cost to close the position is $0 (it expires worthless) and you get the maximum premium for selling the next-dated options.

Figure 5.1 **DELTA CREDIT PREMIUMS AT VARIOUS ITM SCENARIOS**

Stock Closing Price	Delta Credit Premium	April Premium (Closing Cost)	May Premium	Return on Investment
$90.00	$3.75	$0.00	$3.75	4.17%
$89.50	$3.40	$0.60	$4.00	3.80%
$89.00	$3.10	$1.10	$4.20	3.48%
$88.50	$3.00	$1.60	$4.60	3.39%
$85.00	$0.50	$5.10	$5.60	0.59%

Flash Dance: Doubling Up, Doubling Down

If you have sold a naked put or covered call that clearly is well OTM approaching expiration, you can "double up" your position for the short period of time prior to expiration by writing the option again for the next available expiration date. In this way, you are effectively getting decay for both options and saving commissions by not buying back the option that is presumably about to expire worthless. For example, if you earlier sold September $45 strike price puts on a stock that is trading at $47 per share the day before expiration, you may opt to sell October (or whatever the next options expiration date is) $45 strike price puts even before the September options expire. When you are the seller of premium, the longer the premium is on the books, the more time is working on your side. By selling the next month's options on the Thursday before expiration, rather than waiting until Monday post-expiration, you get an additional three to four days of time decay working for you. All things being equal, the next month's option will probably lose ten to fifteen cents' worth of premium between Thursday and Monday (which could easily be 10% or more of the position). If your goal is to squeeze intelligently every penny of profit (and who does not have that goal?), then doubling up is a good idea. The same applies to doubling up on short calls that are well OTM going into expiration.

POWER TIP

When to Hold 'Em, When to Fold 'Em

Sometimes your options hand is strong, sometimes it is weak. It is important to take the right actions to optimize your profit potential. Here are two scenarios. If you hold an ITM short put that is approaching expiration and the option becomes less ITM for some reason, you are well served to use this strength to roll the option to a later-dated strike price. While you might get lucky and the underlying stock continues to rise so that the option ends up worthless at expiration, it is best to take advantage of this strength to roll and get the large delta premium credit while you can (prior to expiration). If the stock does continue to rally, you will be making money on your later-dated short puts. If, however, the stock heads back south prior to expiration, you will have lost the opportunity to get any meaningful delta premium credit. Thus, rolling on strength provides only upside while hesitating can lead to a situation in which little to no premium credit is attained as the options become increasingly ITM. Discipline, as always, is key. Conversely, if the short put is slightly OTM approaching expiration, it is okay to hold the position until expiration approaches as the option will at best expire worthless (stay OTM) or at worst get closer to ATM or even slightly ITM—in which case substantial delta premium credit will still be available.

As with all investing and trading, however, it is important to know what your true risks are and to manage them accordingly. Stock prices can move quickly and dramatically, often when you least expect it. It is not uncommon for even large-cap stocks to move 5% or more in a single day. It is one thing to dash to your bathroom without any clothes on in the privacy of your home; it is another thing entirely to run down the street naked.

When selling additional farther-dated puts on top of the puts you are already short—the ones about to expire—you are adding incremental long exposure to your portfolio. You need to be prepared to act very quickly if the stock goes against you, or to take on the additional exposure if the stock price that was well out-of-the-money on Thursday suddenly falls below the strike price on the Friday of expiration. Again, this does not happen often, but it does happen. Knowing what is on the calendar—earnings announcements, Fed meetings, and the like—is vital, as these events might drive near-term stock movements. Having an alert system in place is also critical so that if the stock hits a certain predetermined target you are able to close out the option that is about to expire before it starts losing you money. One good technique is to establish an e-mail alert that notifies you when a stock on which you have doubled up on \$22.50 puts hits \$23.50. Depending on how close to expiration it is (and how averse you are to being assigned on the puts such that the size of your effective position doubles), a trigger of 2% to 5% away from the strike price is a good range. That way, you can close your about-to-expire \$22.50 puts while they're still profitable.

If you are unable to monitor the position, then do not double up on options prior to expiration; it is simply not worth the risk that the one time you are unable to act quickly a dramatic market or stock movement will take place. A single material event can result in a loss that wipes out your other gains and then some. After selling incremental options on about-to-expire positions, you will soon get a feel for the relationship between the number of days left until expiration, how far OTM the option is, and what trigger price should cause you to close out the about-to-expire option while still preserving your position profit. Clearly, the closer to expiration, the closer the stock price can be to the strike price and allow you to double up. If expiration is due in a few minutes and the stock price in question is 2% or more from the strike price, you can pretty safely sell the incremental calls/puts, although you should be prepared to monitor the position until close to be certain, because even a quick flash can get you in trouble. Similarly, the farther away the stock price is from the strike price, the more room for error you have in doubling up, and the farther from expiration time-wise you can double up (always with an alert in place). As with all trading, this is part art (pattern recognition, a gut feel for stock movements, and a sense of time decay) and part science (doing the math), and only with experience will you develop the necessary skills.

***Figure* 5.2 MANAGING OPTION POSITIONS**

	Option Near Expiration	Option Far from Expiration
Stock Far from Strike	OPTIMAL Doubling Up OK	Moderate Risk Monitor Doubling via Alerts
Stock Near Strike	Moderate Risk Monitor Doubling via Alerts	DANGEROUS Focus on Risk Control

In supervising options positions around expiration, other risk considerations include total portfolio exposure, net exposure, and position size. Let's say you have purchased 500 shares of Company X for $23 per share and sold five of the September $25 strike price calls. Soon after you purchase the stock it falls to $21 per share, so you take this opportunity to **layer in** more long exposure by selling five of the $20 September puts, bringing your total notional long exposure to the equivalent of 1,000 shares long excluding the OTM short calls, which reduces your net position exposure slightly. For this example, assume that your portfolio size is $1 million so that your notional long position size is 2.05% (500 shares at $21 per share, the current price, plus 500 shares at $20 per share via the short puts). Of course, your delta adjusted long exposure is less than 2.05% since the delta on the puts about to expire is close to zero and your short calls reduce your long exposure, but for the purpose of this analysis, it is best to use the more conservative notional exposure calculations (for many accounts, short puts are secured by cash meaning that the brokerage firm sets aside the notional value of the option and reduces margin availability commensurately).

If, shortly before expiration, the stock is trading around $22 and you are confident that the short September put position will expire worthless, you might elect to sell five October $20 puts before September expiration to take advantage of additional time decay. In this case, your notional long exposure will increase from 2.05% to 3.05% (500 shares at $21 per share plus ten short puts at $20 per share). An important variable to consider for risk control is the total position size on a notional basis. Remember, when selling options, you have to think the same way as the buyer or seller of a stock: How are the fundamentals of the business? What is the valuation? In terms of portfolio construction, how big is the position? When calculating the latter figure—and, indeed, for ongoing portfolio construction and managing purposes—using delta adjusted figures is perfectly legitimate. When making incremental exposure decisions, however, you are best served by focusing on the more conservative notional exposures. Remember, the purpose of risk control is to consider what will happen in the worst-case scenarios should the proposed position work against you. It is not a matter of if, but when, you will experience a dramatically adverse move, so you need to plan accordingly and not end up with unintentionally large single-company positions.

It is one thing if the total notional short put exposure for the position is 4%, via doubling your puts prior to expiration; it is another matter entirely if the sale of the additional puts increases the notional position size from 5% to 10%. In this case, you are likely better served by waiting to write additional puts until you are nearly, if not totally, certain that the September puts will expire worthless—waiting until just before close Friday or even until the following Monday post-expiration. *When in doubt, choose the conservative approach, which is to hold off on selling the incremental puts.* Remember, your goal is to optimize overall portfolio performance, not to maximize every trade. Attempting to maximize every single position might lead to a suboptimal total outcome over time.

At times your short puts will continue to go against you so that you have to keep rolling them as they get deeper and deeper ITM. Once a short put gets deep ITM, approximately 9% or more, delta approaches 1.0 and you are effectively long the stock.

***Figure* 5.3 ITM Short Put Deltas**

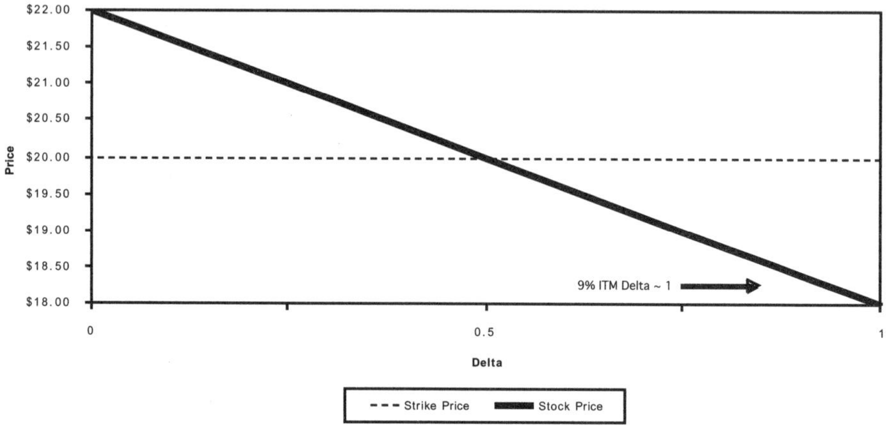

Since you are effectively long the stock, you might want to sell short calls at the same strike price to hedge the position and add incremental profits to your portfolio. Remember, however, that your short puts provide no profit potential above the strike price, so your short calls will become naked if the price of the stock goes above the strike price. Furthermore, you will likely have to go out sixty days, ninety days, or more since your short calls have to be so far OTM (you will be selling calls at the same strike price as your ITM puts, which are now, by definition, deep ITM). In this case, you must place premium on the books as soon as possible to get time decay working for you. Of course, the downside to selling the short calls so far out in time is that the underlying stock might rebound in the interim. Thus, I tend to sell short calls selectively against my deep ITM short put positions, and set alerts so that if the stock gets to within approximately 5% of the strike price (depending on how far from expiration), I can close the short call so that the net exposure on the position will not become negative if the underlying stock price continues to rise. Alternatively, you can put on a partial hedge, specifically selling fewer short calls than puts that you are short. A 2:1 ratio of puts to calls is a conservative way to go and will ensure that the combined position stays net long except and until the underlying stock increases dramatically, at which point your alert would have long since notified you to take action accordingly.

Figure 5.4 ALERT SETTING: SHORT CALLS AGAINST ITM SHORT PUTS

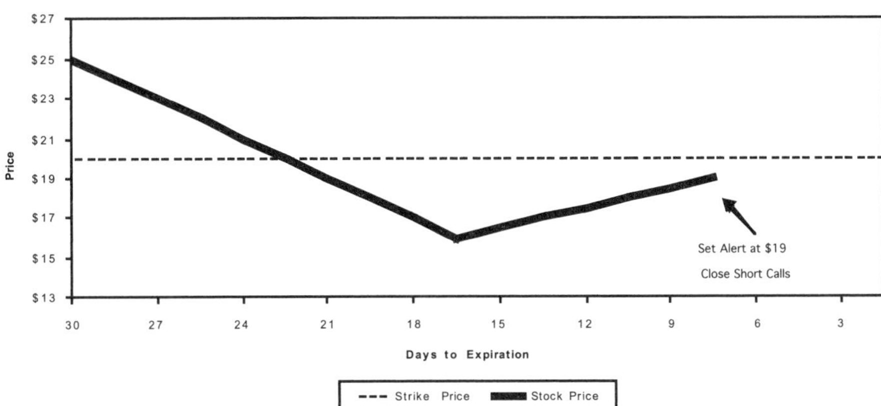

When you are short both puts and calls on a given security (without any direct ownership), another way to look at your effective net position exposure is to examine absolute premium dollar levels rather than, or in addition to, delta adjusted exposure levels. These premium levels can be a good proxy for delta adjusted exposure levels. Thus, if you have $3,200 of short put exposure and $800 of short call exposure, you still have a net long position (even if you have more short calls on the books than short puts on a notional contract basis).

Getting Top Heavy: Ratio Call Selling

There are times when you own a stock long against which you sold a call that subsequently dropped materially in value due to the substantial decline of the long stock position. If VIX is high or the volatility of the underlying stock is significant, opportunities to sell calls on a 2:1 or even 3:1 notional basis will arise. This is sometimes called **ratio call selling**. Let's say you purchased 1,000 shares of Company X on March 1 for $28 per share and immediately sold ten contracts of the June $30 calls that are about three months out for $1.55 per contract. Halfway through the options cycle (day 45) the stock is trading at $24.50 per share and your call options have collapsed in price to $0.40 due to time decay and directional decline. You still believe this is a quality company, and it pays a dividend that you are collecting. One strategy is to write additional calls seventy-five to ninety days farther out, in this case ten contracts (or fewer, to be more conservative) of the July $30 calls for $1.10. Since deltas will be very low on the way OTM calls, the net position will still be long—up to a point. With time decay on your side, anything short of a massive, sudden run-up in the underlying stock will put you ahead by having double short call exposure on the books. As stocks do run up quickly from time to time, always use a good alert system so that you can close out of the incremental calls at a profit if need be. In this case, an initial alert price at approximately $27 per share will allow you to still close out the June $30 options at a profit. (In general, you want to close out the premium at 50% of the original sale price at most, in this case approximately $0.80 per contract.) Certainly, as June expiration approaches and the June options begin to decay dramatically, you can slowly increase your alert price to $28 and then ultimately to $29. The trade-off for selling the incremental calls is that you gain more by getting later-dated premium on the books than you might lose by having to close out your nearer -dated options at a higher price. Short of a takeover (which does happen periodically, so be prudent), this is a fairly conservative way to gain incremental market exposure and profits, as long as you are disciplined with your alerts and buybacks.

A scenario you will face often occurs when you have purchased stock long and sold call options which you believe are about to expire worthless. You decide to do a little flash dance and sell the next-dated October options to get additional exposure on the books. Let's say your covered calls are Septembers which expire in a few days and the stock starts heading north rapidly. Which options should you close? Since the October calls you just sold still have substantial time premium in them whereas the September calls have virtually none, you are better off closing the September calls rather than the October calls.

In essence, the trade-off of doubling up on calls is that the incremental premium gained by selling the later-dated option prior to expiration rather than after expiration outweighs any potential gain in the stock that would (1) cause you to have to close your about-to-expire option or (2) would have allowed you to sell the option for more premium at a later date (due to the rising stock price having increased the later-dated premiums).

***Figure* 5.5 Ratio Call Selling**

March 1, 2008

1 Buy 1,000 shares Co. X at $28/share
2 Sell 10 June $30 Calls for $1.55

Portfolio
Stock: $28,000
Short (June) Calls:($12,600)

Net Exposure: $15,400

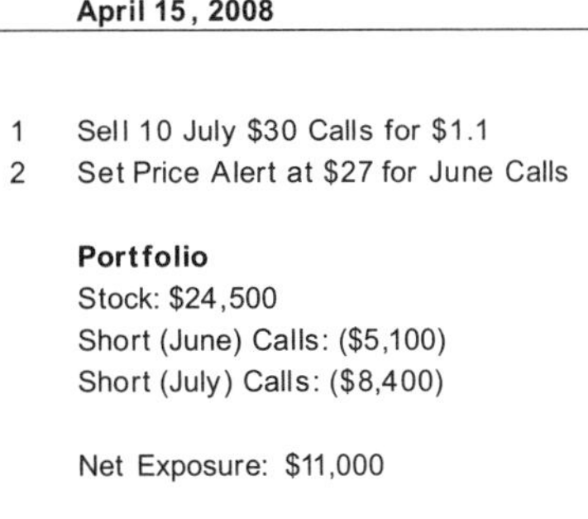

April 15, 2008

1 Sell 10 July $30 Calls for $1.1
2 Set Price Alert at $27 for June Calls

Portfolio
Stock: $24,500
Short (June) Calls: ($5,100)
Short (July) Calls: ($8,400)

Net Exposure: $11,000

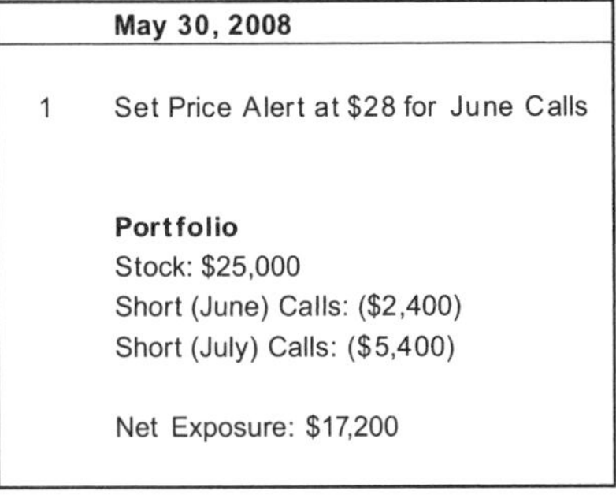

May 30, 2008

1 Set Price Alert at $28 for June Calls

Portfolio
Stock: $25,000
Short (June) Calls: ($2,400)
Short (July) Calls: ($5,400)

Net Exposure: $17,200

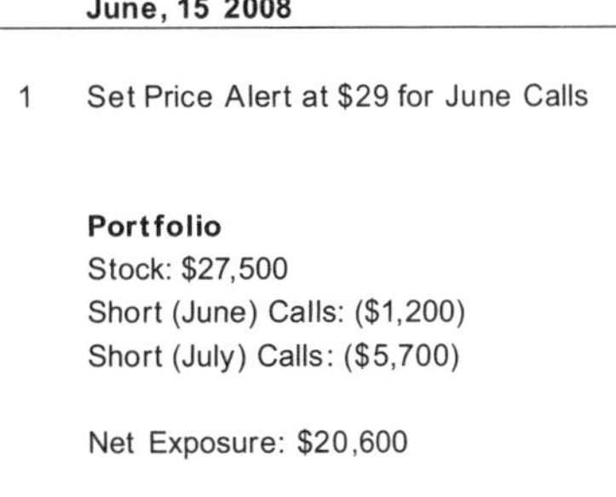

June, 15 2008

1 Set Price Alert at $29 for June Calls

Portfolio
Stock: $27,500
Short (June) Calls: ($1,200)
Short (July) Calls: ($5,700)

Net Exposure: $20,600

If indeed the stock does "pop," don't make the mistake of hoping the stock will come back down and allow you to hold both the September (to full expiration) and October calls. You might get lucky with the stock closing below the strike price at expiration, but this possibility is not worth the risk. If you do not close out your September calls immediately, your stock may be called away upon expiration, leaving you with October naked calls. At this point, you are effectively short the stock. Since your portfolio should be full of only top-quality companies, that would mean that you are short a great company that is trading at a reasonable valuation and that's not a good position to take. Assuming the sale of puts is done on quality companies at good valuations and your total notional exposure is such that the position size is reasonable, doubling up on short puts can be an effective way to squeeze out incremental profits prior to expiration because the downside associated with doing so is limited with time on your side. But the sale of incremental short calls prior to expiration should be done carefully and selectively—and if the position begins to work against you, it should be unwound immediately.

THE IMPACT OF EVENTS ON PREMIUMS

As noted, often such companies as Google announce their quarterly earnings right around expiration time. Individual stock volatility can heighten dramatically in the days before earnings releases, only to collapse once the figures have been made public. Because earnings are an important variable in determining whether a stock will move through a given strike price, the anticipation of this data point and its release has a big impact on options premium levels. Accordingly, the main variable to consider when contemplating options moves around expiration is whether the temporarily high premium levels driven by earnings uncertainty will outweigh any directional gains or losses after earnings release.

Assume you own a stock long that is trading at $33.20 on a Tuesday in April before the company is to release its earnings on Thursday before the open. Friday is options expiration day. You are short the $35 April calls, which are now trading for only a few pennies. One move is to take advantage of the enhanced premiums associated with the pending earnings announcement and sell the May $35 calls now (either closing your April contracts concurrent with the sale of the May options, or doubling up on the calls with a very tight alert around $34 in case earnings come in above expectations and the stock rallies hard on Thursday). The sale of May options with the concurrent closing of the April contracts would be the conservative trade. If earnings are disappointing the stock will either be flat or down and you will have maximized the premium you received for selling the May $35 calls as they will likely trade down based on the combination of: (1) time decay (the fact that a couple of days have passed), (2) directional decay (the fact that the stock has declined in price), and (3) reduced volatility (the fact the volatility-induced premium has dropped with the announcement of earnings).

Under the scenario in which you have sold May calls prior to earnings being announced (and maintained your April calls) and the company announces favorable earnings—both historical and projected—you need to act quickly to close out your April calls. While this would not be the optimal outcome relative to your timing of May

POWER TIP

The Battle of the Ages

The way to think about the counterbalancing forces of time decay and the strengthening of the underlying stock price is as follows: As we age we lose a certain amount of physical strength and endurance. After the age of approximately thirty-five, if you do not exercise at all, you lose a given percentage of your strength and aerobic capacity each year. If you exercise, this exertion helps to offset the natural deterioration of the body. To make the analogy clear, think of physical exercise as an increasing stock price and time as . . . well, time. In the case of a stock rising rapidly just prior to expiration, the company is working out very hard. However, time is against its about-to-expire options, the ones "near the end." For the farther time-dated options, the ones with a longer life ahead of them, the increase in stock price, just like a good workout program, can have a positive impact on the options' price and health. For options nearing the end of their life, however, time tends to win the battle. You can work out as much as you want, but if you are on your deathbed, exercise has little effect. So, too, with options that are about to expire; a dramatic increase in stock price does not forestall the inevitable demise (read: worthless expiration) of an OTM option about to expire.

If Company X's stock price increases approximately 5% to $34.80 per share, the April $35 calls will only gain a few pennies. However, the May calls will gain much of what the underlying stock gains (the May $35 contracts likely gaining close to $1), the delta typically being higher and, more important, the theta lower for the later-dated options, especially for ATM options. (For way OTM or ITM options, delta varies little regardless of how long dated the options is.) Under this scenario you would get the double benefit of near-term options decay and farther-dated increased premium in the May $35 calls. On an absolute basis, the increase in stock price—or workout to complete our analogy—disproportionately "benefits" those with longer to live than those near the end of their lives.

call sales, assuming you close out your April calls before the stock rises too highly it is still a favorable outcome for your portfolio as a whole.

The more aggressive trade would be to wait until earnings are announced and adjust your options concurrently with the subsequent stock reaction. If earnings are strong and the stock rallies, you will generally be able to buy your April calls back for pennies (since time decay is so dramatic in the last day or two approaching expiration), and get maximum premium for May options to boot, given the increase in price of the underlying stock. Thus, options give you the flexibility and precision to have predetermined outcomes based on your thesis about upcoming events.

Figure 5.6 **Varying Effects of a Rising Stock Price on Options**

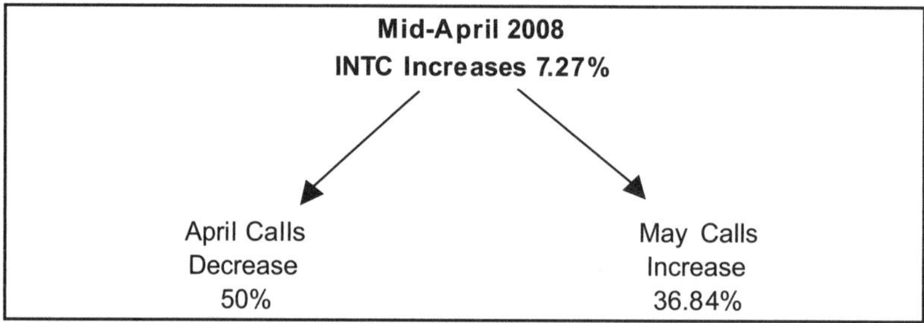

On April 16, 2008, Intel Corporation (INTC) increased 7.27% from $20.91 to $22.43 on positive earnings news. This caused May calls to increase by about $0.35 to $1.30 per contract, whereas April options due to expire in two days actually declined $0.10 to about $0.09. This scenario provides a stark example of near-term options decay.

From time to time, earnings come in so far ahead of expectations that an otherwise winning position can quickly turn into a losing proposition if you are doubled up on calls and effectively become short the stock. Even large, well-established companies can have single-day (or worse, overnight) moves—when the market is closed and you are unable to adjust your positions) of greater than 10%. If Company X stock rises to $37, an 11.5% increase from its previous closing price of $33.20 per share, then a combined long equity/double short call position has become net short, the delta on the about-to-expire (and expected to be worthless) $35 strike price calls jumping from near 0 to 1 within minutes. At this point you need to close either the about-to-expire or the later-dated, incremental calls unless you want to be effectively short the stock via the later-dated short calls which would be your sole position post being assigned on your covered calls. If you maintain a naked call position and the stock closes above $35 at expiration time, you will end up short the stock outright; the assignment of naked short calls leads to a short equity position, which is a dangerous game with unlimited downside potential. Being short a stock that recently announced better-than-expected earnings in the hopes that the price will eventually go back down is a tenuous proposition. If you get caught doubling up on calls and the underlying stock price increases dramatically and unexpectedly, you are better off acting quickly and closing out the near-term options so that you will not be potentially assigned the stock in the near future. In that way, you will live another day, the stock perhaps closing below $35 at the next expiration period—and allowing you to sell additional later-dated premium. Or you can sell $35 strike price puts as a means to maintain exposure if the stock closes above $35 at the next expiration period.

POWER TIP

Optimization Defined

I have frequently used the term "optimize" rather than "maximize." This usage is not accidental. As investors and traders, we make decisions regularly. Absent risk/reward considerations, we would likely always think in terms of maximizing our results. If you are naked some way OTM calls going into expiration, the maximized result is to let them expire worthless—and thus not have to pay the nickel and commission to buy the options back. However, this maximizing choice might not be the optimal approach. Remember, our portfolio is the aggregate of our investment and trading decisions over long periods. Therefore, many times nonmaximizing choices lead to overall optimal outcomes. Keep this in mind when you are trying to squeeze every penny out of a trade—or when you hold a given position only because you feel you need to "beat" the market and not lose the battle against this stock. Focus on the war, not the individual battles, and you will come out ahead in the end.

CALCULATING ROI ON OPTION SALES

How can you best calculate the return on investment on options positions? For covered calls, the answer is simple. The ROI is the sum of the capital gains, premium received, and any dividend collected (minus margin interest paid if the stock was purchased using leverage) divided by the stock purchase price. For example, if you purchased Company X for $43 per share and simultaneously sold the $45 strike price calls for $1.10, your return upon assignment would be $3.10 ($2 capital gain plus $1.10 premium collected) divided by $43, or 7.2%. If you collected a $0.50 dividend as well, your gross (also known as absolute or raw) return would increase to 8.4%.

You can look at this return on an absolute basis (the actual return on a percentage basis) or an annualized basis. Assuming you held the position for three months (the calls you sold simultaneously with the long equity purchase were ninety days out), then the annualized return would be approximately 34%, depending on whether you look at this on a compounded or additive basis. Be careful, however, about annualized return claims as they assume the particular position is replicable every time period held. Traders who are new to options often comment that they were told by firms selling options-related trading software that they can make X% (usually 4% to 6%) monthly via a covered call options strategy. While it might be true that for any particular position for a given thirty-day time period the potential return is 5%, repeating this return profile on the same security every thirty days is virtually impossible. By their nature, stocks rarely close right below the strike price at which you sold the option (which would yield the highest possible return for the time period), making it possible for you to rewrite the option for additional maximum premium. If such a stock did close month after month at or near a given strike price, it would have a very low volatility profile and the premium you would receive for selling options against such a stock—and, in turn, the return potential for said position—would drop over time. To be sure, high-volatility stocks are typically cited in claims of 5% monthly return potential, and volatility cuts both ways. Only one significant drop in a company's stock price is needed to quickly eliminate the following month's 5% return potential.

For short put options, the calculations are a bit more complex if not inexact. Simply stated, there is no universally accepted approach to calculating ROI on the sale of put options. For easy math, assume the portfolio in question is valued at $1,000,000. Ten OTM puts are sold on IBM at $100 strike price for $1 per contract, providing $1,000 of premium. What is the ROI for this position if the option expires worthless and the maximum profit of $1,000 is reached? Let's examine four possible calculations, all done on a raw (not annualized) basis and determine which methodology best represents true returns:

1. ROI = $1,000/$1,000,000, or 0.10%. This calculation expresses the position profit over the total portfolio/capital base. I think this is *not* the best way to look at the profit of the position as the ROI should relate to the position-specific capital "outlay" and not to the total portfolio. Ultimately, we want to see how profitable the position is—not how much profit it adds to the portfolio (though portfolio profitability relates to total capital amounts at the beginning and end of any given time period).

2. ROI = $1,000/$100,000, or 1%. This approach examines the premium received relative to the notional value of the short puts (ten contracts X 100 shares per contract at $100 per share, or $100,000). The notional value of the short put position is the amount of capital outlay needed if the option were assigned, or full attribution of capital. Hence, in this case the ROI would be 1% raw.

3. ROI = $1,000/margin capital used up. For most brokerage accounts, depending on how far OTM the put is, and on other variables, the sale of a naked put will use up about 25% of cash available on a notional basis, so in this case you are using up about $25,000 of "gunpowder" (25% of $100,000). Thus, the return here is $1,000/$25,000, or 4% raw.

4. ROI = incremental profit or infinite profit. This is an interesting way of looking at the profits. The rationale here is that you have your core portfolio, perhaps even 100%, invested. On top of that you layer in "incremental" OTM put positions that add to the P&L ad infinitum.

> Clearly there is a limit, however, to the number of puts one can sell based on capital levels and margin requirements, so I don't think you can take this line of reasoning to the extreme. The profit is neither "free" nor unlimited from a cash-available or risk standpoint, so I don't think one can truly say that the ROI is infinite. There has to be a base by which to divide the profit. In a declining market, this theoretical "infinite profit" can become a very real loss; the idea that the sale of OTM short puts is "free money" and adds infinite incremental ROI to a portfolio is a tenuous one at best.

While there is no right or wrong answer per se, the most "accurate" calculation of ROI is probably #3, or some blend of #2 and #3. At the end of the day, what matters is the return of a total portfolio within the context of risk taken. That should be your focus, though you should certainly consider the ROI for any given option position for risk management purposes and position sizing.

The Day After the Day After Tomorrow

Some people like to use an options-writing strategy with a single broad-based ETF like the SPYs. The thinking is that you are getting enough diversification with the S&P 500, which is easier to track, and that you don't need to worry about individual stock selection. While these are valid points, and for long-term buy-and-hold investors a portfolio with a small number of low-cost, broad-based ETFs or mutual funds can be a great approach, for the more active trader looking to add incremental profit to a portfolio, there is a far superior strategy. Let's use DIAs in our example. As a starting point, you buy the DIA ETF and sell calls against it at whatever level OTM meets your objectives (tight calls for more income and downside protection, farther OTM calls for more capital gains potential). Thirty days later the ETF closes just below your given strike price and you repeat the cycle. That all sounds good…except that in most cases the DIAs will close well below the option strike price or perhaps even well in-the-money. What do you do then? If you bought the DIAs for $82.50 and sold the next month's $83 calls for $2.20 and DIA closes at $76.40 so that the following month's $83 calls have virtually no premium in them, then what are your alternatives? You can sell an option that expires in thirty days at a strike price low enough to give you decent premium, for example the $78 calls. This, however, locks you into a loss should the DIAs rebound and force an assignment. Alternatively, you can sell the $83 calls but at an expiration date that is six months or farther away. In either case, you are tied to the semirandom closing price of a single security. You might have to wait several months, not selling and collecting options premium in the interim, until the ETF price "comes to you" thus allowing you to begin to sell options premium again at strike prices that fulfill your gain objectives.

Compare the purchase of a basket of stocks (even the thirty securities contained in the Dow Jones 30 Industrials). In a twenty-to-thirty position portfolio, some positions invariably close near the strike prices (which is optimal in terms of maximizing future premium sold). Some close ITM so that you are called away and thus the profit potential drops from, say, 5% monthly to 0% since this position is no longer in the portfolio. And other stocks close at an expiration cycle well OTM, the next month's premium for the same strike price being low or nonexistent. An example of this latter scenario is if you bought non-dividend–paying Company X for $34 per share on the Monday following expiration and received $0.70 of thirty-day premium for the $35 strike price so that the return potential is 5% monthly. It would not be uncommon for the stock to close at $31 per share at time of expiration. In this scenario, the next month's $35 calls will have little or no premium, therefore your ability to use options as a means to generate 4% to 6% monthly returns has been eliminated on this particular position. Given that you have a basket of stocks, however, you can sell the same strike price puts on your buy-write positions that have closed ITM for the next month to maintain exposure to the security. For the stocks that closed slightly OTM, you can sell the same strike price for a later-dated option and maximize premium earned. For those long equity positions for which your call expired well out-of-the-money, you could capture capital gains by owning the stock unhedged or wait until the stock price increases to sell additional calls. You could even add incremental shares and simultaneously lower your average purchase price by acquiring additional shares at $31 and selling the $30 ITM calls or slightly OTM $32.50 options. Simply put, the Monday after options expiration offers all sorts of opportunities to profit when you are working with a basket of stocks that have closed at various levels relative to option strike prices that expired two days before. To be sure, part of you will want Monday to open up on weakness so that the stock that was assigned away over the weekend can be bought back at lower prices. Other parts of you will hope for strength so that call premiums will be richer on stocks for which OTM calls have just expired. In any case, you will invariably have a variety of opportunities to optimize profits within this dynamic portfolio, one of the many advantages of maintaining a portfolio with twenty to thirty positions rather than just selling options against a single or few broad-based ETFs. Because I have alerts set up to inform me in real time if a particular stock price has gone down to a certain price or if a certain security has reached a sale price, I know that stocks have either opened sharply higher or lower, and I am ready to take advantage once again of whatever near-term prices the market has to offer when I wake up Monday morning.

POWER TIP

Only the Shadow Knows

A shadow short is one way to look at an OTM put. If you sell a put with a strike price of $20 when the underlying stock is trading at $23 per share, you have a "shadow short" between $23 and $20. Unlike a real short, you do not profit from a decline in the stock, but you do not lose money if the stock rises. On the contrary, you make money as the stock price increases. By selling the OTM put, you are saying that you are not a buyer of the stock until it gets to your strike price; hence you are holding a shadow short.

ADDITIONAL OPTIONS TRADING TIPS

Below are some frequently asked questions about situations that arise when trading options.

If I am bullish on a given stock but I am looking to just make a trade as opposed to investing in the company for the long term, am I better off buying the stock long and selling a call or selling a put with the equivalent notional exposure?

The risk/reward ratio of entering a covered call position versus a naked put position depends on several variables. First, in general, puts offer more premium than calls that are equally OTM. Therefore, if a stock is trading evenly between two strike prices then the sale of a put will generally offer a better return potential on a risk/reward basis whereas the buy write has greater total gains potential.

Selling Put versus Buying Stock/Selling Call

Specifically, assuming Company X stock is trading right between two strike prices at $21.25 a share, selling the $20 puts will provide you $1 per share of return potential and lower your effective purchase price to $19 per share (reduce risk). The purchase of shares long combined with the sale of a $22.50 call for $0.90 per share will provide for a return potential of $2.15 per share but your breakeven will be $20.35, or nearly 7% higher than under the put sale scenario. Thus, if you have more conviction on the stock, enter a buy write whereas if you are looking to be more conservative, sell the puts. Given the deltas associated with the OTM puts, you can actually sell more puts to generate similar profits as the buy write setup. You would have to approximately double your notional exposure (sell twice as many contracts) to generate the same absolute profit as buying the stock long and selling an equally OTM call. Thus, you are ultimately looking at risk reward ratios. Another consideration for those who qualify for higher options levels is the amount of margin used in entering the transaction. The purchase of long stock uses up margin capacity dollar for dollar, whereas the sale of short puts will initially only require approximately 25% of the margin for the same notional position. A further nuance is whether the position is considered a core holding versus a special situation. If the latter, then the put sale should be favored, whereas if you are looking to potentially hold the position indefinitely, then buying the stock long and selling a call that you are okay with expiring worthless (meaning that you would continue to hold the stock and simply have made incremental portfolio profit from the sale of the call option) is the optimal path. Related, if the company is a dividend payer and you would like to begin to accumulate payouts, then you need to own the stock long to be entitled to future dividend payments.

If I have sold a put on Company X for $1 and now the option is trading for $0.20, should I buy the option back to lock in a profit, or should I maintain the position?

By definition, the original option trade premise is working, so you should be reluctant to exit this position. As sellers of options, we have time on our side. Most often we are getting paid for waiting patiently. Usually the sale of a conservative put represents an attempt at hitting a single rather than a home run. All things being equal, it is generally worthwhile to run all the way around the bases so that you avoid the transaction costs associated with closing out the position. That said, a good rule of thumb is that if you have received 80% or more of the potential profit on a given position (if an option you sold previously is now trading for 20% or less of the original price), and especially if this collapse in options premium has occurred in a short period of time, then you should close out the position. For example, if the option you sold has an expiration date sixty days hence and it is down by 80% or more after only three weeks from the time you sold the option, then you should consider closing out the position. Another factor that would suggest that you close the naked put would be if the position size is uncomfortably large on a notional basis. In this case, you could close half the position. Furthermore, if your portfolio net long exposure is very high and you are looking to reduce some gross long exposure, short puts that have collapsed in a brief period of time are good candidates to take off the books as the upside/downside ratio is skewed to losses over gains. In any case, if the underlying fundamentals of the business appear in jeopardy, or if there is a company-specific event like an earnings announcement due between now and expiration, you should look to close out the position as it will possibly go against you and you have already largely achieved the position's profit potential.

On the call side, if you have sold a call against a long position and the underlying stock price drops (causing the short call option to decrease in price), you might want to consider buying the option back with the goal of reselling the call at a higher price if the stock price rebounds. A scenario in which this might happen is if a stock-specific or macroeconomic event is on the near-term calendar like an earnings report or a Fed meeting. Here are some of the many considerations. Let's say you sold a call on a stock as a means to generate additional income or profit, but you also think the company is a strong one and, unless there is some negative change in the company's fundamentals, you would like to own the stock for the long term. In this case, taking advantage of near-term stock price weakness to buy back the short calls at a profit could be wise because doing so eliminates the possibility that you could be assigned on this quality company. Alternatively, if you are perfectly happy selling the stock at the strike price at which the options are written, then holding the options is worthwhile in order to squeeze out any and all profit opportunities, be they additional options premium decay, stock capital gains, or dividend payment—or some combination thereof.

Generally speaking, I do not try to get too tricky with options once the position is established. For instance, I do not often attempt to buy back short call options with the goal of reselling them later at a higher price. I will regularly buy back short put and call options at a profit in order to permanently exit the position for the reasons described above. Trying to close out a position in the hopes that you can resell the option at a higher price later is a difficult task at best. Time decay, spreads, and transaction costs are all working against you, especially with near-term options. Stock prices have to move quickly and dramatically to allow you to truly profit from this tactic. Remember, an option trading at \$0.50 X \$0.60 has a 20% spread; this alone makes the profitable and repeated entry/exit of this derivative security difficult. In most cases, you will not be able to resell the option at a higher price once you have closed it out at a profit. Therefore, let your underlying objectives dictate your actions rather than attempting to time the market or a particular short-term stock price movement. You will get lucky sporadically and nail a stock drop and sudden rebound just right with your short calls, but you will lose more often than you will win. Stick with consistently winning strategies.

If I purchased a stock and sold ATM calls concurrently, and upon expiration the stock is well below my original purchase price (and option strike price), should I sell calls again for nominal premium or wait for stock strength, to try to get more premium later?

This is a scenario that happens frequently. You buy a given stock and sell ATM or slightly OTM calls, and the long stock position declines so that upon expiration there is little premium in options that expire within ninety days. The question is whether you reach for that nominal premium, sell later-dated options (e.g., 180 days), or wait for stock strength in the hopes that the nearer-dated options will gain premium that you can sell for greater profit. The variables to consider when deciding the optimal tactics include whether the company pays a dividend, what its **beta** is, whether the stock is trading at the low end of its valuation, and what your total portfolio net exposure is, as described in the following figure:

Figure **5.7 Variables to Consider for Selling Options**

	Yes/High	No/Low
Dividends	Sell Call	Wait
Beta	Wait	Sell Call
Position of Stock on Valuation Spectrum	Sell Call	Wait
Portfolio Exposure	Sell Call	Wait

The more conservative alternative is to get short premium on the books today. If you end up with what I call a "luxury problem," in this case the stock rising above the strike price, then you will have made money in the form of options premium (twice), dividends, and some level of capital gains, depending on how far OTM the original call sale was. This is not a bad outcome. In the other scenario, where the stock does not hit the strike price prior to expiration, you will be glad that you added incremental profits to your portfolio via the short call sale.

What should I do if a stock I own with covered calls rises and the calls become ATM or ITM?

The optimal move in this scenario depends on a few variables, including how far OTM the call was when you sold it originally, the time left to expiration, and your objective with the underlying stock. Let's look at these considerations in detail, starting with the two extreme scenarios. In scenario one, assume you bought Company X for short-term trading purposes and sold a far OTM (4% or more) short call option with an expiration date thirty days out. Fast-forward a few weeks and the stock is now trading ATM. In this case, you have captured most of the upside potential associated with this position, having received both the highest capital gain as well as most of the time decay in premium sold. Since the goal was a near-term trade, you are best served by closing this position out since the options provide little downside protection at this point (premium would be very low as expiration is near). With the stock ATM and options expiration just around the corner, the upside associated with the position is very limited, whereas the stock could collapse due to company-specific issues or broad market declines. Be disciplined; the position was entered into as a near-term trade and it worked. Get out and move on to other ideas (or reenter if the stock later declines to a point at which it becomes attractive again).

Examining the other extreme, if you bought Company Y for longer-term investment purposes, sold a near or ATM call to expire in thirty days, and the stock price rises in the near term—as in soon after you purchased it—then you are best served by holding the position since most of the gains associated with this position relate to time decay and only a few days have passed. In this case, your short call premium is still large, and it offers both greater downside protection and time decay profit. If the stock is about to go ex-dividend and your short calls are ITM, that is an extra incentive to hold the position in order to capture both additional option time decay and the dividend.

The guidelines for what to do as an option becomes ATM or ITM are as follows: You should be more inclined to close out the position the more the position is a trade, the closer the option is to expiration, and the farther OTM the original option was. You should be less inclined to sell the more the position is an investment, the farther it is away from expiration, and the closer-to-the-money the option was at time of sale.

For short puts, the optimal time to roll options that are approaching ATM is before the option becomes ITM.

Do option prices reflect dividends to be paid on the underlying stock? If a company is paying a large special dividend (as Microsoft did in 2006 when it paid a onetime $3-per-share dividend), will options prices be adjusted to reflect the dividend payment?

In general, options prices reflect the fact that a stock will go ex-dividend between today and expiration. There is no free lunch; it is not as though you get both the benefit of the dividend payment and the entire dividend amount built into the options price. (Arbitrage situations that arise from time to time are beyond the scope of this book.) For example, if you buy Company X stock long on July 3 for $54.20 per share and concurrently sell the July $55 call options, the price in these call options will reflect any dividend payment to be made prior to expiration—or, more precisely, an ex-dividend date prior to expiration as the actual dividend payment might occur later. If the July calls trade for $0.65 per contract, this pricing already reflects a $0.50 dividend payment that you will receive if you hold the stock to the ex-date. Note that if you hold stock long and the short calls become deep ITM approaching an ex-date, often you will be called away (assigned) and will be forced to sell the stock before the ex-date, depriving you of your dividend payment. Keep this in mind when you own stocks long that are covered by ITM calls approaching ex-dates. If you want to continue to own the stock and capture the dividend, you will need to close or roll your call option to either a farther-dated expiration date or a higher strike price (that is OTM), or both. By definition, an OTM option will not be prematurely assigned and rarely are options that have thirty or more days left until expiration assigned, even if they are fairly ITM.

As for the issue of options adjusting, options chains certainly do get altered to reflect new ticker symbols, stock splits, and the like, but they are only adjusted for special dividends representing 10% or more of the underlying stock price. For example, if you sell a LEAPS, often the option ticker chain will change when the option is six or nine months out (versus twelve months or more at the time of sale). Similarly, if you have sold options on a company that does a spin-off, the option pricing will be adjusted for the spin-off (just as the underlying stock price adjusts) and you may end up with multiple options representing both the original security as well as the spin-off.

Popular ETFs like DIAs and SPYs typically go ex-dividend on the last day of trading before option expiration. Often you will be exercised on ITM short options prior to the ex-date by those who are long the options and want to own the underlying security prior to the ex-date so that they will be paid the dividend. In general, your decision to hold or exercise an option should be driven by your confidence in the underlying security because the stock will drop by the amount of the dividend being paid. Any additional movement in the security will affect your profit.

Should I sell an entire option position at once, or layer in as I occasionally do with equity positions?

If your plan is to purchase a stock long and sell a short call against this long position for hedging purposes, you are better served by selling the call at the time you buy the stock long rather than by trying to wait to sell the call on subsequent strength. You might be right on the direction of the stock. Perhaps the stock does go up not long after you buy it and prior to your selling the call. More often, however, time decay will have erased any advantages gained by the increase in stock price, and the premium you get from selling the calls will be less than if you had opened the short call position at the time you purchased the stock long. Remember, as we learned with VIX, rising stock prices tend to correlate with reduced volatility levels, so time decay plus reduced volatility-induced premium loss are all working against you.

Do not confuse this lesson with selling calls on strength in general. The scenario described above is one in which you buy a stock long with the intention of immediately selling calls against that long position to generate additional profits and to hedge your position. A related scenario is using calls to hedge a position that has experienced a material run-up in price. In this latter scenario, you might have bought the stock long at $28 per share with the intention of maintaining the position as a long-term holding and over time the price has increased to the high $30s. Perhaps valuations at this level are frothy, but you still believe in the stock for the long term, so you decide to sell the $40 strike price calls just to provide some near-term hedge. In this case you might hedge only a portion of the position, for example selling five calls on a 1,000-share position. If the stock continues its upward trajectory, then you sell out on half your position at $40 per share plus premium earned with the possibility of repurchasing the shares sold for less than the $40 in the future (or via the sale of five $40 short puts). If the stock retraces prior to expiration, then you have made incremental profit on the short calls that are now worth less than the amount for which you sold them.

If you are layering your long purchases, then by definition you will be selling calls at different times (perhaps even at different strike prices), which is perfectly suitable. For example, if your goal is to purchase a 1,000-share position in Company X but you intend to buy in two tranches if the stock trades lower, you might purchase 500 shares at $27 per share and immediately sell the $27.50 calls. If the stock subsequently falls to $24 per share, you purchase your second lot of 500 shares to dollar cost average down, and in turn sell the $25 calls. Upon expiration, if the stock is trading around $24.50, you might sell the next month's $25 strike price calls on half the position but sell the $27.50s that are ninety days out, the other tranche given insufficient premium in the near-dated $27.50 calls. When I have part of a position with room to run (in this case the original 500 shares purchased for $27 per share now trading for $24.50), I generally sell a tight call on the incremental shares I purchased knowing that getting assigned on the lower-priced shares is a good problem to have—since I will still be making money on the shares that are not hedged as tightly. Instead, if you have attained strong premium in your first round of options selling and feel bullish on the stock, you could decide to sell ten of the $27.50 calls for further capital gains potential on the 500 shares for which your effective purchase price is likely around $23 ($24 purchase price less premium collected). This example once again shows the strength and flexibility of options as precise tools to achieve your evolving objectives.

In the case of naked short puts, you can layer them in just like you might layer in stock purchases, acquiring less than a full position at first (via equity purchases in the case of buying stock long, or in the case of naked puts selling less than a notionally-based full position) and adding more contracts if the stock trades lower. That said, because commissions as a percentage of the total position size are so much larger for options than for stocks, and because bid/ask spreads are generally so much wider for options than for stocks, layering in options is not as cost efficient as layering in stocks. Ultimately, the process for layering in is best viewed as a risk control measure more than anything else.

What moves can I make when naked put options sold are about to expire—either worthless or for potential assignment (ITM)?

There are a number of possible approaches:

1. Let options expire worthless and do not reestablish a position. In this case, the premium collected is your profit. You would take this course of action if your fundamental analysis indicated that the underlying stock on which you sold the put short was no longer a viable investment candidate. You might also choose not to resell options if your total portfolio exposure is such that you are "overexposed" to stocks. In other words, while you still feel good about the underlying position, your total portfolio exposure could be too net long and you might decide not to sell additional short put exposure so as not to increase incremental long exposure on an already long-biased portfolio. This is smart portfolio risk control.

2. Let options expire worthless and resell new options (either before expiration or post-expiration on the same position—see the section on "doubling up")—either at the same strike price or a lower strike price—to make the position more conservative, depending on where the stock settled at expiration time and VIX levels and market levels. If you feel bullish on the stock, you would sell the same number of contracts (or more contracts for higher exposure) at the same strike price on a later-dated option. If you are less bullish on the stock, or if your total portfolio composition is such that you do not want this much long exposure, you can sell fewer contracts, or, if the premium allows for it, you can roll down a strike price. For example, if you sold ten put contracts on Company X with a strike price of $22.50 and

the stock closed at $23.10 at expiration, you could either sell fewer contracts at the next-dated $22.50 option (e.g., five, which would halve your notional exposure), or sell ten contracts at the next-dated $20 strike price or some combination thereof. In the latter case, you might have to go out more than one month in order to reduce both notional and delta adjusted exposure this way since selling ten contracts of the $20 strike price puts reduces your notional long exposure to $20,000 from $22,500. In either case, any time you can get a similar amount of premium that you collected from selling the previous short puts by selling a smaller number of new puts or the same number of puts at a lower strike price, you are improving your risk/reward ratio and this path should be pursued. The advent of $1 rather than $2.50 strike price increments makes this rolling-down process easier as you can still find decent premium in lower strike prices without having to go so far out in the calendar. This is also known as rolling "down and out." In this way, you are able to reduce notional and delta adjusted exposure.

***Figure* 5.8 Percentage Gaps Given Strike Price Increments**

Strike Price Increments	% Gap
$20.00	
	12.50%
$22.50	
	11.11%
$25.00	
	10.00%
$27.50	
	9.09%
$30.00	
	8.33%
$32.50	

Strike Price Increments	% Gap
$20.00	
	5.00%
$21.00	
	4.76%
$22.00	
	4.55%
$23.00	
	4.35%
$24.00	
	4.17%
$25.00	

3. If the option is in-the-money approaching expiration, you can roll the option to a later-dated expiration for the always sought-after delta premium credit. Note that the deeper ITM the option is, the lower the delta premium credit will be because deep ITM options provide very little time premium (only intrinsic value premium). Furthermore, ITM equity (American-style) options approaching expiration are subject to premature assignment. Thus, if your goal

is to keep the short put option, as opposed to close the position entirely or be assigned the stock, you should roll the option as it approaches ATM, and certainly before it gets too deep ITM. In being proactive, you will optimize the delta premium credit you collect and also avoid having to "take," or be assigned, the stock.

4. Let option get assigned and hold stock long. If you sold a short put position, you were willing, if not wanting, to own the stock long. In selling an OTM put, you have entered into this position at a lower price than the stock was trading at when you sold the option. In this case, you can hold the stock unhedged as part of your portfolio with the goal of profiting from capital gains and dividends (in the case of a dividend-paying stock). Alternatively, you can immediately sell calls against the assigned stock in order to profit from options, but this time on the call side rather than the put side. If it is clear you are going to be assigned on or near expiration day, you can presell your calls in anticipation of being assigned. This will allow you to capture additional days' worth of short premium (see the section on "doubling up").

When in doubt, look at your total long exposure (your long stocks, short puts, and long calls) relative to your short exposure and if you are "overexposed" on the long side, take your short put profits (either by buying back profitable short puts or by letting them expire without reselling additional puts) as a matter of discipline. If stocks go up, you will make money from your long exposure. If stocks drop precipitously, you will be glad you did not add incremental long exposure, which you can always add later at a more attractive price.

TAKING DOWN THE HOUSE—LONG OPTIONS TRADING STRATEGIES

The great majority of options expire worthless, just as most insurance policies expire worthless. To be sure, it is always better to be the house; betting against those who control the game and make the rules is generally a loser's game. Selling options, when done intelligently and tactically, can be a great way to hedge, generate income, and add to profits.

What about buying options long? In purchasing options, you have to be accurate in the event, direction, magnitude, and timing. For example, if you purchase an OTM call to expire within thirty days in hopes of profiting from an earnings beat, you have to be right on four counts: that the company exceeds its earnings (the event), that the market reacts in the way you believe it will (the direction), that the subsequent gains are sufficient to cross the break-even hurdle on the OTM purchase (the magnitude), and that this all occurs prior to expiration (the timing). You could be right on two or even three of the four necessary variables and still lose money. Having a call option that was a bet on a pending takeover expire worthless on a Friday only to read in Saturday's paper that a deal was announced after market close (and thus too late) is a painful experience. While 98% of the time I am the house (since in selling options you can be "wrong" on multiple counts and still profit), in certain circumstances being long options can provide strong profit or hedging opportunities. Let's examine how to maximize option ownership to your advantage.

If you believe a company represents a good long-term investment opportunity and your goal is to own more of its stock for a long time, you are best served buying ITM long-term options (LEAPS). The deeper in-the-money an option is, the less time value premium there is, most of the premium being intrinsic value premium. With LEAPS, you will get virtually the full benefit of any appreciation in stock price over time while minimizing the negative effects of time decay. In other words, the longer the expiration period and the deeper ITM an option is, the more it behaves like the underlying stock, as delta is near 1.0. The benefit to you of owning ITM options, versus the stock outright, is that you have to shell out less capital to control the same number of shares, and you are paying less for time value premium than if you owned OTM calls.

As an example of an optimal time to use ITM LEAPS for the purchase of an otherwise high-quality company, assume Company X reports weak earnings, sending its stock down 10% or more after the investment banks finish their downgrades. If a trader concludes that the market overreacted, and maintains a long-term bullish position on Company X, but either does not have or chooses not to lay out the capital for buying shares outright (and does not want to hedge via covered calls, given his belief in the strong upside of the stock), the purchase of ITM calls would potentially be a good way to profit. Usually, the sweet spot for buying ITM calls in terms of balancing capital outlays and minimizing time value premium costs is one strike price below where the stock is trading. With the company being quoted at $32 and change after its earnings miss, the in-the-money $30 calls would be a good entry point. How far out should you go time-wise? The later-dated options cost more due to more time value premium being embedded in the option, however, they allow for more "recovery" time for the stock to rebound from its sell-off. A time frame of six to eighteen months, depending on your assessment of how long it will take the company to turn around, is usually a good range to consider (your fundamental analysis will help you determine the appropriate time frame).

Figure 5.9 **ITM Long Call Break-Even Analysis**

Options	Premium	Break-Even Stock Price	% Gain to Break Even
Jan. 2009 Calls; $30 Strike	$4.50	$34.50	7.81%
Jan. 2010 Calls; $30 Strike	$5.80	$35.80	11.88%

Assume Company X stock drops to $32 a share from $36.40 in the second quarter of 2008. At this point you can either buy the January 2009 $30 strike calls or the January 2010 $30 strike calls. In order for you to break even on the 2009 contracts, the stock needs to increase to $34.50 (the $30 strike price you will pay plus the $4.50 premium you paid when you bought the option). Because the option expires in January '09, you would have nine months for the stock to recover 7.81%. If you buy the 2010 January calls, the stock needs to increase 11.88% in order for you to break even. However, you now have twenty-one months to accomplish this.

When would you want to buy near-term OTM options containing relatively little total premium but substantial time value premium (no intrinsic value premium)? The time to do this is if you believe a very near-term event such as the announcement of greater-than-expected earnings will move the stock significantly upward prior to the option's expiration date. You must have a specific reason to believe the stock will go up enough to justify the premium paid, otherwise you are merely giving money to the house. Remember, unlike equity ownership, the purchase and sale of options is a zero-sum game of winners and losers. When you lay out cold hard cash for the purchase of an option, you are lining the pocket of someone else on the other side of the transaction. One of you will win, one of you will lose. I have found that the sale of options described in this book—transactions from which you will benefit regardless of outcome—is the best use of one's money (preferably someone else's).

***Figure 5.10* OTM Long Call Break-Even Analysis**

Options	Premium	Break-Even Stock Price	Required % Gain of Stock
$27.50 strike	$1.15	$28.65	7.91%
$30 strike	$0.38	$30.38	14.43%

If Company X stock price is at $26.55 and you think that the stock will move upward in the near term, you can buy OTM calls. The likely suspects are either the $27.50 strike or the $30 strike, both expiring about thirty days hence. Buying the $27.50 strike means you are closer to ITM and the stock has a shorter distance to move for you to break even. However, premium on these options is more expensive. If you buy the $30 strike, the stock has farther to increase for you to break even. However, the premium is cheaper. In either case, an advantage to buying a call option long rather than buying the stock outright is that your downside is limited to the premium that you have paid for the option. This preset downside limit is an important risk control in and of itself.

Disaster Movie

We have discussed at length the sale of puts. When, if ever, do you want to go long puts? Consistently making money by using puts for market-timing purposes—to bet against the market in the near term—is a difficult undertaking at best. Sure, you may get lucky from time to time but you have decay and general market trends working against you (markets go up over time, not down). Consequently, you should only go long put premium for three reasons. One, you want to hedge your portfolio at large and are willing to lose the premium to hedge. In this case, you would buy ITM, long-dated options. As discussed, ITM options have a higher delta, thus declines in the broad market will largely be reflected in the price of the put options. You should determine how much of your total portfolio you want to hedge and buy enough options contracts notionally to provide the appropriate hedge. Also, be certain to pick a broad market index that closely resembles your portfolio (e.g., the Russell 2000 if you own mostly small caps, DIAs if you own predominantly large-cap industrials). This is not a market timing bet; it is truly a hedge, a form of portfolio insurance. A good time to employ this tactic is after a big run-up in the broad markets and a decline in the VIX to low double digits. As with any position, the purchase of a broad-based index put serves a purpose, namely to protect you against a calamitous event. Thus, if such an event occurs, *be sure to cash in on your insurance policy.* If you total your car, you don't wait until you have a new car to cash in on your policy; you get your totaled car paid for, less the deductible, and you buy insurance again once you are driving a new and safe automobile. So, too, it is important to exercise your long puts once the event you were protecting against happens. That discipline is important, otherwise you are just throwing premiums away. While you will not know when the market has been "totaled," you can certainly use your judgment about the value of the long puts and whether they will increase even more in price before expiration. Time is against the option holder, so if stocks drop quickly, causing a dramatic rise in your long put position, cash in.

Two, you own a specific stock on which you have gains that you want to protect. You have no particular reason to believe that the stock is about to stumble, but you want to buy insurance on this stock to protect your gains. Perhaps the stock represents a large percentage of your portfolio and you want to hedge against concentration risk while you extend your holding period to gain a tax advantage (a holding period of one year or longer). In this case, the purchase of slightly to moderately OTM long puts is the best course of action as this will provide you the direct protection you seek.

Three, contrary to the above example, you have a very specific reason to believe a stock will drop significantly in the near term. Perhaps you think a company will miss earnings or delay a product launch. Long put options give you a low-risk way of profiting from the decline in a stock as your maximum loss exposure is the amount of premium paid. This approach is generally better than shorting the stock, which has unlimited downside potential should you be wrong and the stock goes up instead of down. To determine which strike price to purchase, calculate how large a decline the stock might face, factor in the premium you need to pay in your break-even analysis, and purchase the option accordingly. The key is using options in the right way at the right time, especially when you go long options and time is *not* on your side.

When it comes to put buying, the underlying message is the old adage "Do things when you do not have to." The best time to raise money for a company is when the company does not need the money. Call a friend or associate "just because"—not when you need something from her. Shop around for a new mortgage long before your ARM approaches its fix date. Buy your long puts when everything in life seems good and you have no worries. This is very difficult as the feelings associated with a severe bear market are acute and naturally cause us to want to take action, whereas when the market is rallying we just assume that this is the way it is supposed to be and our guard drops just before the market is about to land an uppercut to the chin. Don't buy fire insurance when you smell the first whiff of smoke. Make your purchase during the rainy season when no one is interested in fire protection and rates are cheap. Making a financial move when you *have to* will be more expensive, if not too late, to provide the protection you seek. Yet most people, especially when it comes to investing, are reactive by nature. While investors' collective memories are short, equities do go through bear markets from time to time, and just as they tend to overshoot on the upside (think 1999–2000), they have a propensity to undershoot on the downside and last longer than they "should." The purchase of a broad-based put option is a great way to protect against the twenty-five-year flood that hits once or twice every decade. Bear markets, like the one experienced in 2008 and 2009, can be ugly and painful, so if your portfolio has seen good times lately, take out your checkbook and buy some broad-based stock market disaster insurance so you can sleep well at night. This is especially true if you are approaching the end of your equity-investing time frame (if you need the funds in the next few years) when near-term losses would have an even more damaging effect. And this is also true when a company comes out with bad news, the stock collapses, and *then* investors rush to buy put insurance to protect against a slide in the stock price. It takes tremendous discipline and foresight to buy an umbrella when it is 82 degrees and sunny. But if you own a stock that has gone up a lot in price and you feel compelled to protect against the downside, buy puts *then*. Take a step back and realize that a storm could be just around the corner. Buy your insurance early, and on the cheap.

SHARK INSURANCE: A LESSON IN OPTIONS AND INVESTOR IRRATIONALITY

As we have learned, it is almost always better to be the house—to be the seller of insurance. But when is the optimal time to be the seller of put premium? *When everyone is scared of the event they are trying to protect against and premiums are high.* If such a policy existed, and to make the point vis à vis financial tools available, I would be the guy down at the beach selling shark insurance when *Time* magazine had its every-other-year cover story about shark attacks in the United States.

Here is how it works. Shark attacks cause fewer than 100 deaths in the United States each year—an infinitesimal number compared to annual car-crash deaths. Usually the attacks are spread out, random, and not newsworthy to anyone but those directly involved. But every few summers, three attacks will occur in the same week; at least one will be in a fairly prominent place, and one will involve a cute surfer girl who makes great daytime talk show television. Statistically speaking, the number of shark attacks—or the likelihood of a swimmer being attacked—has not increased. But major periodicals will run headline stories about the prominence of shark attacks, and these headlines make otherwise rational and intelligent people choose not to go into the ocean. *That is the time to sell shark insurance.*

When people are willing to bid up the price of insurance for what is still a highly unlikely event to unreasonable levels, that is when you want to sell as much of the stuff as you can. Of course, sharks do attack and kill from time to time, as investors learned during the 2007–2009 financial crisis. If you are on a shark-watching tour and the captain is throwing chum in the water to attract Mack the Knife, and there is a scuba-diving class just down the coast, that might be one of the rare times when the sale of shark insurance is not a prudent business proposition. You still need to do your fundamental research on a given company combined with a wise dose of macroeconomic and technical analysis.

While not as extreme or as dramatic, opportunities exist every day to sell "shark insurance" to so-called investors in the stock market. An otherwise great company experiences a short-term, nonfundamental problem, the stock drops, the investment banks lower their price targets (after the fact, of course), and only once the stock has already gone down do people rush in to buy puts, thus bidding up the price of this insurance dramatically both in terms of directional and volatility-induced enhanced premiums. When there is blood in the stock market waters, that is when you will find the best put selling opportunities, especially for your special situation positions. Fortunately, the stock market is a large and diverse body of water and, as a result, there are many, many opportunities to take advantage of people's overreactions based on emotional responses to events—and to happily accept the premiums that they are willing to pay for that will likely end up worthless to them and highly profitable for you. Naturally, you still have to do your company analysis to be sure that the decline in the stock price is not due to a fundamental issue. Furthermore, you should expect that the decline will last longer than it "should," as most fear- and greed-driven trends do. But, if you do your homework, you will eventually be proven right and be richer for it.

A real-life example of how this works was when the Great One (and I'm talking about neither Jaws nor Wayne Gretzky) announced his company's (Berkshire Hathaway, Inc., BRKA) earnings in 2006. A big part of the strong gains came from nothing else but the sale of hurricane insurance post-Katrina—at high premium rates you can be assured. Now, your immediate reaction might be, "How can people take advantage of others' misery?" Save it. If you want to be a successful investor, you have to put your emotions aside, you have to grow your pointy Vulcan ears, and you have to use an "IV" to put ice in your veins. *When I read that Berkshire made money selling hurricane insurance at great rates for the seller, I smiled a pearly-white smile, like Mack the Knife.*

CHAPTER 6

Constructing a Portfolio: Risk Controls, Idea Generation, Position Sizing, and Other Relevant Parameters

I hate to lose money. Actually, I'll take that back; hate is a pretty strong word. I hate *hate hate hate* to lose money would be a more accurate way of putting it. However, in order to attain real investment returns, you must take on some level of risk and be subject to short-term declines. In the immortal words of Thomas Crown, "Do you want to dance or do you want to *dance?*" Similarly, there are losses and then there are *losses;* there are mistakes and then there are *mistakes.* Knowing the difference, and using smart risk control to avoid the latter, will put you on the path to superior investment returns over time. Thinking you are immune to the 100-year flood that invariably arrives every few years will put your portfolio permanently underwater.

In this chapter we will focus on how to properly construct a portfolio. It is one thing to be able to pick good stocks. It is another thing entirely to build and manage a portfolio that will provide superior returns over time. When you assemble a collection of dividend-paying (and occasional non-dividend) securities, coupled with effective options strategies, you end up with a portfolio that not only credits your account consistently and regularly with dividend payments and premium sales, but also provides consistently superior returns. Let us examine in more detail how this is accomplished.

RISK: DEFINITIONS AND CONTROLS

Anything worthwhile in life involves taking some level of risk relative to the potential reward. Want to run a marathon? You risk getting injured. Want to find that perfect person? You risk getting your heart ripped out. Want to get into an Ivy League school? You risk being rejected. Risk is one of the most important considerations in portfolio construction. Yet risk is also one of the most misunderstood—if not misused—concepts in money management.

The definition of risk that you hear used regularly by brokerage firms, market commentators, and financial advisors relates to volatility: how much a given investment is likely to go up or down over a certain period, usually twelve months. In fact, how much someone can stomach the ups and downs of the market is often the dominant consideration for investment professionals attempting to determine how to construct client portfolios. Every day, all across America, financial advisors ask a series of questions aimed largely at determining a client's comfort level with risk as defined by volatility. But is this really the best definition of investment risk? Is it even a good one? A useful one?

Imagine a personal trainer having an initial conversation with a client whose goal is to lose thirty pounds over the next twelve months:

> "So, you want to lose thirty pounds by this time next year? That is an excellent long-term physical goal. I think I can help you a lot in achieving this objective. I just have a couple questions for you. First, do you weigh yourself regularly?"
>
> "Yes."
>
> "Okay, how do you feel about weighing yourself—do you like doing this?"
>
> "No, I hate weighing myself."

"Would you say that it is emotionally challenging to see your weight going up and down?"

"Absolutely. That is why I hate weighing myself!"

"Okay, then," declares the trainer. "We will adjust your training program accordingly."

No! This is exactly the wrong issue on which to focus; it is letting the tail wag the dog! In the case of portfolio construction, why let an emotional aversion be the dominant factor in constructing a plan that must be rigorous and objective to succeed? This is, in effect, the outcome for many investors who are unable to overcome their emotions—and for advisors who are unable or unwilling to do the hard work necessary to educate investors and convince them to do what is right for their pocketbooks, not what feels the most comfortable. Just as the effective personal trainer should counsel his client to only weigh herself every month or so to check the progress toward her twelve-month goal, and to focus instead on the important elements of the plan (consistency in workouts, quality diet, etc.) so too should the professional money manager guide his clients away from checking stock prices at frequencies inconsistent with their investment time horizon. And certainly the advisor should not alter the plan to cater to the nervousness of the client by, for example, over-allocating to bonds to smooth out the ride at the cost of ending up at the destination with fewer Bobby De Niros to spend.

Daily headline noise should be the last thing driving the portfolio construction process. Rather, the first line of discussion should relate to time frames associated with the investor's financial objective. The goal of investing is to allocate X amount of capital today in order to have X + Y capital at a future date. If the money is intended for retirement, for example, and the investor is in her early forties, what happens today, tomorrow, next week, next month, or even next year is irrelevant—just as, with our slightly overweight friend who wants to lose thirty pounds over the next twelve months, day-to-day weight fluctuations should not be the focal point. To be sure, results and progress should be reviewed from time to time, but at reasonable intervals relative to the goal.

POWER TIP

The Ticker Gave In

Imagine if the day after you moved into your new home, a house you planned to sell in the distant future, the abode "went public" and you could track its current price no differently than you can track stocks. UP $10,000! DOWN $13,000! In addition to having access to minute-by-minute vacillations of the price (not value, mind you, but price), you also have the privilege of continuous broadcasts telling you with authority the causes for yesterday's gain or loss. "Your house lost $18,000 yesterday because your neighbor's kids left their toys out on the front porch thus causing broad losses throughout the block." All of this useless input and after-the-fact analysis would drive you crazy. Even though your heart is where your home is, you would quickly "de-list" your house so that you would no longer be subject to monthly, weekly, daily, and even hourly price quotes. In doing so, you would live in peace knowing that you had bought a quality home in a good neighborhood at a reasonable price. Five or ten years hence—perhaps a year or so before you intended to sell—you would begin to check the market and see how your home is priced. But in the meantime, you would not pay attention to near-term price fluctuations.

Since we know that short-term volatility is not an adequate characterization of risk, let us examine some true sources of portfolio peril.

Risk Comes from Not Knowing What You Are Doing

To me, this is the best definition of risk. Is a scalpel risky? In the hands of a toddler, yes. In the palm of an experienced surgeon, it is a potential life-saver. How about being dropped a mile offshore in the ocean? To the person who had never learned to swim, this situation is full of risks. To the athlete training to swim the English Channel, his downside risk (not making it to shore safely) is very small given his skill set. Indeed, to build his endurance and achieve his objective, he *has* to undertake such activities. Relative to his objectives, *not* placing himself a mile offshore—not training appropriately—is risky. In practically every situation, the risk we take is a function of our skill sets. Risk is rarely an absolute; it is almost never the same for everyone, given individuals' different competencies, mental makeups, physical abilities, and so on.

When it comes to investing, people take risks every day that relate quite simply to their not knowing what they are doing, to their not being adequately informed. Why? Because it is so easy to do. The barriers to entry are low and access to information via sources like the Internet is easier than ever. This reality makes the stock market less efficient in the short term, not more efficient as many had predicted. The theory that the market would become ultra-efficient as more and more people started investing and trading on their own behalf assumed that the players in the market would act rationally, and use the complete information available. This has not been the case. Time and time again, investors buy stocks based solely on a tip, or on the fact that they saw the price go up recently, or because they heard the name mentioned on a talk-radio financial show. And is the disposition of stock always based on the latest and most comprehensive information available on a given company? Certainly not. Sometimes an investor sells because he needs the money for that month's mortgage payment! The average investor chases returns, buying more when the market is up and less when the market is down. The average investor also does not know what he is investing in; he has not researched the fundamentals of the underlying business. Thus, it is not surprising that the average investor's returns over the last twenty to thirty years have been about one-third of what the market has returned over that time (the average investor having earned a little over 3% versus approximately 9% for the market).

All other risks are essentially a subset of this first risk. If you know what you are doing, you will likely not make the other mistakes that are the main source of investment risk.

Risk Comes from Not (Truly) Knowing Anything About the Companies You Are Buying

Think of the classic scene in a movie in which a man, having unknowingly slept with a mobster's wife, is then informed by a friend that he is dead but doesn't even know it yet. When you buy the stock of a company you know little to nothing about, you are financially dead and you don't even know it yet. Or to paint a less gruesome picture, you are like one of those cartoon characters who has been chased off the edge of a cliff; your feet are still moving but the next direction is straight down. You might get lucky and the stock might work out, but relying on luck or hope or tips for investment profits is a way to ensure inferior returns if not permanent capital losses. Without question, the elimination of your three biggest mistakes/losses in a given year—primarily through the discipline of taking no action—will add more profit to your portfolio than your three biggest winners will.

Many people "playing" the market buy stocks based on a ticker symbol or a slick software package that is flashing green or red, up or down, rather than on thorough company analysis. Rarely do they know *what* they are buying. Basing investment decisions solely on price is like saying yes when someone asks you if you would like to buy water for $1 and not knowing whether the water is a gallon of Evian's finest or an ounce of polluted, disease-filled river water. The price per share tells you nothing about the company, its total enterprise value, its true worth, or its competitive position. Yet many investors use this as their main, if not sole, source of information when it comes to investing, often looking in the rearview mirror and assuming that if the stock has been ticking upward it will continue to do so regardless of valuation, or that because the stock was once trading for $20 and is now selling for $12, it *must* be a bargain. Or, conversely, investors will hold on to a $25 stock as it becomes a teenager because they psychologically want to sell it once it gets back to breakeven, their "anchor" price, regardless of what the company is truly worth. If you do not sincerely comprehend the underlying fundamentals of the companies to which you are allocating capital, then you are taking real risks that have nothing to do with the daily ups and downs of the market but will likely have a real impact on your account balance over time.

Bottom line, if you do not have the time and inclination to dedicate the resources necessary to increase your probability of success, stick to broad-based indices that will minimize any material downside—or else find someone you trust who manages money professionally on a full-time basis.

POWER TIP

There Are Losses and There Are Losses

As the Oracle himself, Warren Buffett, has said many times when it comes to investing: *Rule #1: Don't lose money. Rule #2: Don't forget Rule #1*. But many people misinterpret this message and pay the long-term price of inferior investment returns for the error. Buffett is specifically *not* saying don't lose money *ever*. On the contrary, he is also quoted as saying you should be prepared to lose as much as 50% on a given stock post-purchase. How do you reconcile these seemingly contradictory concepts?

The answer is subtle and simple, but powerful.

When Buffett says don't lose money, he is referring to *permanent capital losses*. He is saying, in effect, do not make stupid investments in the stocks of low-quality companies that you know nothing about and that might see their price go to zero...permanently. But having the stock of a quality company go down 30%, 40%, 50% due to uncontrollable market forces before heading back north to the land of profits? No problem. (After buying GE in 2008, Buffett experienced near-term losses of more than 50% in a matter of weeks.) Expect it, welcome it, for you can then buy more stock at a lower price, a common practice of the superior investor.

If experiencing a temporary decline in stock prices is not considered an investment mistake, what breaches of investing discipline should we be avoiding in order to improve portfolio returns? Here are some additional common mistakes that can truly have a permanent negative impact on your portfolio.

Risk Comes from Mismatching the Time Frame Associated with Your Investment Objective and the Type of Investment You Are Using to Achieve This Objective

As the saying goes, time heals all wounds. When it comes to investing, time is on your side—if you manage it correctly.

Money market mutual funds are one of the least risky investments, right? You will hear again and again that if you want to avoid risk, you should put your money in a stable money market fund as it is virtually assured to maintain its 1.0 net asset value. Again, this places the emphasis on volatility. What if your goal is to save for the college tuition you anticipate coming due in twelve years? If you had the choice between putting $10,000 in a money market fund and investing the same $10,000 into the S&P 500, which would be riskier? Looking at this scenario in terms of the investment objective and time horizon—which is how risk should be measured—putting the $10,000 in a money market fund is by far the riskier bet, as the money will likely be worth less on a real, post-inflation basis twelve years from now. Compare this outcome with that of putting the funds in the S&P 500. Will that index see large declines from time to time over the subsequent twelve years? You bet. There is a great probability that the index will periodically drop 10% or more from peak to trough given the index's historical **standard deviation** of approximately 15%. But, given the twelve-year time horizon, this volatility is essentially meaningless. Interim ups and downs only matter if you need the money in the interim. Match your investments to your time horizon and volatility becomes your friend.

If I could garner only one piece of information from a new client, it would not be the misapplied concept of "risk tolerance." It would be the simple question of: When do you need the money back? One year? No problem, we'll invest accordingly. Ten years? That requires a different portfolio entirely.

Many investors track their long-term holdings on a monthly, weekly, or even daily basis. The media does not help matters by presenting investing and financial news as though it were a terrorist alert. One financial news show has even displayed a countdown clock to when the U.S. markets closed that showed how much time was left "on the clock" to the *hundredth of a second!* Investing in stocks should be more akin to running a marathon than a sprint. I will never forget a particular image from an adventure race in Baja California that my adventure sports magazine covered in the late 1990s. The final twenty-four hours consisted of a 100+ mile "hike" across a desert in the middle of summer. When the gun went off, dozens of racers *sprinted* into the arid wasteland. Fast-forward about eighty miles, twenty hours, and 110 degrees later and fewer than one-third of the competitors were still in the race. The rest had succumbed to exhaustion. *They had mismatched their exertion levels to the distance necessary to reach the finish line.* Match your investments with your time horizon and you will greatly mitigate a source of financial risk.

Risk Comes from Taking on Too Much Leverage

Every year or two, like clockwork, a high-profile hedge fund or major financial institution blows up. What are the two most common themes in these meltdowns? You can bet one of them relates to leverage. The more leverage you take on, the smaller your margin for error—and the less you are able to withstand temporary fluctuations in portfolio values that otherwise would pose no problem. Take $1,000 to Vegas and if you end up down 10%, you walk away with $900. Not a great outcome, but not devastating enough to ruin your weekend. Take the same $1,000, leverage it up 10X with the house's "easy" money so that you now have $10,000. Lose a few bets so that you are down 10% and your entire capital, the $1,000 with which you came to Vegas, is obliterated. A 20% loss at that level of leverage wipes out your capital and leaves you in hock to boot. That is the destructive power of leverage.

If used correctly—if the cost of the leverage is low and, more important, if the holding time horizon is sufficient to ride out the inevitable ups and downs, and if the user of the leverage is not beholden to the supplier of the leverage for continued access to that capital in good times and bad—then leverage can be a productive source of return enhancement. Leverage is the essence of the United States real estate mortgage industry. However, even those industry dynamics changed with real estate "investors" taking out short-term loans, putting little or no money down (read: higher than historical leverage; the difference between 20% down and 5% down can easily mean the difference between riding out the storm and foreclosure), and looking to make near-term gains by flipping houses (read: speculating rather than investing). This short-term, highly leveraged game works as long as the music is playing, but as soon as it stops, the "house" wins and you lose, with leverage magnifying the damages.

Risk Comes from Attempting to Short a Company or the Market as a Whole Without Proper Expertise

Shorting stock—borrowing it, selling it, and hoping it goes down so that you can repurchase it at a lower price and pocket the difference in profits—is a dangerous game. Undoubtedly, the shorts have their day in the rain from time to time, but the financial odds are stacked against them. Stocks go up over time, so right off the bat you have the long-term trend working against you. To short stocks means borrowing costs. Strike two. Your upside is limited (a stock price cannot become negative) whereas the downside is unlimited (you could have shorted Google at its seemingly overvalued IPO price and the stock might never see that level again). Strike three.

Shorting the market at large is a form of market gambling. Once in a while you will be right; in most cases you will be wrong. If your investments match your time frame, then the fact that the market goes down in the interim is irrelevant. Do not try to be too tricky and short the market. Losing money when the market is going up—experiencing permanent capital losses—is a financial sin, not to mention a disaster. Own a quality dividend-paying company, and if the market and the stock price of this company go down, no big deal—you can collect the dividend check and reinvest it; you don't need the capital today anyway. Let the long-term market, economic, and financial forces work in your favor for long-term gains. Betting against a quality company based solely on valuation, or on the market at large, is a loser's game.

Shorting should be left to people who dedicate their professional lives to finding specific companies that are likely to go to zero due to scam situations or dramatically deteriorating financial fundamentals—the very things you need to avoid on the long side (indeed the shorts are *selling* stock to *you*). If you have some very specific and in-depth information about a company and why it is likely to see material decline in its operations, perhaps you should consider dedicating a small amount of capital to shorting the stock. Or, for a more broad-based hedge, you can short an index ETF and hedge the short by creating a sell write. Like any position, this should not represent more than about 10% of your total portfolio. Bottom line, shorting equities is a full-time job, not something to play around with in your spare time. Otherwise you may soon be asking people if they can spare some change.

Risk Comes from Lack of Liquidity

The other common theme in financial blowups is that of liquidity, specifically the lack thereof. When you sell because you have to rather than because you want to, you sell from a position of weakness. When the market for the given investment has dried up, you will likely take a beating. Certain assets are inherently less liquid than others. Golf courses are harder to sell than shares of IBM. There are fewer potential buyers and thus, if the market is turning south, the law of supply and demand works against you. Often integrally related to the risk of lack of liquidity is the risk of concentration. If a good chunk of your portfolio is in that golf course and you need to raise cash, you have few options in what to liquidate and those on the other side of the transaction will use that to their advantage.

In these scenarios, if the market is heading in your favor then the inherent risks are masked. During the rainy season, you don't notice the risk of your house catching on fire. It is when the downside comes that true risks are exposed. The key is to remember that the weather will turn hot and dry eventually and to take action before it is too late. Protect yourself against worst-case scenarios and the permanent loss of capital by not over-leveraging and having an overly concentrated portfolio.

Risk Comes from Overpaying for a Good Company or, Worse, Buying a Bad Company

There is risk-taking that may lead to near-term losses and then there are outright permanent losses. Suppose you bought Coca-Cola in the late 1990s when it was trading at over $80 per share and selling at a P/E ratio of over 50X (versus a price per share of approximately $45 and a P/E ratio in the mid-teens ten years later). In this case, you committed the crime of overpaying and you "paid the price" accordingly. But you bought a quality, dividend-paying company rather than the likes of JDS Uniphase or, worse yet, one of the many companies taken public in the late 1990s that are now worth $0 per share. While an investor should have a strong value orientation, always looking for high-quality companies at reasonable prices, an investor would rather make the mistake of overpaying for a quality company than buying a bad company that might experience permanent capital loss. In the case of Coca-Cola, while you were waiting patiently for the company's earnings to catch up to its valuation (and, indeed, Coke was earning nearly triple per share in the late '00s versus what it earned ten years prior), you were getting paid an ever-increasing dividend that was being reinvested at lower and lower prices. *Never forget that the reinvestment of dividends, especially at lower prices, is one of the most powerful sources of wealth generation there is.*

When stocks are expensive today, the probability of superior future returns is lowered dramatically. Conversely, when stocks are cheap by objective financial metrics, future return potential goes up. Buying stocks is no different from buying any asset. If you buy a 16 oz. bottle of water at Wal-Mart for $0.50, you will likely be able to resell it later at a profit (e.g., for $1.00). Buy that same bottle of water for $3.50 at a Las Vegas casino kiosk after a night of gambling and you will likely find few takers at a price that will provide you a reasonable ROI. Your "entry price" is too high and the same bottle of water can be found down the street at 7-11 for less than half the price. Maybe in ten or fifteen years the price of water will catch up to what you paid, but plenty of quality $0.50 bottles of water are out there, so why overpay and take the risk? Avoid making the mistake of overpaying, even for a high-quality company, and whatever you do, don't take on the risk associated with purchasing the stock of inferior companies that might give you nothing but permanent capital losses in your portfolio. If you are patient, you will be surprised how often high-quality companies go on sale.

Risk Comes from Not Knowing Who Your Money Manager Is

If one were to ask 100 otherwise intelligent people with decent-sized portfolios who is the person making investment decisions on their behalf, who is the one deciding how their hard-earned money is allocated, the vast majority could not name that person. Most people can name the mutual fund company in which their 401(k) or brokerage account is invested. But name the manager making the decisions? Good luck. Of those who know that some often-in-the-press money manager is the one pulling the trigger for their mutual fund, only a few will ever have met this person, had an in-depth conversation with him or her, or discussed goals, objectives, and time horizons. Those who have money with the big brokerage firms have typically only met their "financial consultant," who is nothing more than a salesperson. These folks do not make investment decisions on their clients' behalf. The actual money manager is typically several layers away operationally and geographically far removed from the client. Imagine never getting to meet the person making important decisions for you in law or medicine. Would you find it comforting, not to mention effective, if your child's pediatrist lived 3,000 miles away and never interacted directly with you or your child? Most investors should be concerned about the fact that they do not even know the name of, let alone anything else about, the person managing their hard-earned money. Without regular, direct contact between the client and the money manager, how can objectives be monitored and updated? How can changing circumstances (a new child or a new job) be factored into the investment plan? Get to know the person making decisions about your financial future and reduce the risk associated with the lack of a relationship between client and money manager.

People over-attribute risk to market elements beyond their control and underestimate the risk associated with factors within their purview, namely their own actions and behaviors. At the end of the day, risk is not volatility, as it is traditionally defined in the stock market, rather it is not knowing what you are doing; making investment decisions based on emotion rather than hard facts; over-leveraging; paying too high a price for your investments or, worse yet, purchasing bad companies; and being overly concentrated.

Now that we have a better handle on risk and how it relates to portfolio construction, let us look at some specifics in terms of how to use equities and options in creating a portfolio that can tap into the power and magic of compounding.

PORTFOLIO CONSTRUCTION

The investing and trading style espoused in this book can be characterized as disciplined and value-hedged. Consistency and self-control are keys to superior performance and long-term success. As noted in several sections of this book, deviating from your investing and trading strategy—from your predefined rules—even for a short time in order to squeeze out a few extra dollars of profits is a surefire way to incur losses that will be difficult to recover within a reasonable time frame. The superior investor must know more than how to pick a great company, as a single stock does not a portfolio make. Rather, one must know how to continually generate good investment ideas, how to enter into and build positions, how and when to sell, how and when to hedge—and how many positions to hold and in what proportions. In this section we discuss these vital elements from start to finish.

Idea Generation

I am often asked where I get my investing and trading ideas. The resources I use for equity possibilities and analysis (macro, industry, company) are largely as follows:

- General observation: having an investor perspective when I am out and about in life, listening to people and conducting commerce.
- Company annual reports, 10-Ks, earnings releases, conference calls, and other company-specific information.
- Objective news sources, such the *Wall Street Journal, Barron's,* and the *New York Times.*
- Industry periodicals.
- Colleagues whose views I trust (not for stock picks, but for informative discussions).
- Value Line (an objective company information source).
- Standard & Poor's (an objective company information source).
- Argus (an objective company information source).

- A few investment bank research groups (to check in with their thinking; they are often contrarian indicators).
- Some proprietary sources to which I have access.

One source noticeably absent from my list is the financial talk shows that have become popular lately. The fact is that doing the hard work is time-consuming and difficult, which is why most people don't do it. Listening to someone take three seconds on TV to talk about a stock is useless at best. When these commentators are asked if they own what they have just screamed that everyone is crazy not to own, nine out of ten times they answer no. Remember, commentators are paid to commentate (or entertain), not to manage your portfolio!

Core Holdings and Special Situations

Having identified good idea sources, you must next predefine your criteria for equity selection. That way you will know quickly whether a company that comes across your radar screen is even a candidate for consideration. One effective way to do this is to put your stocks into two separate buckets, **core holdings** and **special situations**. Core holdings should consist of quality dividend-paying companies that meet your valuation metrics and dividend payout ratios. These are typically intended to be longer-term holdings that you either hedge via short calls or hold long unhedged to take advantage of potential capital gains and dividend reinvestment.

Special situation stocks can be defined as companies that pay little or no dividends but that are otherwise quality companies that, temporarily and for nonfundamental reasons, have fallen on hard times. Special situation stocks tend to be shorter-term trade-oriented, often with the goal of taking advantage of a spike in put premium associated with a quick drop in the stock. Special situation stocks are often "bad news" stocks or sectors (by industry or geography). I typically track several dozen companies and ETFs and if on a given day one of them drops dramatically, or meets some predetermined price threshold, I will attain exposure, often via the sale of short puts. (Much of my short put exposure is attributed to special situations.) Basically, whenever there is bad news, I become interested because put premiums have been inevitably bid up.

Mergers are a good example of special situations and a good, understandable representation of **arbitrage**. At its essence, arbitrage is the taking advantage of discrepancies based on either distance or price or both. Before the proliferation of information, products, and services, an enterprising young man could have purchased Pop Rocks in Arizona where they were first introduced and sold them to his fellow 8th graders in Illinois for a premium. Today price arbitrage is more common when the bid for a security differs even infinitesimally from one market to another. These discrepancies are increasingly more difficult to capture given advances in technology. But in the case of merger arbitrage, such gaps between price arise, in this case the dimension being that of time. Often there is uncertainty associated with whether a given takeover will occur. Consequently, the premium in the puts can be quite large. An example of this was when Tribune, Inc. (TRB) was in the process of being taken over by Sam Zell in 2007. The expected take-out price was $33 per share, however, the market was uncertain as to whether or not the transaction would take place, and thus the stock traded in the $26 to $31 range for several months. The premium associated with the $25 strike price puts was unusually large for a very long time period.

Figure 6.1 **ENHANCED PUT PREMIUMS ASSOCIATED WITH MERGER ARBITRAGE**

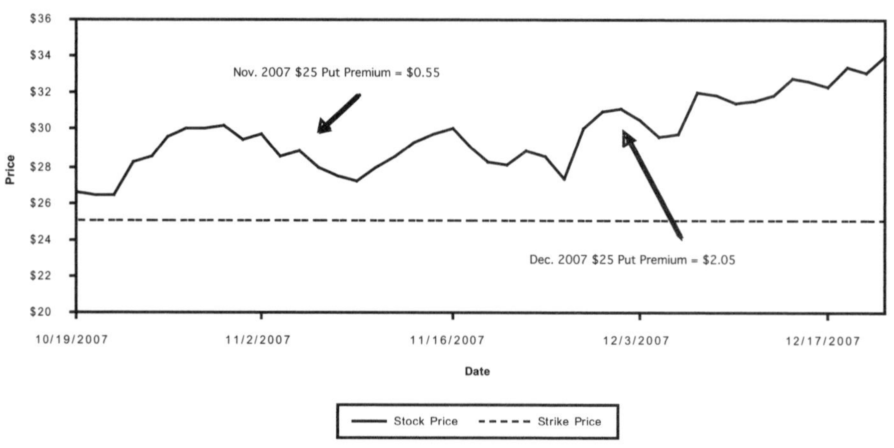

SOURCE: MARKETDATAEXPRESS.COM

Of course, if the deal does not get consummated, the stock will likely trade down to its pretakeover levels, so you need to be willing to own the

POWER TIP

She's Got Legs (So Know How to Use Them)

Like a shark, I am attracted to blood in the water that represents an otherwise quality company that has been beaten down. Learn from my mistakes, however, and refrain from entering a position the day that bad news is released. While a stock that has fallen will occasionally rebound quickly, that is the exception. The first thing to occur after a company's stock falls is that most of the investment banks issue downgrades, adding further selling pressure to the stock. Then, the big mutual funds that have mandates to sell any stock that misses its earnings begin their drawn-out selling process. Finally, a bottom will form days or even weeks after the event that led to the decline. To be sure, the stock's volatility will be at its peak on the days following the negative event. But this is one of the few times when putting premium on the books (assuming the position is entered into via farther OTM short puts) is often best done only after the dust settles. This is so you can be certain that there is no more bad news (which is not an uncommon phenomenon for truly broken companies—first they crack, then they crumble). The benefits to avoiding such an outcome greatly outweigh missing a few points of premium were you to act upon the release of the bad news.

stock at the strike price at which you are selling the puts. You can always hedge your short put position by buying farther out-of-the-money long puts at the next strike price or by establishing a put bull spread. As discussed in the options section, such a position limits downside risk to the spread between the two strike prices (usually $2.50). Merger arbitrage is a field unto itself, so tread carefully if you are using takeovers as a source of profitability.

Special situation stocks tend to be smaller positions, in the 2% to 4% range on a notional basis in terms of short put exposure.

To Hedge or Not to Hedge, That Is the Question

How much hedging you employ is largely driven by your investment

POWER TIP

Returning That Special Delivery

If you have taken a position—either via direct equity ownership or by way of the sale of a short put—in a special situation stock that is not a core holding, consider employing a tight stop-loss sell discipline of 10% or less. While, as my good friend Huey says, Cool Is The Rule, it is true that sometimes Bad Is Bad.

objectives and time frames. The shorter the investment time horizon, the more an investor should hedge her portfolio, and the tighter the hedges should be. By "tighter" I mean that, all things being equal, call options sold should be closer to ATM, as opposed to far OTM. The longer one's investment horizon, the less hedged a portfolio should be. If you are in your forties and managing a retirement account, hedging should be done very selectively. (Remember, the sale of calls is first and foremost a profit-generating trading technique; it can certainly be used appropriately within the context of longer-time-horizon accounts, but it must be employed more discerningly.) This retirement account has a very long time horizon, and one potential downside in selling calls that are too tight, or sold on weakness rather than strength, is that the upside potential associated with equity appreciation can be curtailed if one is too aggressive with call sales. On the investment objective side, the more growth-oriented an account is, the less hedging should be employed, whereas an income orientation is well suited for dividend-focused stocks coupled with option sales. Depending on stock and volatility levels, you can often generate 1.5X to 3X in options premium over what is paid in the form of a dividend. For example, if you buy Company X that pays a 5% dividend, you can reasonably generate another 7% to 15% of incremental income annually through the sale of options. During high VIX environments the amount of income available from options sales can easily exceed 20% annually. In short, you can certainly create a portfolio with superior return potential that is absent of options—for example, a long-term portfolio such as a child's 529 college savings plan, which needs little incremental trading in order to achieve its objectives. But for appropriate accounts and for those willing to dedicate the time to learn and monitor positions accordingly, the use of options on top of dividend-paying stocks can be thought of as equities on steroids.

Figure 6.2 **Hedging Strategies Associated with Investment Objectives**

	Growth	Income
Long Time Horizon	Little to No Hedging	Moderate Hedging
Short Time Horizon	Moderate Hedging	Most Hedging

A final consideration for the level of options selling that you should include in your portfolio is that of stock valuations. If the market has taken a beating so that P/E ratios are on the low end of the historical range, you should hedge less—regardless of time horizon and investment objective. The sale of a call is a form of a short, and depressed markets are a time to buy, not sell. (This would be a good time to enhance returns via more aggressive put sales, especially given that a depressed market is typically associated with a high VIX and thus rich put premium levels.) Conversely, if the market as a whole, or a single stock holding in your portfolio, has risen so that the valuation is flush—although not so much that you want to exit the position—the sale of a call can provide some near-term downside protection, and in the case of an assignment, it will "force" you to sell when the stock is trading at a premium. In many cases, the stock price will retrace and you will have the opportunity to repurchase the stock at a lower price post-assignment.

Battle Royal: ETFs versus Mutual Funds

Let's discuss mutual funds as a vehicle for investing and trading. For the small accounts of passive investors, a low-cost mutual fund can be an excellent vehicle for wealth creation over time. The same holds

POWER TIP

Fire and Rain (Keeping Your Gunpowder Dry)

Maintaining at least some cash level, or available equity-buying power, along with a "wish list" of stocks that you would like to buy if prices become attractive enough is an excellent way to create wealth. A cash level of 10% of your total portfolio represents a good starting point. When things get ugly, selling begets selling, and often quality companies see their stock prices cut to unreasonably cheap levels. This is when you want to be the buyer and not the seller. These opportunities might not present themselves for years, but when they do you need to have the ammunition necessary to shoot the fish in the barrel. Maintain the discipline of having your target list and the means to buy them at fire-sale prices. When people need to raise cash, they will sell at virtually any price. That is where you step in. Remember, since your portfolio likely has exposure beyond your long stocks by way of short puts and short calls, even though you have 10% of your capital in the form of cash, your total portfolio exposure may well exceed 100%. This is another advantage of using options in your portfolio; it allows you to maintain high levels of exposure to the market while still keeping your gunpowder dry for future opportunities.

true for the investor who is adding small amounts to his account at regular intervals. Most mutual funds will let you purchase additional shares in very small increments without sales charges; thus, for those putting money away monthly from their paycheck, for example, mutual funds can be a good investment vehicle. By definition, a set monthly investment achieves dollar-cost averaging—buying more shares when the market is down and fewer shares when the market is high—and maintaining this disciplined approach is important. Too many people turn off their automatic investment plans just when they should be increasing them, namely when the market is down. He who buys at the lowest price wins, so you are *always* better off putting money to work when broad indices are down rather than when they are up. Don't fall prey to novice investor mistake *Numero Uno,* which is to buy high and sell low. Start a plan, focus on keeping costs low, and stick to it. That is the very best way you can tap into the power of compounding.

Mutual funds, however, have certain inherent disadvantages over ETFs and individual stocks. The first is that of liquidity (frequency of trading). While for investors with very long time horizons, intra-day trading is not essential, for traders looking to take advantage of near-term fluctuations, the once-a-day pricing of mutual funds represents a negative. By contrast, ETFs trade throughout the market day. And even if you are not concerned about trading a fund throughout the day, you could be discouraged to have entered your mutual fund order in the morning when the market was up, only to discover when you confirm the sale order the next day that your price was much lower than expected because the broad market sold off late in the day. Furthermore, the portfolio holdings of mutual funds are stale, with position updates quarterly at best. The fund manager could have made material changes to the portfolio between the time the holdings were last published and the time you bought into the fund, so you cannot be certain what you are buying. ETFs, on the other hand, have essentially fixed portfolios, the contents of which are available for review and analysis at any point. You know more and you have more control over what you are buying.

Another advantage of ETFs is that they can be sold short; you can bet that they will decline in value. This adds additional flexibility in terms of risk control and portfolio management. ETFs tend to be more cost effective; actively managed mutual funds can have expense ratios of 1.2% or more, versus an expense ratio of around 0.3% for most ETFs. As mutual funds are traditionally actively managed, trading costs are another important consideration. Commissions can potentially add fifty basis points (0.50%) or more to the expenses associated with mutual funds. Taxes are another reason to choose ETFs over mutual funds, the latter often paying out large capital gains even to those who did not participate in the earnings themselves. Getting the tax status on mutual fund holdings is often challenging, which can lead to nasty surprises and large tax bills for those who buy into a given fund just prior to distributions (these usually occur toward the end of the year). ETFs, on the other hand, do not typically have any embedded taxable gains. An additional subtle, but important, differentiation between ETFs and mutual funds is the impact of capital flows. A fund that is going through a hot streak, whether due to the skill of the manager, or luck, or the fact that the sector on which the fund is focused (e.g., a particular geographical region or industry) is hot, will often see very large capital inflows after publishing impressive results. As the typical retail investor often chases yesterday's large returns, the fund will invariably experience large capital inflows just before—or just as—the securities in which the manager is investing are peaking in value. The manager feels compelled, and indeed is paid, to put this money to work almost regardless of security valuation. Think of all the large-cap growth managers who received literally billions in their coffers in the late 1990s and who were essentially forced to buy stocks they often recognized were overvalued lest they take heat from angry investors whose funds underperformed when their manager held on to new cash to wait for reasonable stock valuations. All of this exacerbates the trend in the near term, making the music last a little longer before the party ultimately is over.

Conversely, if a manager has a cold spell, or more typically gets into a sector that she feels has good long-term prospects but is subject to short-term capital **depreciation**, the resulting underperformance will often cause assets to flee. It is not uncommon for mutual funds to go from many billions of dollars to only a couple of billion in assets. All those investors clamoring for their money back are expecting a check in the mail (from time to time mutual funds provide securities rather than cash; this does not make mutual fund investors very happy), and that triggers massive selling by the mutual fund manager, which in turn sends portfolio holding prices even lower in the near term. Thus, there is quintessentially a "prisoner's dilemma" phenomenon with mutual funds in that the actions of one participant (say the short-term trader) can have a material impact on another investor in the same pool. The same reality does not apply to ETFs, as they have a mechanism in place to facilitate redemptions without having to sell the underlying shares en masse.

The final important factor when considering ETFs versus their mutual fund cousins is the ability to sell options against the underlying securities. Simply put, there are no options on mutual funds. There is no way to directly hedge or take advantage of your mutual fund's holdings by generating income through call sales, for example. By contrast, many hundreds of ETFs have options that trade against them.

Bottom line, for sophisticated investors ETFs and individual stocks are superior to mutual funds when it comes to structuring and hedging a portfolio.

Figure 6.3 **Advantages of ETFs over Mutual Funds**

ETFs	Mutual Funds
Trade throughout the day	Trade 1X per day
Have lower costs	Often have higher costs
Able to short	Cannot short
Can sell options against	Cannot sell options against
Real-time holdings known	Stale portfolio info—as much as six months old
Tax efficient	Can be very tax inefficient
Not adversely affected by fund flows	Affected by fund flows as big capital infusions force the manager to buy more stocks. Similarly, big withdrawals force the manager to sell stocks, causing adverse tax consequences as other investors are forced to over the fixed expenses
Portfolio fixed	Managers often buy "hot stocks" at the end of the quarter, dump their losers just to "mark up" their books to look better in the eyes of investors—chasing after "winners" for appearances only

Portfolio Size: Using Individual Stocks versus ETFs

Whether to use individual stocks as opposed to ETFs depends on several variables. The first factor for consideration is portfolio size. Some level of diversification within your portfolio is important, and while a low-six-figure portfolio size is a good starting point for the use of individual securities to achieve return objectives, it is difficult to get adequate diversification using individual stocks if a portfolio is under $100,000 in total value. A portfolio of under $100,000 should contain primarily ETFs in order to get equity exposure. Fortunately, there are hundreds of ETFs covering virtually all segments of the market, including industry-specific, geographically focused, stock-capitalization segmented, and the like, and options trading is available on many of them. This allows for the building of a sophisticated portfolio even with lower amounts under management. No longer do you have to rely on active mutual fund managers who have no direct knowledge of your financial objectives, nor do you have to rely on a few broad-based ETFs like SPYs or DIAs as was the case not long ago.

For portfolios between $100,000 and $500,000, a combination of individual stocks and ETFs is advisable. If a particular sector looks as though it is becoming attractive due to price declines, but is not an area in which you have expertise or the time to do proper research, ETFs allow you to participate without the risk of stock selection. The same holds true for geographical exposure. Most countries have only a limited number of securities that trade on the major U.S. exchanges via **American Depository Receipts (ADRs)** or **American Depository Shares (ADSs)**. Even if one could build a reasonable portfolio via a particular country's ADRs, you are often better off buying the "S&P 500" of the country rather than selecting individual stock positions. For example, if you want to get exposure to the Japanese market you can buy the EWJ ETF. Similarly, the XLYs will allow broad-based exposure to the discretionary consumer sector for those who think that this is a good segment in which to invest. The market can be sliced and diced in virtually any way via ETFs, making them an effective way to gain exposure to various segments without having to acquire enough individual securities to attain adequate diversification within that sector.

Accounts of over $500,000 are large enough to merit almost exclusively individual securities; however, you must consider whether you have sufficient time to do the research necessary to avoid fatal investment mistakes. ETFs mitigate individual stock purchase exposure risks. Thus, if your time to properly research and follow individual companies is limited and you still want to invest and trade actively (as opposed to buying index funds or actively managed mutual funds), you are well served to use ETFs predominantly. That said, be certain that a given ETF is well diversified. For some ETFs, the top two or three holdings can represent 20% or more of the ETF; in that case you are largely making an individual stock bet. However, the top ten portfolio holdings and their respective percentages of the total ETF makeup are easily researched, and most ETFs are fairly well diversified.

For option sellers and buyers, another consideration is whether options trade on a particular ETF. Not all ETFs have options associated with them, and even for those that do, often the volumes traded are so low that bid/ask spreads can be very wide. Examine closely options volumes and associated liquidity before placing orders. For options sellers, especially call sellers, this is less of a consideration in that if the bid is priced so that the amount of premium collected represents a good profit potential, then a wide spread is not that meaningful. For options purchasers looking to exit the transaction at a profit, though, wide bid/ask spreads can be a big inhibitor to profit generation even if your initial thesis is correct and the option price moves in the desired direction.

Another trade-off to using ETFs rather than individual stocks is that the diversification benefit inherently associated with ETFs is offset by their lower volatility and options premiums. By their nature, ETFs are less volatile than individual stocks, and accordingly the premiums a trader can get from selling options on ETFs will be less than he can receive for selling options on a similar basket of individual stocks.

Number of Positions and Position Sizing

When it comes to portfolio construction and risk control, position sizing is an important element of optimizing the risk/reward profile. Generally, you should have twenty to thirty core long positions plus another five to ten special situations in your portfolio with the largest positions—those core holdings in which you have the greatest conviction—sized in the 4% to 6% range; special situations tend to be smaller position sizes. That said, anything less than a 1% or 2% position is not worth your while, whereas a single position should not be materially larger than 10%. Given that some of your positions will likely be ETFs, a portfolio with thirty to fifty positions will be more diversified than the number of positions suggests.

A portfolio with this number of total positions appears to be the

POWER TIP

Know the Score

At times, even with good liquidity in an option, spreads will be wide in both puts and calls. This is especially true when VIX is very high. You may have a spread on a call, for example, that is $2.70 X $3.50 on an option that under normal conditions has a spread of only $0.10. Your approach during these times is simple. First, always place limit orders rather than market orders as you might very well be able to get better than the bid for your order. Second, calculate your risk-reward ratio with the bid (or limit order) price in mind only. Do not worry about the high ask price; this is merely a function of extreme volatility. Finally, recognize that immediately after selling the option the position will be in a loss as the pricing for the position will reflect the higher ask. Again, this is not a concern because your profit profile is locked in. If you need to show period results (e.g., monthly or quarterly), then take this into consideration as you approach the end of a reporting period.

ideal balance to allow for sufficient diversification and "randomness" of stock price relative to strike price at time of expiration while avoiding having so many positions that you cannot monitor them effectively. Or, worse, your portfolio effectively becomes the market as a whole.

The number of short option positions—calls and puts—will be dependent on your objectives. The active trader who uses the full spectrum of tools available will often have as many option positions as stock and ETF holdings, so that the entire portfolio has forty to sixty positions or more at any point in time. This might sound like a lot, but the typical mutual fund can have several hundred holdings.

In order to construct and oversee such a portfolio, you will need to research and analyze as well as monitor approximately seventy-five to one hundred companies at any given time.

In terms of industries, it is important not to allow any one industry segment to represent more than approximately 30% of your total portfolio. That said, I am generally agnostic as to industry preference. Instead, I focus on the quality of the company, its fundamentals (including valuation), and its position and competitive strength within its industry.

Whether your portfolio is predominantly ETFs, or stocks, or somewhere in the middle, you should have a solid, diversified representation of various industry and geographical sectors that are attractive investments or trades. (You do not need to have exposure to an industry just for the sake of diversification. If a particular sector or geographical region is overvalued in your opinion, you can pass on exposure in this area for now and wait until the investment opportunity is more compelling.) At any point in time, some of your positions will be weak, some will be strong, and some will be middling. Many factors drive stock prices in the near term, some of them random (near-term noise) and some of them specific to the company or industry—for instance, macroeconomic news such as employment or interest rates, or company-specific fundamental news, like earnings announcements. Combine these ups and downs with the artificial construct of options expiration calendars, and for any given options cycle you will have some positions within your portfolio that close well below strike prices, some

POWER TIP

Don't Get the Wrong Notion

It is important to calculate your short put position size on a notional rather than delta adjusted basis for risk control purposes. There will be times when your short puts are way OTM and you will consider their effective position size to be negligible. This will be a mistake. You must make the assumption that your portfolio is subject to rapid and large declines, thus a delta adjusted 2% position by way of a short put can turn into a delta adjusted position of 8% very quickly as deltas accelerate in value due to a declining stock. Your portfolio can go from being conservatively positioned to highly leveraged (by way of premature short put assignments) in a matter of days. Do the conservative, disciplined thing, which is to calculate short put option position sizes on a notional basis for risk control purposes.

POWER TIP

Optimizing Dividend Reinvestment

While the reinvestment of dividends is one of the greatest sources of wealth accumulation, you are better served by taking your dividends in cash at times. Fortunately, with today's trading and portfolio-management tools, you can "turn on" and "turn off" the dividend reinvestment feature with a click of the mouse. In general, if you have purchased stock long and sold tight calls (near- or at-the-money), then dividends should not be reinvested as this position is meant for a near-term gain with the goal of getting assigned on the short call—and there is no need to pay the commission on the small number of incremental shares purchased by way of the dividend when the underlying position is assigned. For instance, if you are long 1,000 shares and short ten ATM calls and a dividend is paid, you are better off simply keeping the dividend in the form of cash rather than investing the cash for a small number of additional shares which you will be left with if and when the 1,000 shares are assigned.

If, however, you have entered said position and the underlying stock goes down so that the short call expires worthless and you choose not to sell any additional short call premium (either because you cannot get enough premium without going too far out time-wise or you are fine with the position being a longer-term hold), then you are well served to have these and future dividends reinvested for potential capital gains. First, your position is intended for the long term. Second, the stock price is now far from the strike price at which you might be selling calls. Finally, the current stock price is lower than your entry point, and you are always better off buying more stock when it is low and selling stock (or buying less of it) when the price is high. You can reassess every few months whether you want the next quarter's dividends reinvested. Remember, you need to turn on or off the dividend reinvestment feature prior to the dividend being declared. If you wait until the stock has gone ex-dividend (but the payout has not yet been made), it will often be too late for your brokerage firm to execute your new instructions.

that are trading near-the-money, and others that are well ITM. With a well-constructed portfolio, you will have the opportunity regularly to make optimizing decisions about options moves vis-à-vis your stock and diversification to realize material gains over time.

Remember, a portfolio is a dynamic, organic entity; it is not a static stock pick. There are many variables to consider in constructing a portfolio that will serve you and your investing objectives well over time. You can be right in terms of stock selection and wrong in terms of investment management if you do not pay close attention to factors like position size, industry concentration, and hedging levels. Love each child individually, but do not forget that family dynamics are also vital to long-term success.

POWER TIP

A Penny for Your Thoughts

There are times when you will want, if not need, to buy back options that are trading $0.00 X $0.05 for the sole purpose of freeing up margin availability. Though the option might be way OTM and about to expire worthless—and you would rather not spend the money to buy it back—it is worth doing if this frees up capital that allows you to sell other options. For example, if you are short way OTM Google puts leading up to expiration, these are likely to be eating into a great deal of margin equity. Thus, rather than selling stock, close this OTM option to free up buying (or option-selling) power to allow you to enter into a new, more profitable position.

CHAPTER 7

On Becoming a Great Trader and Investor

What color is your parachute? I hope the answer is "the color of money," but in any case it is important to get a realistic sense of what type of investor you are. To do so, some definitions are in order. First, let's define **investor** (or **investing**) versus **trader** (or **trading**). I think of investing as allocating capital with a time horizon of a year or more with the objective of gaining a return on that money. Trading would be defined as allocating capital with a time frame of one year or less with the goal of getting a return on that capital. Trading is associated with risk-taking and with gambling, but I believe that speculation and gambling are functions not of time frames but of mind-sets and one's knowledge basis. You can intentionally have a position in place for a matter of only days—let's say with the objective of profiting from an impending earnings announcement—and be a trader rather than a gambler. Conversely, someone could allocate capital to an investment that has an inherently long-term time horizon, such as private equity funds (which typically have time frames of three to seven years), and be approaching said investment as pure speculation by virtue of his lack of knowledge of the underlying investment, or with a mind-set that labels the allocation "play money."

You can be both an investor and a trader at the same time. If you put money to work in a private equity fund, you are very likely investing. Conversely, if you are buying or selling options that expire within a short time, that is a trade. You can trade around an investment to add incremental profits by buying more on weakness and selling off shares on strength, either outright or via options.

The key is to know which hat you are wearing, and to act accordingly. Most people think they are investing but really they are trading. They go into a situation with the long term in mind, but they invariably exit the position in its entirety in the near term if the stock price spikes or if a seemingly better, "sexier" opportunity comes along. Alternatively, many market players enter a position with a certain time horizon in mind and end up holding on to the position for far longer than they intended to if the price of the stock is lower than their purchase price. Why? Basic emotions; anchor-priced inertia (the need to "get back to even"). When you are putting money to work in the market, be disciplined about whether the allocation of capital is intended to be an investment or a trade. You can make money both ways—*especially if trading is effectively combined with investing*—but only with a disciplined, purposeful, proactive approach, not a reactionary one. The bottom line is that we are all both investors and traders. It is just a matter of what end of the spectrum we are on for any given capital allocation.

Furthermore, market conditions change. During the 1990s you could buy a few growth mutual funds and make 30% or more per year derived largely if not exclusively from capital gains. But equity environments vary, and like great companies, superior investors must incrementally refine their approach. There are times when markets seem to whipsaw daily. The decade following the Internet bust was one such period. The buy-and-hold investor would actually have lost money from 2000 to 2009, especially after factoring in taxes and inflation. While the market went nowhere from point to point, it went plenty of places in between, like the characters in the film *Jumper,* where fluctuations that used to be measured in months or years were suddenly occurring in weeks, days, or even hours. Movements that the nimble trader could take advantage of to his financial benefit. While no one can predict with certainty what the next ten years will hold, gains from dividends, option sales, and nimble trading could easily make up the majority of profit potential, with long-term capital appreciation coming in a distant fourth.

Once we recognize the four main sources of potential profit and understand that during various market cycles you need to shift your emphasis from one to another, the next consideration for superior stock returns relates to that in which we invest. Clearly, if you buy the market as a whole (however you define that), then your returns will be the market minus whatever fees you pay, be they commissions, fund fees, advisory fees, or other investing or trading-related expenses. But what are the main ways superior investors outperform the market? These include: which subset of the entire market you buy (stock selection) because even in down markets some stocks increase in price; when you buy what you buy (which is really another way of saying price) because two investors owning the same stock could have dramatically different returns, point of entry being key to returns; what your position sizes are; when you sell (having a disciplined selling methodology is important for superior returns); and the ability to hedge and trade.

The next question is whether you are an **active** or **passive** investor. Though these two terms might seem to relate to how frequently we conduct transactions, the more nuanced and perhaps more useful definition relates to our belief in our ability to outperform the market over time. A passive investor believes that the markets are efficient, and thus does not attempt—either directly or via a professional money manager—to secure returns above those of the market. Active investors or traders believe that markets are not entirely efficient, or that they possess a methodology or process that can lead to returns that are superior to the market.

The reality is that no one is a purely passive investor. Even if you do not think about it in these terms, everybody makes timing and allocation decisions.

When you decide to put money into a large-cap U.S. mutual fund or an international bond fund, you are making an active decision to allocate capital to those sectors or market cap categories, as opposed to one of the other investment opportunities available. Even if you are investing in an S&P 500 index fund in your 401(k) via an automatic salary deduction plan—a seemingly passive investing approach—you are making decisions about which investment you will allocate your funds to and at what time. You cannot invest funds you do not have, but you can choose not to invest funds you do have—or to invest later at a possibly lower price. Whether consciously or not, whether intentionally or by default, anyone investing in the market is continually making timing and allocation decisions. It is only a matter of degree.

Figure 7.1 **INVESTOR/TRADER MATRIX**

	Short Time Horizon	**Long Time Horizon**
Seeks to Add Value	Active Trader	Active Investor
Believes Markets Are Inherently Efficient	Passive Trader	Passive Investor

Bottom line, you can make money investing, you can make money trading, you can make money being passive, and you can make money being active. The important element is being honest with yourself. Realistically assess your level of competence and your ability to commit the necessary time—your parachute color, as it were. Know when you have your active trader hat on (perhaps taking advantage of the temporary weakness of a stock) and when you have your passive investor hat on (putting money in a long-term qualified savings account like an IRA or 529 plan that you don't want to monitor aggressively for years on end).

While most people think of Warren Buffett as a buy-and-hold-only investor, and the typical view of Jim Cramer is that he is a lightning fast trader, these two money men are not as far apart in terms of style as it would appear. Buffett is constantly getting in and out of positions, be they equities or special situations, from commodities to currencies, to everything in between. Similarly, while Cramer is undoubtedly more active than Buffett in terms of equity holdings, he maintains many positions for years, as long as the fundamentals stay strong. Simply put, the very best money managers are both investors and traders, and they know which hat they are wearing at any point in time and, more important, *why*.

GREAT INVESTORS

You know who they are. They are the ones who always seem to avoid what are in retrospect "obvious" mistakes and focus on the correct sectors at the right time. When markets are booming, they are just average investors, but when equities suffer, they shine like a thousand lights and their emotional fortitude comes to the fore. They are, simply put, the great investors.

The Talented Mr. Ripley (It's Not Your Fault)

Me: "It's not your fault."

You: [blank stare]

Me: "Really, it's not your fault."

You: "Stop saying that."

Me: "It's okay. I understand. You can't help it; it's not your fault."

You [breaking into tears]: "I know, I know. I can't help it!"

Scene fades . . .

After Warren Buffett donated some $30 billion to the Gates Foundation, he said, in effect, that his investing success was not a function of being good at reading annual reports or performing complex mathematics. *Rather, it was due to how his brain was wired—his ability to process information and then act or behave in certain ways.* Investment prodigies are no different from masters in music or sports. The reality is that without certain innate physical talents and the right mental makeup, no amount of training can make you an Olympic gold medalist marathoner. When it comes to making regular, fundamental investing mistakes, it really is not your fault. You were not "wired" to make consistently superior investment decisions.

Money has a sizeable emotional component to it. Despite what efficient-market theorists espouse, near-term equity prices are driven by millions of market participants who are subject to the psychological quirks that are embedded in human nature. Are you going to be subject to the detrimental consequences of letting emotions drive your investing and trading decisions, or are you going to take advantage of the inability of the masses to separate their emotions from their financial choices?

Navigating the Market Waters: Characteristics of Great Investors

I spent many years sailing competitively. In sailing there are two concepts called *true wind* and *apparent wind.* As the names imply, true wind is how the wind is *actually* blowing, whereas apparent wind is how you *perceive* the wind to be blowing. Using the example of an automobile, if a stopped car is facing north and the wind is coming from the south at 20 MPH, a passenger in the car putting his hand out the window will feel a breeze coming from behind (the south) at 20 MPH. In this case, the true wind and apparent wind are the same.

Now the car begins to move, heading straight north. As the vehicle speeds up, the wind will appear to shift direction at a new speed. The true wind is still a 20 MPH wind from the south, but as the car starts going faster and faster, the wind will feel as though it were coming more and more from the north until, once the car is going fast enough (e.g., 100 MPH), the apparent wind will be directly from the north. Between the car accelerating from being at rest to the car moving at 100 MPH to the north, the apparent wind has slowly shifted 180 degrees. And the true wind did not change one bit. (I recommend only trying this experiment on an isolated road.)

In the stock market, there are apparent winds, sometimes of hurricane strength, blowing every day from many directions, masking the true wind. The apparent wind is what the market is temporarily valuing a company at, while the true wind is what the company is actually worth. Sometimes these are in line; most of the time they are off slightly; and once in a while they are far apart. What drives these apparent winds? You name it. Sometimes investors mix up ticker symbols. I remember one instance in which investors heard rumors that the company TeleCommunication, Inc., known as TCI, was going to be taken over. Ticker symbol TCI jumped the next morning. The only thing was, the company with the ticker symbol TCI *was not* TCI but some other company. Whoops. So much for academic theories about perfectly efficient markets based on the free flow of information. And while the academics might say that this and countless other examples of inefficient market behaviors driven by apparent winds are exceptions, all you need is a few exceptions a year to achieve superior returns.

Figure 7.2 **True and Apparent Winds**

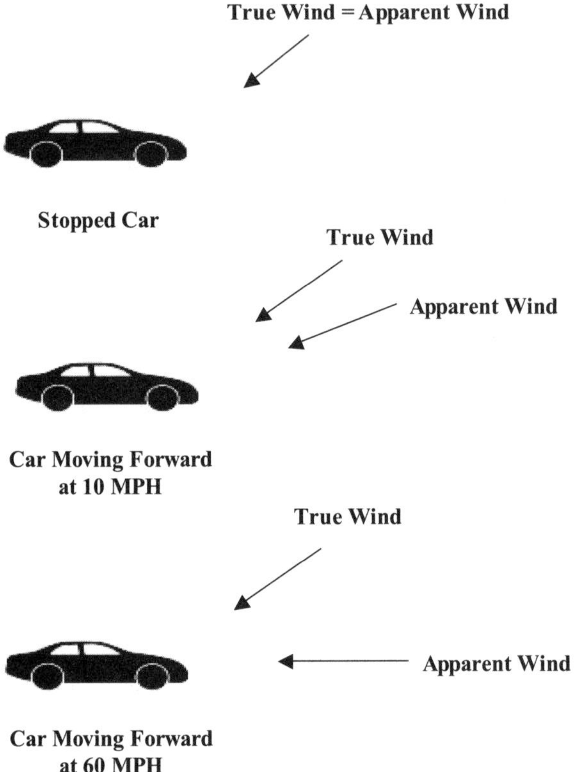

In reality, the exceptions in the marketplace, the times when the true and apparent winds diverge, are more frequent (if not more subtle) than the above example; you have to know how to perceive them. Maybe the manager of a big mutual fund retires and the new portfolio manager does not like a certain position, so he sells the fund's entire stake and the stock drops on big volume. There's been no change in the company fundamentals, only a big shareholder deciding to sell. Or perhaps a bunch of people buy a stock one day because they see it going up, or because they received an e-mail touting said stock. From day to day, the reasons for movements are as varied and indiscriminate as the millions of people making the buy/sell decisions—little apparent wind shifts every day.

Once in a while the market at large is driving backward at 80 MPH so that much of the market appears to have a huge wind at its back. But these forces eventually stop, the car runs out of gas, and the true wind rules again. The late 1990s was one such period.

When great investors make investment decisions, they do so within the context of what they know at the time and with a discipline that is consistent with their stated investment objectives. It is vital that you have and hold a conviction that will yield the optimal (and superior) risk-adjusted returns even though this position might not immediately lead to the perfect result. Too often investors are quick to look back at a situation and state, "Of course stock X was going to go up; it was so obvious." But hindsight is 20/20 if not 20/15, and memory tends to fade quickly when it comes to the situations in which our all-knowing investor got it wrong. The goal is to stick with a style that will do well in virtually all market conditions, and not feel as though you have to be number one in every market environment. It is the performance at the end of the race—as defined by your time horizon—that ultimately matters. This is not the Tour de France, where you will be awarded bonus points for intermediate sprints.

How do the great investors navigate such waters? What separates them from the masses who are unable to distinguish true wind from apparent wind? The first thing you might point to is financial acumen, the ability to read balance sheets and such. You would be decidedly wrong. The monumental irony of investing is that financial analysis is not the core skill that separates the great investor from the average investor. Lots of people took Math 101, Finance 202, and Stock Analysis 303, which yield more than enough quantitative and analytical skills to be a great investor. *It is psychology, behavior, and temperament that separate the great investors from the masses.* This means the ability to take a step back and objectively, sans emotion, separate the true wind from the apparent wind. Great investors have the discipline to not get caught up in the latest trends, the rigor to invest only when their criteria are met, the self-control to only invest in things they understand—a discipline that is built into their investing DNA. They also have patience, the ability to *not* take action, to sit back and wait for the market or a particular stock price to come back to them.

Great investors also have the ability to think and act in long-term ways. Our society, via the media, pushes short-term fixes and instant gratification. As more and more of the public has started investing in stocks—because the costs of doing so have come down and the ease of doing so has gone up (largely because of the Internet)—the short-term, emotionally driven behaviors that people exhibit in their personal lives spill over into the stock market, creating apparent winds all over the place. Eventually, as the true wind comes back, earnings and valuation ultimately win out. But in the short term, crowd behavior can have material near-term impact on market prices. The great investor must have the discipline to stick things out.

POWER TIP

Pop! On Being There When a Stock Moves Big

Most stocks move 30% or more trough-to-peak during a given year, even if their net return is in the single digits. This is a surprisingly regular occurrence, even for large-cap companies. A stock trades within a range for weeks, months, or even years. You watch it regularly and it seems to go nowhere. (If it is a quality, dividend-paying company then at least you are getting paid dividends that you are either investing elsewhere, spending, or reinvesting to purchase more shares in the same company.) Then, one day you wake up after having not monitored the stock for a while and it is up 25%, 30%, or more. Be patient, be *there* for these inevitable moves.

When I talk about having the patience necessary to be there when a stock pops, I am not talking about little companies with typically volatile stock prices. I am talking about the stock prices of some of the biggest companies in the world: Walgreens, Microsoft, and others. Seemingly overnight, the stock can go from $40 to $50+, as Walgreens did in a short period in mid-2006 after having traded in a tight range for years. What caused this surge, a movement that can amount to several years' worth of gains in a matter of months or weeks? In most cases, absolutely nothing.

***Figure* 7.3 Large Stock Moves in Short Periods**

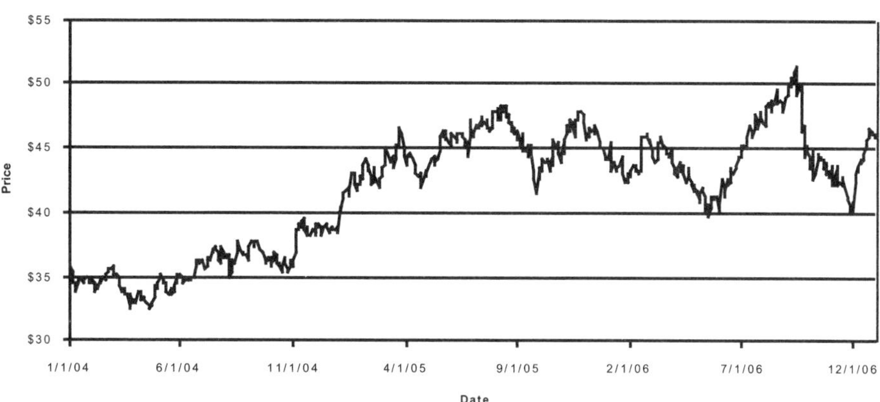

SOURCE: FINANCE.YAHOO.COM

Look at Walgreens more closely. Nothing fundamental about this company had changed yet the stock gained nearly 30% in a short period, adding billions of dollars of market cap value. This is not some start-up; Walgreens has been around and at the top of its game for decades. It has consistently paid out dividends since 1933. If you looked at the chart you would think the company had made a major announcement that caused the stock to jump. Yet all Walgreens did was what it has done month in and month out for years—provide good products and services to its customers in a way that allows it to consistently increase revenue, earnings, and dividend payments.

The point is that you need to be there when a stock moves. It can happen at any time for any reason—or for no reason at all. You have to be patient. Generating income via a nice dividend certainly helps with that (psychologically especially as it gives you the sense that something is happening), which is one of the many reasons why I like dividend-paying stocks.

Most people recognize on an intellectual level that great investor behavior is how you should approach investing, but in most cases there is a disconnect between knowledge and action. Investors know that they should buy low and sell high, but time and time again, people become interested in making an investment only after the prices have run up and the stock has made the cover of *Business Week*. Then, when the price begins to fall and the investor can't stand it anymore, he sells in frustration. Eventually, prices rebound and the investor has his interest piqued again. Once the surging prices are the headlines, and only after he can no longer stand hearing about his neighbors making so much money, does he jump back in and continue the cycle. Taking advantage of the average investor's conduct is what gives great investors profit-making opportunities. Let me say that again. *Great investors take advantage of the behavior of the masses who play the market rather than invest in companies.*

Great investors are able to do this because they focus on true wind while being aware of apparent wind. They make sure not to get blown around by it, but from time to time they profit from it when the downside associated with doing so is low. Here's how it works in sailing, and here is the lesson that transformed me from a national-level sailor to a world-class competitor. I now apply this vital lesson to investing.

There are waves on most bodies of water. We have all seen them. They crash near shore, but farther out at sea they pass or roll by. These waves are not as dramatic as breakers pounding against the shore, but they are every bit as real. A boat can rise and fall five feet or more from the peak to the trough of a wave. Waves usually come from the direction of the wind, as air currents are an important component of wave generation. Let's say that the wind is coming directly from the north, or twelve on a clock. As you probably know, a boat cannot sail directly into the wind, but rather it must sail at an angle to the wind. A boat can sail at ten (starboard tack) and two o'clock (port tack) when the wind is coming directly from the north.

To make a complicated subject simple, a boat very subtly slows down while climbing the face of the wave and speeds up again while going down the back side of the wave as it sails against the wind and the waves. This makes intuitive sense: You go slower when gravity is working against you and faster when gravitational pull is on your side. What did we learn above? When a car slows down or speeds up, that movement affects the apparent wind. True wind does not change, but apparent wind does. Thus, great sailors make rapid and subtle adjustments to their bodies, the angle of the boat, their sails, and the other variables under their control with every movement up the peak of a wave and back down toward the trough. The movement is constant and fluid and done literally thousands of times throughout the course of a race. If you didn't know what to look for, you wouldn't see it. The competitors in the back of the pack make few or no adjustments. They just sail up the wave and back down. This is fine, it will get you to where you want to go—eventually. This is the index fund of sailing, and it serves a purpose. But you won't become a world-champion sailor if you don't take advantage of slight shifts in movement and gravity.

Figure 7.4 **Sailing at an Angle**

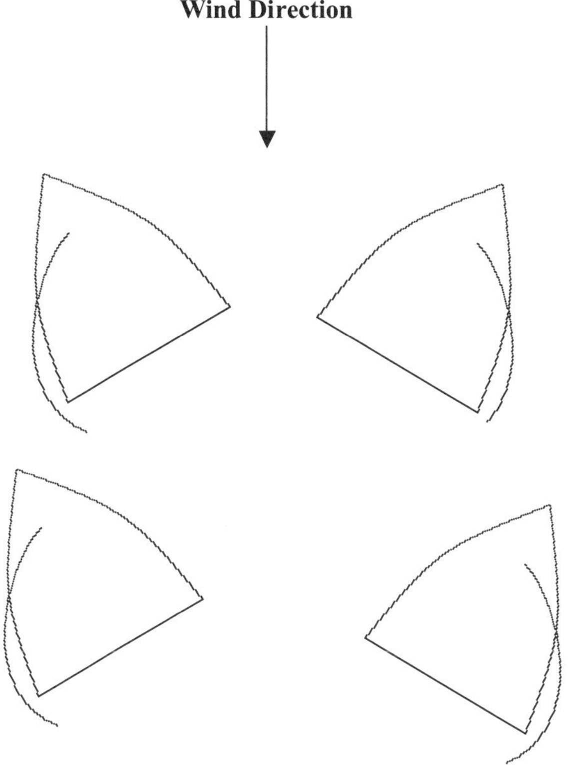

How does this translate into investing? The concept I am about to introduce is advanced and is not for everyone. Many people without the time or focus to dedicate to investing are comfortable with middle-of-the-pack, near-market returns. This discussion is for those who have the time and, equally important, the mental fortitude to take investing to the next level of potential returns.

Stock price trajectories are rarely linear either up or down. Yet, for many top-quality companies, revenues and earnings growth are fairly smooth and steady. In any case, rarely does a company's stock price directly track near-term financial performance. Price, which is what the market says the company is worth, and value, what the fundamentals suggest the company is worth, line up over time, but day to day, week to week, even month to month, the stock price for a company might jump all around even though the company's business has made steady progress during that period. Why does this occur? Apparent winds. I am in no way suggesting that you react to these daily or weekly variations. Doing so is impractical for most people who are professionals in other fields. But not all waves are the same size, and you do not need a rogue wave—a huge disconnect between true and apparent winds—in order to take advantage of subtle shifts and add incremental profits to a portfolio. You should be selective and conservative, but the opportunities are there.

You might make a reasonable argument that, if someone is willing to pay X for a stock or asset, then by definition that is what the market is saying the stock is worth, and therefore price equals value. The market is speaking, as it were, and who is to say that the true value is something other than the price? In any case, who cares, since the price is the price? But this is not the case. Remember, prices are set on the margin—on whatever the last transaction was. The price might be fleeting and the transaction based not on fundamentals but on circumstances. Let's say you were in the middle of the desert and a distant mirage of a lemonade stand turned out to be real. A couple of enterprising kids greet you with smiles on their faces and a hand-painted sign reading, GLASS OF COLD LEMONADE: $25! Given your circumstances, you would shell out that amount of money for a Dixie cup's worth of lemonade. This was a legitimate, arm's-length transaction that set a real price. But does that mean that a glass of lemonade is truly worth $25? Is this price sustainable or aberrational? What is the real value of the glass of lemonade?

While this example might seem extreme, the scenario is not far removed from what was occurring in the stock market in the late 1990s when it came to Internet-based companies. For a brief time there was a clear disconnect between the price investors were willing to pay on the margin for certain stocks and the value of the underlying businesses. In effect, investors were as desperate to own a piece of Company X.com as you were for that glass of lemonade in the desert. But investors' willingness to pay exorbitant prices for Internet companies that lacked profitability and sustainable business models disappeared as fast as a desert mirage, and prices quickly declined to match value. Every day in the marketplace there are disconnects, however fleeting, between the price and the value of assets. Your focus must be on how to take advantage of such disparities.

Let's return to Walgreens, which, like most retailers, reports comparable store sales monthly. This company is by many measures number one in its industry, has a rock-solid balance sheet, and has been paying and raising dividends for decades—all of the financial characteristics we look for in investments. Given Walgreens superior historical performance, it has set a high bar for itself, one that it does not always leap over. Hence, the company occasionally reports monthly store sales that disappoint the market in some way, even though they are almost always strong, even record sales. The stock often sells off the day of the sales announcement, only to climb back over the next thirty days, and then the cycle repeats itself. When this kind of apparent-wind event occurs, an active trader can add incremental shares of the stock on an interim basis. In essence you are buying a slightly larger position than you would otherwise hold. So, if you usually have a 5% position in Company X, increase it to 6% or 7% at moments of nonfundamental weakness. This can be done either by adding to a long position via equity or through the sale of short put options at a level that would increase the position on a notional basis by a couple percentage points. Upon subsequent strength, sell off the incremental long position or let the short puts expire worthless. Ride these waves as long as the opportunity presents itself. If the stock breaks out to the upside, do not force the sale of additional puts at a higher strike price. Either take advantage of strength by selling calls (if you are willing to part with some or all of your shares), or be patient and wait for true weakness before adding additional, incremental shares. If the stock never retraces, that is fine; with a portfolio of twenty to thirty positions, you will have plenty of candidates that will provide you with opportunities to profit from disconnects between true and apparent wind.

Figure 7.5 **Taking Advantage of Natural Market Volatility**

Regardless of what caused a short-term drop in the stock, when the stock comes back—as it likely will, whether in a few days, weeks, or months—sell off the incremental position. In other words, trade around your core positions by adding slightly on weakness and selling slightly on strength. Just as the world-champion sailor makes small adjustments to his sails to squeeze out every advantage, this is how one makes incremental profits in the stock market. This process can be done via adding stock or selling stock, selling puts on weakness, and/or selling calls on strength. "But won't this have tax consequences?" is the usual question. Yes, you will get taxed on your additional profits in nonqualified accounts. You make more money, you pay taxes on those additional profits, and you are better off.

Taking a Flyer: Lessons on Emotions and Investing

I truly believe that my competitive sailing during my formative years (I started sailing about the same time I learned to walk) helped to shape me as an investor. As it turns out, characteristics that make a good sailor—being able to look into the horizon (literally and figuratively), to navigate the short-term waves while focusing on the bigger and longer-term picture, and to deal with harsh realities and take appropriate action—are shared by excellent money managers.

POWER TIP

The Real Deal (Rent to Own)

In Southern California in the early '00s, and for that matter all around the country in the middle part of the decade, real estate investing was all the rage. For those who are more real-property oriented, I like to draw the following analogy to explain the essence of covered calls. Let's say you own a second home for investment purposes only. You paid in cash, so you have no mortgage on the property. To your way of thinking there are two ways you can make money on the property. The first is through price appreciation. That will be our stock capital gains analogy. You can also rent the home out to generate income. That is the equivalent to owning stocks that generate income for you in the form of dividend payments. What if there were an active options market for real estate? Let's set a scenario where you bought your investment property for $500,000 a few years back and it was recently appraised for $1 million. If someone, even your current tenant, were to offer you $100,000 for the right to buy your second home for $1.3 million during the next twelve months if the price were to reach that level, would you be open to selling such an option? Perhaps you were already considering exiting the position if the right offer came along. Using your investment property to generate additional income in exchange for being "forced" to sell it at an even higher price seems too good to be true. This is at the heart of covered call selling. The market for such options is real, the potential profits are real, and the costs for entering into the transaction (time and dollars) are real, but extremely low (unlike the case for real estate).

One of the most profound investment lessons I learned from sailing involved what is called "taking a flyer." Taking a flyer is sticking with a course even though all the wind, current, and other trends are working against you. Think of sailing around a baseball diamond, with the goal of getting from home plate to second base and back. Only in sailing, you can't aim directly at second base and simply sprint there.

Instead, you have to crisscross back and forth—tacking against the wind—pursuing 45-degree angles to your destination. Some sailors stay close to the middle of the course, tacking frequently and taking a conservative path. Others go way out to the right side of the course (first base), and then tack back toward second base. Others will go way out to third base before heading back to their destination. When someone goes to an extreme—all the way to first base or third base before shifting course and heading to second base again—then they are taking a flyer. When they do it not because they think it is the best course of action but because the conditions "force" them to do so, then they are *really* taking a flyer.

When you go way off to the extreme sides of the course, you might end up a big winner, or you might end up at the back of the pack. What causes people to take flyers and how can we learn from that to make ourselves better investors? Sailors typically go to extremes when conditions on their side of the course begin to deteriorate and they are willing to double their bets that eventually the conditions along their "chosen" route will improve. Rather than looking at the field and cutting their losses early by heading back to the middle where conditions are better, most sailors will blindly stay the course. They won't even look—they don't even want to know—what is going on elsewhere on the course. They are too emotionally committed to their choice and they won't even consider an alternative.

When you compete in a major sailing championship, you typically sail about eight races; think of them as rounds in golf. Your scores are added up and, as with golf, the lowest score wins. You could go the entire competition without winning a race, but if your total score across all eight or ten races is lowest, you win. Some sailors have finishes that are all over the map—they'll win a race, then get a 25th place. Other sailors are very consistent: they'll get a 5th, then a 3rd. These are the sailors who win world championships and these are the investors who get good returns. How do these sailors avoid the double-digit scores that invariably drop them down in the overall rankings? They discipline themselves not to take flyers. More to the point, they open their proverbial brokerage statements and they analyze the information with a raw, cold, emotionless calculus. Fortunately, I learned this painful and costly lesson early in my sailing career.

When I first started competing in major championships, I was nervous as hell. I was in my teens and sailing against a hundred of the best sailors in the world—guys I had read about who had represented the United States in worldwide competitions. When I would get on the sides of the racecourse and the conditions were working against me, I didn't even want to know what was happening elsewhere on the course. At first I would be next to some current national or world champion. Then the situation would start looking bleak and five minutes later I would be on my own, farther out on a limb that was getting weaker by the minute. A more experienced and wiser competitor would have assessed the situation and tacked back toward the center of the course, cutting his losses and knowing that the fundamental conditions had irreparably deteriorated on his side of the course. Once in a while my flyer would pay off and I would win a race big, but my inconsistent scores would invariably lead to an overall finish out of the top ten. I analyzed the scores of the top five competitors and noticed tremendous stability. They made fewer mistakes than I did; they cut their losses when the fundamentals changed; they went for singles and doubles rather than home runs (and strikeouts).

I soon changed my ways; I stopped taking flyers. More important, I opened my eyes and assessed the conditions with brutal objectivity before I got into such a situation. How am I doing? How are the conditions where I am positioned? Are they likely to improve any time soon? What do conditions look like elsewhere on the course? This was my first vitally important step toward consistent success.

Your immediate reaction might be to consider the sort of behavior characterized by taking a flyer as irrational. Think, however, about how many times, when the market is falling day after day, you hear your friends say, "I can't even open my brokerage statements and look at how my stocks are doing." (I am sure you have never said that.) The investor who won't even examine his brokerage statement is no different than the sailor taking a flyer.

The Sale Discipline

A good deal of emphasis is placed, as it should be, on factors leading to purchasing or not purchasing a stock and hedging or not hedging

POWER TIP

When to Take the Stairs

We have all been there before. We push the UP button on the elevator and wait. We are late for an important meeting, so each passing minute seems like an eternity. We contemplate taking the stairs but hesitate; we have waited this long; we might as well hold on. The question is: At what point should we take the stairs? The optimal answer is not the intuitive one. For most people, the longer they wait, the more apt they are to take the alternate route (the four flights of stairs to the meeting). In reality, if you need to be somewhere at a given time, you are always better off being decisive immediately. If you have all day, then waiting it out is perfectly fine. But if you have three minutes, and the elevator does not arrive in the first minute and each flight of stairs takes you thirty seconds to ascend, you are best served by taking the stairs as soon as one minute has passed. When trading for the short term, you need to be decisive and take action early to cut your losses.

it. But what about the sale process? Stocks are a means to an end. The goal of investing is not the ownership of securities in and of itself, but rather to achieve objectives (growth and income) across certain time frames (near term, long term) so as to have resources for some future economic event (retirement, home purchase, college expenses). Thus, it is not a question of will you sell a given stock, but when and why. Here are some variables for consideration. First and foremost, selling takes tremendous discipline, whether it is the sale of a given stock based on a predetermined gain objective, or more important—and more difficult—because the fundamentals of a given company are deteriorating. So know that you need to be on your game and put emotions aside in order to optimize the time at which you sell stocks.

The first consideration in when to sell a stock is the easiest—if it meets a target sale price. This might be determined by the strike price for a call that has been sold or, independent of any short call hedge, you might have a percentage gain in mind at which point you will take some or all of your gains. One easy methodology is to have an alert in place so that if your stock reaches the target price, you are informed (usually by e-mail), and you can execute the trade like a machine. Do not become wedded to your stock positions. They are there to serve you, not vice versa. If the stock price continues trending higher after you have sold it, don't look back—you still made the right move. If the price heads south for nonfundamental reasons and you want to reenter the position, you now have the opportunity to do so at a lower price.

The next consideration in selling is a much more difficult one, namely selling a stock for which the fundamentals have deteriorated. This is very different from selling a stock just because the price has dropped by a given percentage. Your fundamental thesis might turn out to be wrong because of changes at the company or industry level, be they management changes (key people leaving), important financial changes (cutting of a dividend or stock issuance), competitive changes, or a fundamental deterioration in the way the industry is functioning. Remember, stock prices can always go lower (unless they are at $0.00 per share), and things can always get worse. It typically takes longer to turn around core problems at a company than most people expect, so if your analysis indicates that fundamentals are heading south, consider being decisive: Take action by selling the position. Clearly, the longer your time horizon with the funds the more time you have to see if the company's problems are shorter term in nature. To the extent that the company pays a dividend—and that the fundamental challenges will not put that dividend at risk—then the potential reinvestment of a dividend at lower prices might persuade you to hold the stock. The more growth-oriented the position and the shorter your time horizon, the quicker you should sell if you sense fundamentals deteriorating. Conversely, the more income-oriented the position and the longer your investment time frame, the more room you have to hold the position for a possible turnaround.

Most people invest with their emotions. If the average investor buys a stock, and then it starts working against him because there is something fundamentally wrong that is unlikely to get better within a reasonable time frame, he often will feel a need to "beat" the stock, to hold on to it at least until it gets back to his purchase price. Worse yet, he will stop looking at fundamental news as the price drops. He doesn't even want to know.

The big lesson here is that you need to invest and compete in the financial marketplace sans emotion. You need to be able and willing to take in any and all information—no matter how bad—and take decisive action accordingly. Most people simply are not wired to behave this way. If you do not have the ability to approach investing with a Vulcan-esque mind-set, find someone you trust who is capable of such an approach and let him or her ensure that you do not take any flyers that your pocketbook will regret. If you do have this ability, you might well have the potential to be a great investor.

POWER TIP

The Lesson on Options Back Dating

It is a sad commentary on corporate America that so many executives were found in the mid-'00s to have backdated options grants to themselves and others. But the fact that there is still malfeasance in the workplace is not the big story here for investors looking to improve their returns. The lesson is the most important aspect of investing, namely to buy low! This might seem obvious, but how many times have you been able to muster the fortitude to buy, buy, buy as the market or an otherwise high-quality stock is heading lower? Most weekend warrior investors know in theory to buy low and sell high, but when times get tough, just when such opportunities best present themselves, just when investors need to have the biggest *cojones* on the block, their emotions take over and they say to themselves, "I can't stand it anymore. I'm going to sell now before it gets any worse and then wait until there is more clarity in the market before I get back in." The effective translation of this is, "Even though the market is going down and mathematically I am better off buying now rather than selling, I will sell now and wait for the market to go higher before I buy again because I am not emotionally wired to do it any other way." Learn the right lesson here: He who pays the lowest price wins.

CHAPTER 8

Moving Up the Experience Curve: Using a Journal and Other Exercises

I live by a simple philosophy, namely that we get good at those things to which we dedicate the greatest amount of time. That said, there are many ways to learn. One is to read about a subject. Listening to a teacher utilizes the sense of hearing. Watching an action being performed is another source of education. An even more effective method of learning a subject is to teach it. (Remember when a friend would ask you a question in Economics 101? It was only when you could explain the concept to someone else that you knew you had the topic down.) To perform the task, however, to gain direct experience, is the ultimate form of learning. There is no worthwhile enterprise in the world that you can master exclusively by reading or listening or observing or talking. You must engage in an activity to truly master it.

You could spend a year with tennis great Pete Sampras, listening to him explain the finer points of stroke technique and court positioning, and you would not come close to mastering the game of tennis. Similarly, you could dedicate years to reading the most detailed manual on how to fly an airplane, but you would not be competent to get behind the wheel of a Cessna without some real hands-on experience. There simply is no substitute.

In my case, I won countless national and world sailing titles before the age of twenty. I enjoyed sharing my expertise with others and started a company called Performance Sailing Seminars. I dedicated weekends to "downloading" everything I knew about the sport to twenty or thirty eager sailors looking to get an edge over their competition. While I certainly believe these students benefited from my teaching—and indeed, several of my pupils and training partners went on to become world-champion sailors—I soon realized that I could not impart the vast majority of what was between my ears and embedded in my muscles. Why did I make a certain move at the start of the race? In some cases the decisions and subsequent actions were explainable—preset maneuvers, as in chess (think of the Sicilian Opening). In other cases, my body and mind seemed to remember that of the 12,123 times that I had been in a similar situation, 73% of the time move X worked better than move Y.

Do the reading, listen to others impart their wisdom, teach a colleague what you know, but above all else, engage in the activity yourself to learn at the highest level.

Every investor, even those with decades of experience like the great Warren Buffett, makes mistakes from time to time. (Buffett has been quoted as saying he should have sold some of his "permanent" holdings in 1999 or 2000 when valuations got so out of whack.) If you are fortunate, you will be making at least some investing mistakes until you are 120 years old as the Talmud says. To enhance or codify the learning process, I recommend that you start an investment journal. You cannot fake experience, but you can accelerate and optimize the process through certain actions, one of which is to write down and study your triumphs, failures, lessons, questions, and observations to increase the likelihood of repeating your successes and avoiding your mistakes. In response to the question, "what is the key to a football team's success?" my NFL veteran cousin replied without hesitation, "the coach's watching the game tape." Now I am specifically not recommending that you watch the stock ticker tape. However, in reviewing your plays, your victories, and your losses, you will improve your game. Remember, making some mistakes is inevitable; the question is whether you learn from errors and have the discipline to alter your methods.

My process is as follows. Throughout the year I make entries into an investment journal. For example, if I bought the stock of a company that met all of my investment criteria but that went down soon after I bought it (thus causing me to call into question the initial investment) only to rebound for a gain, then I make a note accordingly, in this case reaffirming the notions that: (1) you cannot predict short-term stock movements, and (2) always invest in the strongest companies within a given industry. A journal is useful both in noting new lessons and in reaffirming learned concepts (and, with luck, reminding yourself of mistakes made only once). Over the weekend post-expiration, I often look back at my trades from the previous options expiration cycle and see where I optimized positions and where I could have squeezed even more profits. This is akin to a football coach reviewing the game tape on the Monday following a big game, or a fighter examining film from a contest to see where he can improve his technique and form. Here are some typical entries and lessons learned from my own investment journal, which I have been keeping for decades:

- An investment bank I purchased not long ago dropped a little over 30% while other financial companies have been getting crushed, only to rebound above my purchase price within weeks. The lessons here are multifold. First, even very large companies can have large percentage moves in short periods of time—when you least expect it—so be patient, and do not hedge away potential large gains. Also, the company I purchased is one of the best-managed and financially sound businesses in its industry. Own top quality only. Trying to time exact entry points is impossible; focus on the fundamentals of the business.
- Must be able to step back and, when in doubt, do zero.
- Layer in trades, especially in a generally declining market.
- When you have the opportunity to close out a position, let's say you are double hedged and there is weakness allowing you to close out your incremental calls at a profit, take the opportunity. Be disciplined and do not hesitate!

- Always buy best-of-breed companies. Better to buy more of the best companies than gamble with the weak ones. I bought a third-tier financial firm and paid the price.
- Do not think of closing a given position at a profit but rather think of where the stock could go in the future. Small losses can turn into big losses, so assess each position on its own merits as of today, especially if it's not a core holding. Overall portfolio construction and risk controls always dominate "winning" any given trade.

Regular journal entries are, by their nature, brief and informal. Although some of the lessons seem obvious, it is vital to "check in" with the basics periodically to be sure you are maintaining your investing and trading discipline when you are in the midst of battle.

Similarly, taking a step back to formalize a lesson is highly valuable. To that end, every year around the holiday season I dedicate a few days to reflect on the previous year in investing. In addition to being the time when returns are calculated, year-end is often the one time in the calendar when you can truly switch out of business mode for a few days, given holiday-driven market closures. As part of this annual process that I have undertaken for over twenty years, I write about ten pages of notes on investing or trading issues in which I did well, and on areas I need to improve upon. While my investment journal is now approaching 200 pages, there are realistically only ten to fifteen lessons and themes, many of them interrelated, that repeat themselves year after year. Pay attention and certain undeniable investment "laws" will emerge. Here are some summary lessons from over the years, in no particular order:

1. *The "obvious" trades are not always so obvious, and certainly not so certain.* Going into 2006, the so-called smart money was certain that General Motors (GM) was going to crater and Ford (F) was going to be the stronger of the two auto companies. Instead, GM turned out to be the best-performing Dow component stock (gaining more than 50% that year) while Ford went essentially nowhere. This is one of countless examples. Lesson: Don't assume that obvious investment themes, especially those espoused by market commentators, will hold true. Do your own homework and research.

2. *The best time to buy stocks is the hardest time emotionally to buy stocks.* It happens all the time—either the stock market as a whole or a segment thereof—drops precipitously. Out of the blue, whether for an identifiable reason or for seemingly no reason at all, the market tanks. Overnight the world gets a little darker, a bit more dangerous, and there is a little less spring in our collective step. Most of the major Wall Street firms "advise" investors to wait until "some clarity emerges." Now, when has life ever been clear? The other day I heard a market commentator say, in effect, "Unless we get some surprises this year, I see the S&P 500 rising about 10% on the year." Unless we get surprises? He might as well have said, "...if life stops existing as humanity has existed for the past eight million years then my prediction will hold true." Life is surprises, and the market is driven by unknowns. The market is anything but clear and anything but linear. If you live life—investment life or otherwise—waiting for clarity, you will live your life waiting. You will never call the bottom and you will most certainly be "wrong" for a period of time, but if you invest when things look darkest, you will also be wealthier over time. Rationally, mathematically, you are better off buying stock at a lower price than a higher price. "Wait until there is more clarity" is simply code for "Wait until the market has gone back up so that you feel emotionally more comfortable buying stocks even if financially you are worse off." Lesson: When you feel the least comfortable buying stocks is the best time to do so.

3. *There will always be bad things going on in the economy and in the world. You need to focus on the fundamentals of potential investments—earnings and valuation first and foremost.* This theme is related to lesson number two. As an investor you must recognize that bad things happen year after year, decade after decade, century after century—economically, socially, and financially. The year 2006 saw a serious crack in the United States housing market, a major war on two fronts, terrorist activity throughout the world, turmoil in the oil market, corporate scandals . . . and the S&P 500 gained nearly 14%, or double what many very smart investors consider the likely average returns for the S&P 500 over the next decade. In the near term these events will cause prices to rise and fall, but these

events are by definition not predictable, nor is their effect on the market. How many times leading into a Federal Reserve meeting have market commentators made predictions about the Fed's next move and its impact on the market? Even if the pundits get the first step right (e.g., the Fed will raise rates by X%) more times than not the effect on the market is the opposite of expectations. Lesson: Take advantage of inevitable disruptions in the world, the economy, and the stock market—don't be subject to them. At the end of the day, it is valuation and earnings that matter.

4. *Markets can, and often do, move in one direction for longer than they "should" (or longer than you expect them to).* Countless examples of this exist, but I think the example to beat all examples is this one. In 1996 Alan Greenspan—the man who presumably had at that time probably more economic information than any other single human—said that he thought the markets were overbought. The market hiccupped, then quickly continued its march upward for another three years. Some very, very smart investors—like Julian Robertson of Tiger Management Corp.—held major short positions during this time and lost a fortune and their jobs. Lesson: The market couldn't care less about what you think "should" be the case. Market movements can and often do go on for much longer than seems objectively rational. Get used to it, do not get burned by it, do not fight it. Since quality investments go up over long periods of time, be very careful about shorting "the market," as your pockets might not be deep enough or your stomach strong enough to be eventually proven right.

5. *When investment banks downgrade a stock after it has declined (which is typically when the banks downgrade a stock), that is more often than not a good time to buy the stock. Likewise, when mutual fund companies come out with similar products (think of all the Internet-focused mutual funds that came out in 2000, or all the energy-related funds that came out in 2006), that is often a sign to sell that sector.* You might think I am being cynical, that I am taking digs at my distant French cousins, but au contraire, I am talking about real investment opportunities. You must do your homework. And from time to rare time Wall Street-based financial firms actually downgrade a stock because

it has gone up a lot and is now in a good position to sell (what a concept—sell high, buy low). And certainly all the downgrades *after* the company has released bad news and seen its stock decline can put further pressure on the stock in the near term, so you need to be patient. But this is a lesson I have taken advantage of year after year. One of my favorite examples of this is all the downgrades Microsoft received in the middle of 2006 when it announced that the release of its new operating system would be delayed a few months. The stock subsequently moved from the high $20s to the low $20s. Like lemmings named Linux, most of the top investment banks downgraded the stock from buy to sell (or their equivalent, from overweight to underweight) after the damage was done. Naturally the launch of Windows Vista was soon a reality and the stock climbed back to the low $30s . . . and then the investment banks upgraded the stock after a 30%+ run-up. Lesson: You need to know your companies and you need to expect to be "wrong" for some period of time. But a very good time to buy an otherwise high-quality, financially strong company like Microsoft is when a slew of investment bank downgrades are issued in conjunction with nonfundamentally negative news. This is one of the most surefire ways to enhance your returns.

6. *Even big companies can see their stock prices make major moves over short periods of time.* In the Microsoft example above, the stock went from the low $20s to the low $30s in about six months. Microsoft is no tiny company; it is one of the biggest market-cap companies traded, yet its stock price jumped nearly 50% in a relatively short period. The take-aways here are numerous. First, to the extent you hedge your positions using options, hedge on strength, not on weakness (i.e., sell calls after a run-up, not when the stock has declined, as the stock can come back surprisingly fast). Next, as noted above, the best investment opportunities can present themselves when things look bleakest. Even very big cap stocks can move up very quickly for no particular reason other than a cloud has been lifted. Microsoft did not suddenly get into a new high-growth business or start crushing the competition. The bad news merely faded and the stock took off. Lesson: Big gains can come in quick "spikes," so be patient, especially during periods of weakness.

7. *If you are not sure about an investment or trade, do nothing.* This is one of my favorite lessons, and one of the few mistakes I find myself making on an almost annual basis. For various reasons—our mental wiring, our getting caught up in media frenzies, our need for instant gratification—we often take action when taking no action would have been the right course. Put another way, remove your top three biggest mistakes from a year's return analysis and performance goes way up—usually by more than what the top three winners added to your return performance. Lesson: When in doubt, do nothing. This is a version of Warren Buffett's Rule #1: Don't lose money. In investing, often the *best stop-loss program is the stop-buy program.* There will be many other opportunities to get into good investments.

8. *Good companies with strong balance sheets will survive challenging times and will likely continue to increase their dividends while they are sorting things out.* This is the Pfizer (PFE) versus Ford (F) lesson. Like Ford, Pfizer went through tough times in the mid-'00s. In Pfizer's case this included the tainting of one of its major drugs (the Lipitor/Vioxx scandal), the increased threat of generics, and the cancellation of what was supposed to be its savior drug after key patent expirations. Yet during this period, the company raised its dividend by 26% and 21% in 2005 and 2006 respectively. The company has paid dividends for over 100 years and increased its dividend annually for nearly forty years at an average of more than 12% per year. Pfizer's operational challenges are real, but the company faces them from a position of financial strength. Contrast this with Ford. Its balance sheet is weak given its debt levels, and the company is bleeding cash. As a result, Ford cut, then ultimately suspended, its dividend. Lesson: It is the company's balance sheet, not only its income statement, that is important. Every company faces operational challenges. The question is whether a company has the financial muscle to get through those challenges and continue to reward shareholders through dividend increases and stock buybacks. This can mean the difference between the end of the dividend checks that had been landing in your P.O. box and the continuation, if not the increase, in the size of those checks.

9. *Invest in the best company in an industry.* I have reaped the benefit of this lesson time and time again whether in the realm of private equity or in the public markets. Strong companies have a tendency to stay strong, while weak companies have a propensity to continue to struggle. And when times get tough, as they always do at some point, whether due to macro issues beyond the company's control, industry-specific challenges, or even unexpected internal problems, the strong companies with the best balance sheets, the largest market share, and the greatest profit margins will survive the shakeout and emerge stronger. The weak companies in the industry will suffer if not disappear. A lower stock price can make the second- or third-tier companies in an industry tempting, but buying in is rarely worth it. Look at a company like Walgreens which has been paying a dividend since 1933 and increasing this dividend for decades. A natural tendency is to say, "Well, the company has been around for a long time. There is no way I can make money on it now; it has had its run." Not true. Opportunities to own top-quality companies at reasonable prices come along all the time, minimizing the possibility of capital loss and maximizing the probability of getting a good return on your investment. In another example, Warren Buffett did not purchase Coca-Cola until the 1980s, decades after first learning about this great enterprise. The company was mature at that point, yet Buffett saw a great investment window given the company's valuation and international expansion prospects. Lesson: When you have a choice, which you invariably do, favor the leader in an industry and you will likely be rewarded over time.

ARE YOU IN CONTROL?

Before you get too far into your journal, though, I want you to do an exercise. No, not physical exercise, although it would be great if you did that regularly as well. This is more of a mental exercise. The results can change your life for the better in investing and other areas. Get a pen and a piece of paper. Draw a small circle. Then draw a bigger circle around that circle. Around the second circle, draw a third circle. Inside the smallest circle, write "control." In the second circle, write "influence." In the third circle, write "awareness." Outside the third circle, write "unaware." Label the drawing "spheres of control." Draw arrows coming out of each circle heading to the outside of the page.

Figure 8.1 **SPHERES OF CONTROL**

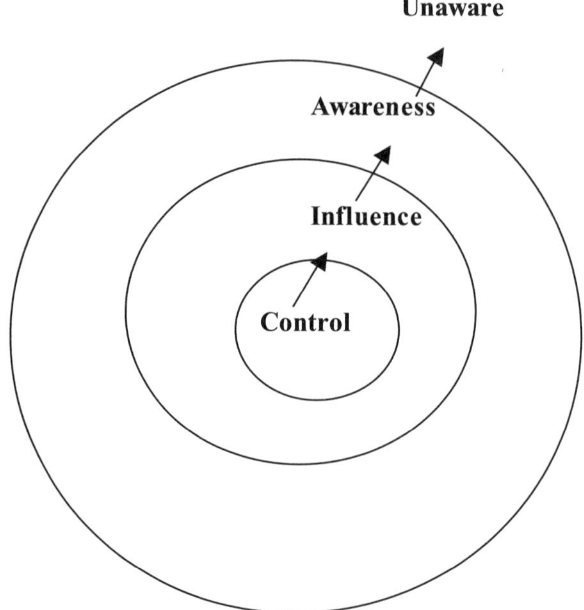

These three spheres represent the various levels of control you have over things in life. Every situation, every circumstance, falls somewhere in your spheres of control, influence, and awareness (and lack thereof). Some things you have total control over; some things you can influence but have no control over; some things you are aware of but can neither influence nor control; and there are some things that you are not even aware of. A given circumstance or set of facts might cross over and transcend the various circles. Our goal is to expand each of these circles over time, to engage in life in such a way that we are aware of increasingly larger amounts of information, facts, and feelings. Being aware of these spheres, being comfortable with them, and being able to deal with them on an emotional and practical level is likely one of the biggest factors that will determine our success and happiness in life.

When you listen closely to successful, happy people, you will hear them use language consistent with an acute awareness, intuitive or otherwise, of these spheres. "Doesn't it really upset you when the fans think you did not give 100% in a game?" Michael Jordan is asked. "I cannot control what others think of me," he replies. "I just focus on doing my best on the basketball court."

Conversely, you will hear people who appear unhappy, unsatisfied, and unsuccessful constantly complain about things over which they have no control. "I am so upset that it is going to rain this weekend. My whole weekend is ruined." Or, worse yet, you will hear them complaining about their jobs or bosses in a way that suggests they are helpless in areas over which they do have some influence if not control. Rather than focusing on matters over which they do have control and maximizing these areas, people dedicate an inordinate amount of time discussing, if not griping about, things over which they have no control whatsoever.

Much of people's attention is focused on aspects of the stock market over which they have no control. Even if you were Warren Buffett, there is not one single thing you can do to influence, much less control, the movement of the U.S. stock market for even a single day. Absolutely nada. Yet people behave as though the stock market is their little domain, their own personal battle that they either win or lose each day. Every day across the United States and the world, otherwise long-term investors open newspapers, turn on the radio, flip on the TV, log on to the Internet, or in some fashion seek information on what the stock market is doing and why. So much thought, so much time, so much communication, so much emotional energy, so much stress, and so much prospective and retrospective analysis is dedicated to short-term movements in the broader market.

Warren Buffett is on record as saying he allocates almost no time to the information that average investors spend hours per day consuming as though their investment lives depended on it. Instead, Buffett focuses on what has and what will always matter, the fundamentals of a given company. This situation is equivalent to Tiger Woods telling the world exactly what he does that makes him a great golfer and the millions of golfers out there fixating instead on the hour-by-hour weather and its effects on grass height and density. Surely Tiger would shake his head in disbelief, knowing that would-be golfing greats are dedicating time to exactly the wrong issues.

The average investor spends most of his time reading absolutely useless commentary about what happened in the market the day before, as though (1) the analyst or market pundit really knows what drove the market that day given the virtually infinite number of variables that drives the stock market in the short term, and more important, (2) it really matters why the Dow went up or down on any given day. In no other industry that I am aware of is so much ultimately useless and irrelevant information produced, sold, and consumed.

Here is an actual quote from a top analyst at a major firm: "There's been enough negative sentiment for days, so any sellers have probably sold. Whether there is another bounce to move us higher from here is unclear." Translation: The definition of a seller is someone who has sold; no one can predict the future. Another classic comment by a TV personality I heard recently was: "There is a big debate about where this market is going. I think we'll have to wait until the market takes its own pulse before we get clarity." No kidding! This guy gets paid big bucks to say in effect, "No one knows where the market will go in the near term but once it has gone wherever it is going to go, then we'll know where it went."

Otherwise smart people get paid a lot of money to make statements like this every day. More surprising, presumably smart people spend time reading and listening to comments like this. Whenever you are tempted to dedicate time to something relating to near-term market movements or financial commentary thereon, break out your Spheres of Control diagram. If the subject matter you are contemplating spending precious time on does not fall at least somewhere in the "influence" or "control" circles, take a pass and go do something productive or enjoyable.

If the average investor dedicated even half the time she spends on market-related matters over which she has zero control—reading about what the market did the previous day or predicting how it will do in the near term—to areas over which she had greater control, such as researching companies or *not* taking action when no action was warranted, then her returns would increase commensurately. Remember, sometimes there are opportunities to make wise investments and trades, and sometimes there are not. You do not have to force the issue; let it come to you. If you feel, however, the need to take action in certain circumstances—and for many people the execution of a trade is a form of attempting to exert power over conditions that are largely beyond their control—then consider the following techniques that might help you save you from yourself. First, put yourself into an environment where you can do no damage (go to the gym or take a walk on the beach). If you still feel the need to take action, buying stock, for example, consider buying more of a quality company that you already own—a core holding. This will tend to cause you to make a smaller purchase (since you already hold some of the stock) and to not buy some inferior company that you have not researched. Finally, if you feel the need to buy some company that you have read or heard about recently, layer into the position by starting with a very small initial allocation. You will be pleasantly surprised at how this series of actions will, in most cases, satisfy your need to take action while limiting the downside associated with doing so in the emotion-driven heat of the moment when the market is presenting nothing but bad news.

If a Tree Cheers in the Forest and No One Hears It . . . Is It Still a Cheer?

The other day I caught a glimpse of a football game in which the quarterback was about to get sacked. At the last second, he threw the ball for an incomplete pass. The crowd went wild cheering the quarterback for spiking the ball without getting tackled, without getting intercepted, and without getting called for intentional grounding. He had neutralized what could have been a very bad outcome.

And I mean the crowd went *really* wild.

This got me thinking. I have played a lot of sports over the years and have had my fair share of people cheering me on from time to time. But when I make smart investments or, more important, when I avoid making bad investments, no one cheers. Not a peep. Not even from the folks who entrust me with their hard-earned money. Not once have I received a call or an e-mail stating, "Hey, Scott, I saw you *didn't* buy Company X today. Good job. Keep it up."

Yet this is the essence of what good investors and money managers do—*they avoid mistakes.* And the stock market provides plenty of opportunities for making mistakes. An investor can buy any one of tens of thousands of different stocks, bonds, REITs, and mutual funds. Yet only a handful of these will make good investments given one's objectives, time horizon, valuation, and prospects for the investment. The vast majority are simply mistakes waiting to happen.

Deciding *against* a particular investment can be of tremendous value. Returns are affected as much, if not more, by the mistakes that we make, the things we did but should not have done, than by the things we did right. Yet no one cheers when I say no to an investment opportunity after much consideration. This is probably the single most important thing an investor can do: not take action when the action contemplated has a likelihood of not meeting his objectives.

Maybe I will buy one of those applause machines and the next time I throw the proverbial ball out of bounds so as not to make an investment mistake, I will push the button and bask in the accolades for a job well done.

THE SECRET SAUCE

Take out a pen and another piece of paper; it is back to high school math with Venn diagrams. Draw three circles that overlap (not concentric circles with the same center, but three circles that overlap in the middle). Label one of them "skill," another "passion," and the third "hard work." Find someone who is engaged in an activity for which he exhibits skill, passion, and hard work, and you will find a successful person. Throw in some competitiveness and a bit of luck and you have someone at the top of their game.

***Figure* 8.2 VARIABLES FOR SUCCESS**

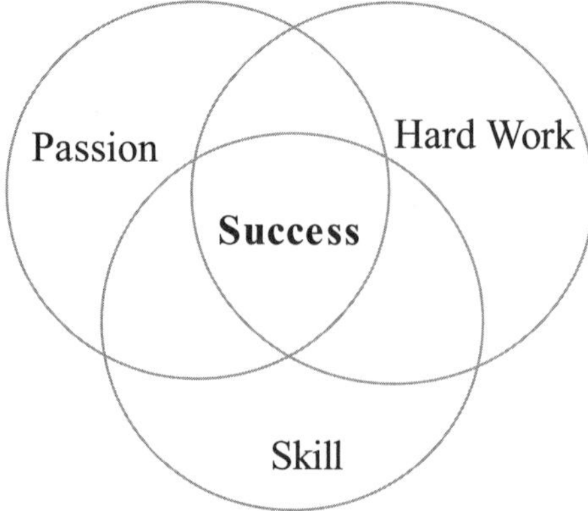

If you can discover something in life for which you have passion and skill—and you work hard at it—you are blessed as you have found the secret sauce of success and happiness. And, of course, these aspects feed each other. You enjoy something and have a love for it so you tend to work harder at it. You work hard and you build skills. You get better and you reap the rewards. And so the circle of success continues. If one of the ingredients is missing, you can do okay, but you won't be the best. I have learned this lesson many times.

***Figure* 8.3 GREATNESS MATRIX**

	Natural Ability	**Lack of Ability**
Hard Work	Achieve Greatness (1)	Those Who Are Admirable (2)
Lack of Hard Work	Those Who Had Potential (3)	Underachievers (4)

I have been blessed several times in life by fitting smack-dab in the center of these three circles (with a *very* large dose of competitiveness thrown in and, to be sure, with the usual luck). I found this in education, in athletics, and with investing. When it came to sailing, I was blessed with natural ability and I worked harder than anyone I knew. I loved what I was doing until the day I retired. Growing up, I could not wait to break the ice on nearby lakes during harsh Chicago winters and sail in any body of water I could. Driven by a deep-down, fundamental love for what I was doing, I developed skills over time. Skills yielded results which enflamed the passion and the virtuous circle prospered. This powerful combination led to several national and world titles.

Compare this with my experience of trying to swim the English Channel. I possessed two of the three ingredients necessary for success. I worked very, very hard on my training. I had the skills, both natural and acquired. But I did not love what I was doing. I tried to force the zeal; I attempted to convince myself that I was passionate about swimming for eight hours at a time in 58-degree water sans wetsuit. Along my journey I read Lynne Cox's book, *Swimming to Antarctica* to motivate myself (she has a serious passion for open-water swimming). But at the end of the day, I was fighting an uphill battle. Not all the forces were aligned. So I fell short in my quest.

Lesson? If you want to succeed at a high level, find an activity for which you have skill, passion, and a willingness to work hard (you won't even think of it as work). Then you will be on the road to success. If you conclude that you need assistance from others to achieve your financial objectives, assess on these three fronts. If someone comes up scoring high in all three elements, you probably have a winner.

However, there are many brokers with whom you do not want to work. (If you are a stock broker you might want to skip the next section.)

EXAMPLES OF INEFFECTIVE BROKER CALLS

For Whom the Bell Tolls

Large brokerage firms often have inherent conflicts of interest when it comes to their stock research, and institutionally driven flaws that you need to be aware of. Here are some of my favorite examples of irrational investment bank behavior and how you can take advantage of it.

In 2007 the esteemed Morgan Stanley came out with an overweight rating on Toll Brothers, Inc. (TOL). To be honest, I have never understood the terminology used by different brokerage firms: accumulate, underweight, outperform, and the like. What exactly do these words mean and how specifically can I act based on these recommendations? What happened to "buy" and "sell"?

Even if "overweight" is not a clear directive in and of itself, at least reasonable investors could conclude that Morgan Stanley thinks the stock is headed up. Unless we are talking about someone's waistline, overweight has to be good, right?

Wrong.

Morgan Stanley's price target associated with this recommendation was $23 per share, over 20% less than the stock price that day.

Huh?

Morgan Stanley issued an overweight rating, yet it thinks that the stock is going to crash? Imagine if Morgan proclaimed that it thought the stock market was going to drop 20%. Investors would start jumping off roofs!

Talk about mixed signals. To be fair, and for full disclosure purposes, Morgan Stanley did say that the overweight recommendation was based on the fact that Toll Brothers was expected to perform better than its peers. In essence: "If you have to own some crappy housing stock that is likely to crash, you should own Toll Brothers." Unfortunately, most people only got as far as the overweight recommendation and made investing decisions that certainly did not make their bank accounts overweight.

Microsoft Finally Gets Its Upgrade

In the fall of 2006 Microsoft traded up over 1.5% on what was generally a flat day for the broader market. Such a big up day for Microsoft was based on some kind of favorable financial or operating news, right? Nah. The company got upgraded to outperform from neutral by Credit Suisse. This was one of several upgrades the company received as it set new fifty-two-week highs. Compare this to what occurred less than six months prior.

In the spring of 2006 Microsoft announced strong earnings and revenues but investors were nervous about how much spending the company was going to be doing in the near term, so the stock collapsed. The same morning, more than a half-dozen brokerage firms downgraded the stock. Read that again. Once the stock had already crashed by over 10%, these brokerage firms *then* downgraded the stock.

Fast-forward a scant six months. Like other great companies before them—companies with superior franchises, strong financials, rock-solid balance sheets, and great management that occasionally go through nonfundamental, short-term challenges—Microsoft came back with a vengeance. Was the low that fateful day in April the final low the stock saw? No. If you "called the low" you were simply lucky.

But it was within a couple of ticks of the final low during that period as the company traded at a reasonable valuation, a key metric for successful investing. Soon thereafter the stock traded up nearly 30% from the April lows. This is one of the biggest companies in the world, up by nearly a third in a matter of months. A relatively brief window to take advantage of this situation existed. The window was foggy and cracked and ugly and likely to cause some bleeding in the near term, but the window was there for those willing to endure some short-term pain for some medium-term pleasure.

If you listened to Credit Suisse, which had a neutral rating on Microsoft while the stock went north from April to the fall—or, worse yet, if you took action based on the downgrades in April, just as the stock was hitting its lows for the year—you missed out on a great investment opportunity. This is not a unique event; this zigging by investment banks while stocks are zagging happens all the time.

Inside the Glass House: Bashing Brokers

Broker guys (the fancy term for them these days is "financial consultants") tend to congregate at the gym in my hometown of La Jolla, California, around 1:05 P.M., just after the market closes. Since their jobs have very little or nothing to do with managing money, or with the markets in general, why they feel the need to be in the office until the market closes is beyond me. I can find out how the market did that day within a few points by reading their body language and listening to their chatter. (Why they are so interested in day-to-day movements in the Dow is also a mystery, but one I think I solved by listening to the following exchange.)

I want to preface this by saying that the following exchange is typical of what I encounter regularly. You might not want to hear this—you might prefer not to know how the sausage is made—but I find this very interesting.

> Broker/Financial Advisor/Sales Guy #1: "Do you know what the market did today? I was on the golf course all morning."

> Broker/Financial Advisor/Sales Guy #2: "Yeah, it went through the roof. Dow was up like 200 points."

> Guy #1: "Awesome. This is a great day to call my clients!"

Guy #2: "Yeah, totally agreed. I'll be making calls after our workout for sure."

The market is up strong, and that makes this a good day to call clients? Let me guess; they will be phoning their clients and saying something along the lines of the following: "Hello, Jim. How's Nancy? The kids? Great. Hey, not sure if you saw it, but the market really rallied hard today. As you know, we think it is important to buy low and sell high. Consistent with the time I phoned you when the market was collapsing and advised you to buy more, now that the market has gone up strong, I would recommend that you sell some of the stocks you hold with us. Put them into cash. Maybe even withdraw some of the funds and invest in art or some other asset class that has gone down lately. I'd be happy to execute your sell orders."

Not!

I would bet my life that the calls these guys were about to make were to let their clients know that the market had just gone up a lot and thus it is a good time to buy.

Imagine any other industry where this perverse "do the opposite of what you should do" behavior takes place. Envision your personal shopper at Nordstrom calling you up and saying, "Hey, got some great news. Those shoes that you have had your eye on the past few months, well I am pleased to let you know that we just marked them up 30%, so now would be a good time to buy them."

The next time your broker calls to tell you that the market is strong and that you should invest more, ask him to phone you back when the market is on sale, when the font size in the *New York Times* is at its largest, when there is blood in the streets. Investing incremental dollars at that point is how you make the real bucks.

Here's another conversation I've overheard:

"Which would you rather own, a stock trading for $40 or a stock trading for $300? Of course, the one trading for $40!" exclaimed broker #1.

"I totally agree," said the second. "It is much easier to sell a stock to my clients that is trading at a lower price than one that is trading for a higher price."

Do not be sucked into this fallacy. The price of a stock in and of itself is meaningless. It tells you nothing about *how much* you are paying for the company that you are buying a piece of. Yet people repeatedly buy stocks of companies that are trading for under $10 because they associate a low stock price with a cheap stock and a high stock price with an expensive stock. As we discussed in the stock valuation section of this book, only when you know what you are buying can you make a good investment decision. Whenever you hear someone talk about stocks that are cheap because their prices are low, run the other way. Something that appears to be cheap on the surface might end up being an expensive investment lesson.

I'll Try Something Unique as Long as Everyone Else Is Doing It: On Using Analyst Calls as a Contrarian Indicator

Investment bank analysts are paid to forecast future stock price movements based on company fundamentals. But more often than not, their recommendations simply reflect what has already happened and thus are less than worthless. And you need to know that many research reports produced by Wall Street in recent years are written by analysts who are making stock recommendations with the underlying objective of winning investment banking business for their firms. If you think this conflict of interest is a thing of the past, read the fine print on these reports. The only difference between today and a decade ago when these abuses came to light is that these conflicts are now spelled out. "This investment bank does and seeks to do business with the companies covered in its research reports. As a result, investors should be aware that the firm might have a conflict of interest that could affect the objectivity of this report." Translation: We are more concerned with earning fees from investment banking business than with giving you our objective view on a company, so be aware. Unfortunately, most investors don't get as far as the fine print; they read the headline screaming BUY and take action accordingly.

Time after time, investment banks tell you to buy a weak company while it is getting clobbered operationally. Then the quarterly earnings report comes out and states what the market already knew—that the weak business is getting worse, not better. On that day, with the stock down 50% or more over the last several months, investment banks do you the great favor of telling you to now hold the stock rather than buy the stock. This is after shareholders who heeded the investment bank's earlier advice have lost over half their money.

If you take the bank's recommendation at face value, the bank is telling you to keep your position. But when was the last time you saw a stock rating change to hold from buy and the stock did *not* drop on the news? We all know that "hold" is a euphemism for "sell"; but if the bank were direct and had said sell, it might risk losing lucrative investment bank business. If you are relying on such recommendations, you are probably buying high and selling low, and experiencing inferior stock returns over time.

POWER TIP

Timing Is Everything—Just Not the Timing They Are Selling You

In an issue of the *Wall Street Journal,* an article discussed the launch of a new international fund by Templeton. In referring to the marketing of the fund, the article noted, "Templeton's timing is better now from a marketing perspective than when it launched its BRIC Fund (Brazil/Russia/India/China). In the third quarter the MSCI Emerging Markets Index rose 4.6% and is up 9.9% year to date. When it introduced the BRIC Fund, emerging markets had just taken a drubbing as the fears of global interest rates in May knocked some formerly highflying stock market indexes down nearly 20%." Translation: When stocks were cheap it was a bad time to encourage people to invest in them, but now that they are more expensive, it is easier to convince people to buy them. This is absurd. Do not fall prey to this psychology, this "marketing" of assets that have already gone up in price and are now more susceptible to declines. In this case, the best time for the company pushing the product to market is not, by mathematical definition, the best time for the consumer to consider buying the product. The lower the purchase price, the greater the probability of making money. Lesson: Whatever the big mutual fund companies are *not* pushing is often a good place to look for investment opportunities. When dozens of new mutual funds spring up around an asset class that has gone nowhere but up in recent times, you can be pretty certain the good times have already passed.

CONQUERING YOUR FEAR: THE ULTIMATE EXERCISE

It is extraordinarily difficult to buy something when it is out of favor. You often don't know about it. It is not making headlines, and the front page is where most investors' research starts and stops. In order to invest in something that is out of favor, you have to look actively for securities and markets that are *not* making the headlines. It is much, much harder emotionally for most of us to put money into something that is falling, or has recently fallen, than into something with a price that has marched steadily upward in recent history. Instead, most people find themselves saying, "Ah, I can't believe I didn't see that as well. It was so *obvious* I should have bought Philip Morris back in 1999 when it was trading at one-third of what it is today and everyone thought the company was going to go down under the weight of litigation."

But we are not mentally wired to do this. Which is strange, because when it comes to purchasing other assets, such as cars or shoes, people are more inclined to buy when the price goes down. Why? Because they have confidence that the great shoes from Nordstrom they had their eyes on are the same at $175 as they were at $250 the week before, only cheaper. However, investors are more apt to buy at $28 and sell at $22 than vice versa. Stocks are one of the few purchases for which the elasticity curve is inverted much of the time.

Everyone has these fearful emotions to some degree. What you do about them is what separates success from failure. One technique I use to overcome the natural fear of investing when stocks are falling is to try to flip the emotion on its head. When fear raises its ugly crown, whether in the final race of a world sailing championship or in the moment before the curtain goes up on a piano concert performance, I embrace the feelings and am thankful that I have them at that moment in time. For me these feelings mean I am challenging myself—that I am putting myself in interesting situations and am pursuing great opportunities and experiences. The absence of such feelings would mean that I am not engaging in life at the highest levels. In the realm of investing, the absence of certain levels of discomfort means that great investment opportunities are not presenting themselves. When things get ugly, when people are getting scared (you included), give thanks that the market is giving you opportunities to get rich.

Pain Is Pleasure

Your gut can be a great contrarian indicator. You just need the mental fortitude to let your mind override your emotions. When you are feeling the worst, when it seems like there will be no tomorrow, when you don't even want to open up your portfolio and see all the red ink, *that is very likely the best time to invest.* This fear is the most acute and recognizable investing emotion; dealing with it, however, is very difficult. Conversely, when you are feeling smug, complacent, even good about yourself and your stock market acumen, *that is the time to take chips off the table via incremental stock sales or tighter hedging.* Having the discipline to sell on strength is very difficult because your emotions are not as urgent as when the market is crashing. Nevertheless, the impact on your portfolio can be dramatic, so listen to your emotions and do the opposite of what your gut is telling you. When you are calm, think through how you should react during various market conditions to optimize your portfolio returns. Having a predetermined process like this can be one of your greatest assets, as it is always more difficult to take action in the heat of the moment. Some indicators that you can use as objective measures include the VIX level, put/call ratios, and consumer confidence. When each is at its worst level, this can validate your painful gut feeling and give you the confidence to take action contrary to your basic instinct that could prove beneficial to your wallet size.

Purchasing superior, dividend-paying companies is the start to an exceptionally profitable portfolio. Combining the reinvestment of dividends with the income generated from the sales of options and compounding these earnings over time can materially increase your portfolio size. In addition, by actively managing your portfolio; by regularly assessing various fundamental, technical, and macroeconomic factors; by taking advantage of natural market volatility; and by leaving your emotions at the door, you, too, can navigate a richer life.

Acknowledgments

Any project of this magnitude is largely a team effort and I owe a great gratitude to the many people who were integral to its completion. Thanks first to Stephanie Manley, Director of Operations at Coastwise, for her assistance in creating the figures and charts contained in this book. Thanks as well to Taylor Wilshire, author of *The Book of Mom,* for her gracious contribution of time and publishing knowledge. David Hough is an editor extraordinaire and I appreciate his red pencil more than he knows. Stacia Decker provided invaluable input early on in the manuscript process and Greg Smith deserves my thanks for his artistic prowess. I must also acknowledge my friend, author, entrepreneur, and winner on *Apprentice,* Dawna Stone, publisher of *Women's Running* magazine, for giving me the idea and inspiration to seclude myself for a week solid in order to complete the book. Without the editorial support of Joclyn Sanford, Director of Business Development at Coastwise and the best team member a manager could ask for, this book would still be a jumbled collection of notes and Post-its. Cyrus Voss gets my expression of appreciation for continuously challenging and forcing me to expand my knowledge and critical thinking vis-à-vis complex options concepts. My genuine gratefulness goes out to my parents, Barbara Battey and Robert Kyle, for their guidance and inspiration when it came to education in general and books in particular; never have I met two people who are more passionate and knowledgeable about the written word.

Additional Resources

BOOKS

I have read hundreds of investment and personal finance books over the years, and here are a few of my favorites, ones I consider worthwhile.

Adventure Capitalist: The Ultimate Road Trip by Jim Rogers. A great book for those who like to combine global macro issues, if not actual travel, with investing.

The Alchemy of Finance: Reading the Mind of the Market by George Soros. Smart guy, smart book.

The Art of the Long View: Planning for the Future in an Uncertain World by Peter Schwartz. An excellent work for those challenged by setting and sticking to long-term goals.

The Art of War by Sun Tzu. Need I say more?

Bringing Down the House: The Inside Story of Six MIT Students Who Took Vegas for Millions by Ben Mezrich. A fun tale of using math and numbers to your advantage in rational ways.

Buffett: The Making of an American Capitalist by Roger Lowenstein. Dozens of books have been written about this legendary investor; I still consider this one the best.

Chaos Theory Tamed by Garnett P. Williams. Everyone should study a little chaos theory. It will actually add some order and security to your life.

The Education of a Speculator by Victor Niederhoffer. Cautionary tales.

Flow: The Psychology of Optimal Experience by Mihaly Csikszentmihalyi. The definitive work on how to get into the zone, or flow. Surprisingly applicable to all aspects of life including athletics, work, trading, and social settings.

Fortune's Formula: The Untold Story of the Scientific Betting System That Beat the Casinos and Wall Street by William Poundstone. Another great examination of numbers and statistics, in this case more directly applicable to investing and trading.

The Intelligent Investor: The Definitive Book on Value Investing by Benjamin Graham. A classic and necessary read for any serious investor.

Mastery: The Keys to Success and Long-Term Fulfillment by George Leonard. A good work on the subject of becoming highly proficient in a given realm.

The Richest Man in Babylon by George S. Clason. This investment classic shows the importance of saving and paying off one's debts.

The 7 Habits of Highly Effective People by Stephen R. Covey. One of the few worthwhile "self-help" books.

Stocks for the Long Run by Jeremy J. Siegel. One of the best investment books out there that demonstrates the importance of maintaining long-term equity exposure.

Technical Analysis of Stock Trends by Robert D. Edwards and John Magee. The granddaddy of technical analysis books, and for good reason.

Zen Mind, Beginner's Mind by Shunryu Suzuki. For those with an inclination toward eastern philosophy, an excellent primer on how to clear the mind for optimal performance.

PERIODICALS

Argus, http://www.argusresearch.com, (212) 425-7500.

Barron's, http://online.barrons.com, (800) 544-0422.

Standard & Poor's, http://www.standardandpoors.com, (877) 772-5436.

Value Line, http://valueline.com, (800) 634-3583.

The Wall Street Journal, http://online.wsj.com, (800) 568-7625.

WEB SITES

www.businessweek.com/investor. Includes a learning center for everything related to finance and investing.

www.cboe.com. The Chicago Board Options Exchange Web site provides great tools and quotes for all things options-related.

www.cbsmarketwatch.com. Good general stock market news.

www.cnbc.com. Excellent source for the latest market news.

www.coastwisegroup.com. A dedicated investment advisory firm whose Web site includes great market commentary and investment blogs.

www.etfconnect.com. A good resource for ETFs.

www.finance.yahoo.com. Excellent research tool, access to chat boards.

www.google.com/finance. Get quotes and research stocks.

www.investopedia.com. Articles, tutorials and a great glossary for anything finance related.

www.ishares.com. Resource for ETFs and other financial products and information.

www.marketdataexpress.com. Here you can purchase and download historical options data.

www.mergent.com. Mergent publishes lists of companies that regularly increase their dividends.

www.msnmoney.com. Stock research and market news.

www.nasdaq.com. The National Association of Securities Dealers Automated Quotations is the largest electronic trading market in the United States.

www.nyse.com. Learn all about the New York Stock Exchange on Wall Street.

www.thepower100.com. Here you will find the Coastwise Power 100 annual list of high-quality dividend-paying companies.

www.thestreet.com. Good general stock market news and commentary.

www.ustreas.gov. Latest news from the United States Department of the Treasury.

Glossary

Active An investment strategy in which the investor believes he can outperform the market by making specific investing and trading decisions. In business, someone who participates in the day-to-day operations and management of a company.

American Depository Receipts (ADRs) Since most other countries do not allow stock certificates to leave their borders, a foreign company may arrange for a trustee (typically a large bank) to issue ADRs (sometimes called American Depository Shares, or ADSs) that represent the actual, or underlying, shares. Each ADR is equivalent to a specific number of shares.

American Depository Shares (ADSs) A U.S. dollar–denominated equity share of a foreign-based company available for purchase on an American stock exchange. An ADS is issued by a depository bank in the U.S. under agreement with the issuing foreign company. An ADS is a single share of the entire issuance known as an ADR.

American-Style Option An option that can be exercised at any time by its owner.

Annual Rates of Change (Per Share) Compound yearly rates of change of per-share sales, cash flow, earnings, dividends, book value, or other industry-specific, per-share figures.

Annual Total Return A compound yearly return to shareholders that includes both stock price appreciation and dividend returns.

Arbitrage The process of buying an asset in one marketplace and concurrently selling it in another at a different price.

Ask Price The price at which someone is willing to sell a security. Alternatively, the price at which an investor can purchase a security.

Assets The total of current assets (normally cash and short-term investments, inventories, and receivables) and long-term assets (typically including property, equipment, and goodwill).

Assignment The process by which the investor is required to buy (in the case of a short put) or sell stock (in the case of being short a call) when options sold short are in-the-money at time of expiration. *See also* Called Away.

At-the-Money (ATM) Used to describe a call (or put) option that has a strike price equal to or near the price of the underlying asset.

Average Annual Dividend Yield Dividends declared per share for a year divided by the average annual price of the stock in the same year, expressed as a percentage.

Average Annual Price/Earnings (P/E) Ratio The average price of the stock for the year divided by earnings per share reported by the company for the year. *See also* Price/Earnings Ratio.

Balance Sheet A financial statement that lists a company's assets, debts, and owner's investment (shareholder equity) as of a specific date.

Basis Point One basis point equals one one-hundredth of one percentage point.

Beta A relative measure of the historical sensitivity of a stock's price to overall market fluctuations. A Beta of 1.50 describes a stock tends to rise (or fall) 50% more than the broad market.

Bid Price The price at which someone is willing to buy a stock or option contract, or conversely the price at which an owner of a stock or option can sell such security.

Bond A long-term debt instrument, typically characterized by fixed, semiannual interest payments and a specified maturity date.

Book Value per Share Net worth (including intangible assets), less preferred stock at liquidating or redemption value, divided by common shares outstanding.

Buy to Close The closing of an option contract, initiated by first selling short.

Buy to Open The act of initiating a contract position by buying a call or put.

Buy Write Buying a stock long while simultaneously selling a call against the long stock.

Call Bear Spread The simultaneous sale of a call at a given strike price and purchase of a call at a higher strike price.

Call Bull Spread The simultaneous purchase of a call at a given strike price and a sale of a call at a higher strike price.

Call Option An option which gives its buyer the right (but not the obligation) to buy a number of shares of an underlying security at a fixed price before a specified expiration date. Call buyers hope the price of the stock will rise. A call option can be sold as a way to generate income and/or provide some downside protection for a long position.

Called Away To be assigned, or required to sell, stock on which calls were sold short.

Cash Flow The total of net income plus noncash charges (depreciation, amortization, and depletion) less preferred dividends (if any).

Cash-Settled Options The owner of this type of option receives cash equal to the difference between the index's closing price and the strike price of the option rather than any securities. Most European-style options are cash based.

CBOE The Chicago Board Options Exchange.

Chain (Option Chain) An abbreviated means for providing relevant information for a given contract. Chains include the underlying security, the expiration date, the strike price, and the type of option (call or put).

Compound Growth The annual rate of growth of an investment when dividends or interest are reinvested.

Contract An exchange-traded derivative instrument that gives the holder of the contract the right, but not the obligation, to exercise the contract and trade the underlying asset at a specified price. In the case of equity options, each contract represents 100 shares.

Core Holdings A significant long-term position within a portfolio which is purchased with the intent of maintaining it for an extended period.

Counterparty Risk The risk that the other party in an agreement will default. This is also known as default risk.

Covered A position that is hedged.

Covered Call *See* Buy Write.

Credit Spread The difference between the amount received from selling an option and the amount paid for buying an option. The spread results in a credit when the price received for selling an option is higher than the price paid for buying the second option in the transaction.

Current Asset An asset on the balance sheet that might reasonably be expected to be converted into cash, sold, or consumed during the normal operating cycle of a business, usually twelve months or less. Current assets usually include cash, receivables, and inventory.

Current Liabilities Financial obligations that a business will have to satisfy within the next twelve months. Current liabilities include accounts payable, taxes, wage accruals, and total short-term debt, or debt due (the sum of notes payable and the portion of long-term debt maturing in the operating year).

Current Ratio The sum of current assets divided by the sum of current liabilities.

Default Risk *See* Counterparty Risk.

Delta The amount an option will change for a corresponding one point change in the price of the underlying security. Delta values range from 0 to 1.0.

Delta Adjusted Exposure Gross, or notional, exposure for a given position multiplied by the position's delta.

Delta Premium Credit The additional premium received by virtue of closing one short option contract and selling a later-dated option with the same strike price.

Depreciation An amount charged against operating profits to reflect the aging of plant and equipment owned by a company.

Dividend A payout to shareholders determined by a board of directors.

Dividend Declaration Date The date a company declares a dividend payable in the future.

Dividend Ex-Date The date by which an investor must have purchased a stock in order to receive announced dividends or stock distributions. If the investor purchases stock on or after this date, he will not receive the dividend.

Dividend Payment Date The date a dividend is paid.

Dividend Record Date The date used to determine which shareholders are entitled to the dividend or distribution. This ensures that the dividend is sent to the correct people and credited to the correct accounts. The date is usually two business days after the ex-date.

Dividend Yield Total cash dividends declared over the previous twelve months, divided by the recent price of the stock.

Dividends Paid per Share The common dividends per share paid (but not necessarily declared) during the calendar year.

Earnings A company's total profit before nonrecurring gains or losses, but after all other expenses.

Earnings per Share (EPS) Net profits attributable to each common share as originally reported by the company, but adjusted for all subsequent stock splits and stock dividends.

Effective Yield The current dividend divided by the original stock purchase price.

Equity Ownership interest held by shareholders in a corporation.

European-Style Option An option that can only be exercised on its expiration date.

Exchange Traded Funds (ETFs) A basket of stocks that trades throughout the day on a major exchange. Each ETF has a unique ticker and trades much like a regular stock.

Exercise To implement the rights of an option holder by buying (in the case of a call) or selling (in the case of a put) the underlying asset.

Expiration Date The date on which a contract ends.

Exposure The amount, or size, of a position. This can be represented in dollar or percentage terms, and on a notional or delta-adjusted basis, and as an absolute number or as a percentage of the total portfolio.

Fill The price at which an order is executed. To complete an order.

Gamma The rate at which delta changes.

Gross Exposure Total value of all positions (long and short) in a given portfolio position on a notional or face-value basis.

Gross Long Exposure Total value of all long-oriented positions (long equity, long calls, and short puts) on a notional or fully assigned basis.

Gross Short Exposure Total value of all short-oriented positions (short equity, long puts, and short calls) on a notional or fully assigned basis.

Growth Stock Stocks of companies with earnings that grow consistently and quickly over time, reflecting the fact that such companies have limited sensitivity to the country's economy as it moves up and down.

Hedge To enter a position that reduces the exposure or risk of an underlying position. To manage risk.

Historical Volatility A measure of a security's or index's past volatility, or change in price, over a given time period. Often measured by standard deviation over a preceding twelve-month period.

Implied Volatility A theoretical measure of a given security's or index's expected or imputed future volatility, usually over a thirty-day period.

Income Statement A financial report that lists revenues, expenses, and net income during a given period.

Income Stocks Equities with higher-than-average dividend yields (often, but not always, stocks with dividends that are likely to be maintained or raised).

In-the-Money (ITM) Used to describe a call (or put) option with a strike price that is less (or more in the case of a put) than the price of the underlying asset. If General Electric common stock is trading at $25 per share, a call option on General Electric with a strike price of $20 is in-the-money.

Intrinsic Value The value of a security, justified by factors such as assets, dividends, earnings, and management quality. Intrinsic value is at the core of fundamental analysis since it is used in an attempt to calculate the value in an individual stock and to then compare that value with the market price.

Intrinsic Value Premium The amount by which an option is in-the-money.

Investor Someone who allocates capital with a time horizon of a year or more with the objective of providing a return on that money.

Last The most recent price at which a trade was executed. In the case of illiquid securities and derivatives, this may differ substantially from a current bid/ask quotes.

Layer In The process of entering less than the intended full position. For example, if your goal is to purchase 1,000 shares of Company X, you might purchase 500 shares today and wait for weakness to purchase the remaining 500 shares.

LEAPS Long-term equity anticipation securities. LEAPS are options that typically have expiration time frames of twelve months or longer.

Leverage The use of various financial instruments such as derivates (e.g., options, futures contracts) or margin borrowing with the goal of amplifying returns. In business, the use of borrowing (usually in the form of bank debt) to finance operations or to enhance ROE.

Limit Order An order placed to buy or sell a set number of shares or contracts at a specified price or better.

Long To enter a position with the objective of profiting from the increase in price of a security.

Long-Term Debt The portion of borrowings (including bank notes, debentures, and capitalized leases) that will be due not in the current twelve months, but in future operating years.

Margin An amount borrowed from one's brokerage firm.

Market Capitalization (Market Cap) The market value of all common shares outstanding for a company, calculated by multiplying the recent price of a stock by the number of common shares outstanding. While there is no single definition accepted, large-cap stocks typically have market values of more than $5 billion. Mid-cap stocks have market values from $1 billion to $5 billion. Small-cap stocks have market values of less than $1 billion.

Market Neutral A portfolio for which net exposure is at or near zero.

Market Order A buy or sell order in which the broker is to execute the order at the best price currently available.

Market Value The price at which a security currently can be sold.

Multiple A ratio, or measure, usually applied to various financial metrics of a company such as its earnings.

Naked To hold a position that is unhedged.

Net Asset Value (NAV) The market value of a company's assets less any liabilities divided by the number of shares outstanding. In the case of a mutual fund, the market value of all cash and securities held within the fund, less any liabilities, divided by the number of shares outstanding.

Net Exposure Gross long exposure less gross short exposure.

Net Profit (or Income) A company's total profit before nonrecurring gains or losses, but after all other expenses.

Net Profit Margin Net income before nonrecurring gains and losses as a percentage of revenues.

Net Worth All the assets shown on the balance sheet, including any tangible assets (i.e., goodwill, debt discount, deferred charges) less current liabilities, long-term debt, and all other noncurrent liabilities. In other words, the sum of common plus preferred stockholders' equity. Also referred to as shareholders' equity.

Notional Exposure The total face value of the option, were it fully assigned.

Open Interest The total number of contracts (for a given strike price and expiration period) that have not yet been exercised or expired, or fulfilled by delivery. This is not the same as volume traded.

Operating Earnings Earnings left after subtracting the cost of goods sold, marketing, and general and administrative costs from sales. Sometimes referred to as EBITDA (earnings before interest, taxes, depreciation, and amortization).

Option A contract that gives the buyer the right to buy or sell 100 shares of stock within a certain period of time and at a preestablished price. A call option gives an investor a right to buy 100 shares of stock at a specified price, while a put option allows him to sell 100 shares.

Out-of-the-Money (OTM) Used to describe a call option with a strike price above the price of the underlying asset or a put option with a strike price below the price of the underlying asset. For example, a put option to sell 100 shares of IBM stock at $60 per share is out-of-the-money if the stock currently trades at $80. Even though an out-of-the-money option has no intrinsic value, it might have market value based on variables such as time and volatility.

Passive An investment strategy involving limited ongoing buying and selling of securities. A belief that one cannot outperform the market as a whole by taking advantage of near-term market fluctuations and/or the temporary mispricing of a given sector. In business, someone who does not play an active role in the management of a company.

Payout Ratio The ratio on a percentage basis of the net income a firm pays to its stockholders in dividends. If a company pays out no dividends, its payout ratio is 0%. If it pays out in dividends the exact amount of its earnings, its payout ratio is 100%. A company with earnings of $2 per share and an annual dividend of $1 per share has a payout ratio of 50%.

Premium The price at which an option trades. The size of the premium is affected by various factors including the time to expiration, interest rates, strike price, and the price and volatility of the underlying asset.

Price The amount at which any asset trades.

Price/Earnings Ratio (P/E Ratio) The most widely used measure of stock valuation. The price of the stock divided by earnings per share for a twelve-month period.

Price/Earnings Growth Ratio (PEG) The ratio of price/earnings per share compared to a company's growth rate. If a given company is trading for 22X earnings and its earnings are growing at 30% per year, its PEG ratio is approximately 0.73. In general, a PEG ratio under 1.0 is viewed as favorable.

Price to Book A stock's total capitalization (market cap) divided by its book value, calculated on either a total valuation or a per share basis.

Price to Sales A stock's total capitalization (market cap) divided by its sales over a twelve-month period.

Put Bear Spread The simultaneous purchase of a put at a given strike price and the sale of a put at a lower strike price.

Put Bull Spread The simultaneous sale of a put at a given strike price and purchase of a put at a lower strike price.

Put Option Gives the buyer the right to sell a number of shares of stock at a price until the option's expiration date. Put buyers hope the price of the stock will fall. Put options may be sold as a way to generate income and/or create an entry point for a stock purchase at a price that is lower than the then-market price of the stock.

Ratio Call Selling The sale of more short calls on a given position than what is held of long stock or deep in-the-money short puts.

Raw Gross, or total, return not converted to an annualized basis.

Real Estate Investment Trust (REIT) A financial intermediary that invests its equity capital and debt in income-producing real estate and mortgages. In general, at least 95% of otherwise taxable income must be distributed to shareholders in the calendar year earned, and specified percentages of both investments and gross income must be related to real estate.

Retained Earnings Net profit for the year, less all common and preferred dividends, when relating to the income statement. With respect to the balance sheet or common equity, it is the sum of net profit in all years of the company's existence, less all dividends (common and preferred) ever paid.

Return on Equity (ROE) A company's earnings divided by its shareholder equity. A critical measure that demonstrates how well a company uses its reinvested earnings to generate additional earnings.

Return on Investment (ROI) For a business, a measure of a company's profitability for a given time period, usually twelve months, divided by total common stock, preferred equity, and long-term debt. How effectively a company uses its capital to produce profits. For investors, the amount of money made divided by the capital deployed for a given investment.

Roll To close one option contract and open up a new contract with the same strike price but a later-dated expiration.

Roll Up and Out To close one option contract and open a new contract with a higher strike price (in the case of a call) and a later-dated expiration.

Sales Gross volume less returns, discounts, and allowances; net sales.

Sell to Close To complete a contract position that was opened up by buying long.

Sell to Open The act of initiating an option contract by first selling it short.

Sell Write To sell a stock short while simultaneously selling a put against the short stock position.

Settlement Price The price established by the exchange at the end (or beginning in the case of index options) of each day for the purposes of determining net gains or losses in a given contract as well as margin requirement.

Shareholder's Equity A balance sheet item showing net worth less the liquidating or redemption value of any preferred issues outstanding. Represents the sum of the value of common stock at par, the surplus of capital received (over par value), and retained earnings (i.e., earned surplus). Retained earnings are the sum of net profits earned in all years less dividends paid in all years.

Short To enter a position with the objective of profiting from the decline in the price of a security.

Short Hedge An investment transaction that is intended to provide protection against a decline in the value of an asset. For example, an investor who holds shares of General Motors and expects the stock to decline might enter into a short hedge by purchasing a put option on GM stock. If GM does subsequently decline, the value of the put option would increase.

Special Situations Otherwise high-quality companies that pay little or no dividends and, temporarily and for nonfundamental reasons, have fallen on hard times.

Spread The difference, or delta, between the bid and the ask.

Standard Deviation A measure of a security's volatility, usually calculated over a twelve-month period. The distance a stock is likely to move from its average.

Stock Dividend The issuance of additional common shares to common stockholders, with no change in total common equity. From an accounting standpoint, retained earnings (i.e., the earned surplus) are reduced and the value of the reported common stock component of common equity (usually called the par value account) is increased.

Straddle The purchase or sale of puts and calls in equal proportion and with the same terms.

Strangle The purchase of both an out-of-the-money put and an out-of-the-money call, each option having the same underlying asset and maturity.

Strike Price The exercise price at which the owner of a call option can purchase the underlying stock or the owner of a put option can sell the underlying stock.

Synthetic Stock A financial instrument that artificially simulates another instrument through the combination of other assets. For example, the simultaneous purchase of a long call and the sale of a short put creates a synthetic stock.

Tau *See* Vega.

Theta The measurement of time decay of a given option position.

Time Value Premium Total premium less intrinsic value premium.

In the case of out-of-the-money options, the entire premium amount is time value premium.

Total Exposure *See* Gross Exposure.

Trader Someone who allocates capital with a time frame of one year or less with the goal of getting a return on that capital.

Value The amount of an asset's true worth based on objective financial metrics.

Vega The amount by which the option price changes when volatility changes.

VIX The implied volatility for the S&P 500 for the subsequent thirty-day period.

Volatility The measure of the amount by which an underlying security is expected to fluctuate in a given period.

Volume The total number of shares or options traded over a given period, usually a day.

VXN The implied volatility for the NASDAQ 100 for the subsequent thirty-day period.

Working Capital The amount of current assets found on the balance sheet, less current liabilities.

Write To sell an option. The seller of the option is known as the writer of the option.

Yield Dividends paid for the previous twelve months divided by the current price, expressed as a percentage.

Index